Economic Growth:
Prospects and Determinants

This is Volume 22 in the series of studies commissioned as part of the research program of the Royal Commission on the Economic Union and Development Prospects for Canada.

The studies contained in this volume reflect the views of their authors and do not imply endorsement by the Chairman or Commissioners.

Economic Growth: Prospects and Determinants

JOHN SARGENT
Research Coordinator

Published by the University of Toronto Press in cooperation with the Royal Commission on the Economic Union and Development Prospects for Canada and the Canadian Government Publishing Centre, Supply and Services Canada

University of Toronto Press
Toronto   Buffalo   London

Grateful acknowledgment is made to the following for permission to reprint previously published and unpublished material: Greenwood Press; International Institute for Applied Systems Analysis; John Wiley and Sons Ltd.; Ontario Economic Council; Methuen & Co. Ltd.; Oxford University Press Inc.; Penguin Books Ltd.; University of Toronto, Institute for Policy Analysis.

©Minister of Supply and Services Canada 1986

Printed in Canada
ISBN 0-8020-7265-8
ISSN 0829-2396
Cat. No. Z1-1983/1-41-22E

CANADIAN CATALOGUING IN PUBLICATION DATA

Main entry under title:
Economic growth: prospects and determinants

(The Collected research studies / Royal Commission on the Economic Union and Development Prospects for Canada,
ISSN 0829-2396 ; 22)
Includes bibliographical references.
ISBN 0-8020-7265-8

1. Canada — Economic conditions — 1945–   — Addresses, essays, lectures.
I. Sargent, John. II. Royal Commission on the Economic Union and Development Prospects for Canada. III. Series: The Collected research studies (Royal Commission on the Economic Union and Development Prospects for Canada) ; 22.

HC115.E25 1985   330.971'064   C85-099631-7

PUBLISHING COORDINATION: Ampersand Communications Services Inc.
COVER DESIGN: Will Rueter
INTERIOR DESIGN: Brant Cowie/Artplus Limited

CONTENTS

HC
115
·E276
1986

When the members of the Rowell-Sirois Commission began their collective task in 1937, very little was known about the evolution of the Canadian economy. What was known, moreover, had not been extensively analyzed by the slender cadre of social scientists of the day.

When we set out upon our task nearly 50 years later, we enjoyed a substantial advantage over our predecessors; we had a wealth of information. We inherited the work of scholars at universities across Canada and we had the benefit of the work of experts from private research institutes and publicly sponsored organizations such as the Ontario Economic Council and the Economic Council of Canada. Although there were still important gaps, our problem was not a shortage of information; it was to interrelate and integrate — to synthesize — the results of much of the information we already had.

The mandate of this Commission is unusually broad. It encompasses many of the fundamental policy issues expected to confront the people of Canada and their governments for the next several decades. The nature of the mandate also identified, in advance, the subject matter for much of the research and suggested the scope of enquiry and the need for vigorous efforts to interrelate and integrate the research disciplines. The resulting research program, therefore, is particularly noteworthy in three respects: along with original research studies, it includes survey papers which synthesize work already done in specialized fields; it avoids duplication of work which, in the judgment of the Canadian research community, has already been well done; and, considered as a whole, it is the most thorough examination of the Canadian economic, political and legal systems ever undertaken by an independent agency.

The Commission's research program was carried out under the joint direction of three prominent and highly respected Canadian scholars: Dr. Ivan Bernier (*Law and Constitutional Issues*), Dr. Alan Cairns (*Politics and Institutions of Government*) and Dr. David C. Smith (*Economics*).

Dr. Ivan Bernier is Dean of the Faculty of Law at Laval University. Dr. Alan Cairns is former Head of the Department of Political Science at the University of British Columbia and, prior to joining the Commission, was William Lyon Mackenzie King Visiting Professor of Canadian Studies at Harvard University. Dr. David C. Smith, former Head of the Department of Economics at Queen's University in Kingston, is now Principal of that University. When Dr. Smith assumed his new responsibilities at Queen's in September 1984, he was succeeded by Dr. Kenneth Norrie of the University of Alberta and John Sargent of the federal Department of Finance, who together acted as Co-directors of Research for the concluding phase of the Economics research program.

I am confident that the efforts of the Research Directors, research coordinators and authors whose work appears in this and other volumes, have provided the community of Canadian scholars and policy makers with a series of publications that will continue to be of value for many years to come. And I hope that the value of the research program to Canadian scholarship will be enhanced by the fact that Commission research is being made available to interested readers in both English and French.

I extend my personal thanks, and that of my fellow Commissioners, to the Research Directors and those immediately associated with them in the Commission's research program. I also want to thank the members of the many research advisory groups whose counsel contributed so substantially to this undertaking.

DONALD S. MACDONALD

INTRODUCTION

At its most general level, the Royal Commission's research program has examined how the Canadian political economy can better adapt to change. As a basis of enquiry, this question reflects our belief that the future will always take us partly by surprise. Our political, legal and economic institutions should therefore be flexible enough to accommodate surprises and yet solid enough to ensure that they help us meet our future goals. This theme of an adaptive political economy led us to explore the interdependencies between political, legal and economic systems and drew our research efforts in an interdisciplinary direction.

The sheer magnitude of the research output (more than 280 separate studies in 70+ volumes) as well as its disciplinary and ideological diversity have, however, made complete integration impossible and, we have concluded, undesirable. The research output as a whole brings varying perspectives and methodologies to the study of common problems and we therefore urge readers to look beyond their particular field of interest and to explore topics across disciplines.

The three research areas, — *Law and Constitutional Issues*, under Ivan Bernier; *Politics and Institutions of Government*, under Alan Cairns; and *Economics*, under David C. Smith (co-directed with Kenneth Norrie and John Sargent for the concluding phase of the research program) — were further divided into 19 sections headed by research coordinators.

The area *Law and Constitutional Issues* has been organized into five major sections headed by the research coordinators identified below.

- Law, Society and the Economy — *Ivan Bernier and Andrée Lajoie*
- The International Legal Environment — *John J. Quinn*
- The Canadian Economic Union — *Mark Krasnick*

- Harmonization of Laws in Canada — *Ronald C.C. Cuming*
- Institutional and Constitutional Arrangements — *Clare F. Beckton and A. Wayne MacKay*

Since law in its numerous manifestations is the most fundamental means of implementing state policy, it was necessary to investigate how and when law could be mobilized most effectively to address the problems raised by the Commission's mandate. Adopting a broad perspective, researchers examined Canada's legal system from the standpoint of how law evolves as a result of social, economic and political changes and how, in turn, law brings about changes in our social, economic and political conduct.

Within *Politics and Institutions of Government*, research has been organized into seven major sections.

- Canada and the International Political Economy — *Denis Stairs and Gilbert Winham*
- State and Society in the Modern Era — *Keith Banting*
- Constitutionalism, Citizenship and Society — *Alan Cairns and Cynthia Williams*
- The Politics of Canadian Federalism — *Richard Simeon*
- Representative Institutions — *Peter Aucoin*
- The Politics of Economic Policy — *G. Bruce Doern*
- Industrial Policy — *André Blais*

This area examines a number of developments which have led Canadians to question their ability to govern themselves wisely and effectively. Many of these developments are not unique to Canada and a number of comparative studies canvass and assess how others have coped with similar problems. Within the context of the Canadian heritage of parliamentary government, federalism, a mixed economy, and a bilingual and multicultural society, the research also explores ways of rearranging the relationships of power and influence among institutions to restore and enhance the fundamental democratic principles of representativeness, responsiveness and accountability.

Economics research was organized into seven major sections.

- Macroeconomics — *John Sargent*
- Federalism and the Economic Union — *Kenneth Norrie*
- Industrial Structure — *Donald G. McFetridge*
- International Trade — *John Whalley*
- Income Distribution and Economic Security — *François Vaillancourt*
- Labour Markets and Labour Relations — *Craig Riddell*
- Economic Ideas and Social Issues — *David Laidler*

Economics research examines the allocation of Canada's human and other resources, the ways in which institutions and policies affect this allocation, and the distribution of the gains from their use. It also considers the nature of economic development, the forces that shape our regional and industrial structure, and our economic interdependence with other countries. The thrust of the research in economics is to increase our comprehension of what determines our economic potential and how instruments of economic policy may move us closer to our future goals.

One section from each of the three research areas — The Canadian Economic Union, The Politics of Canadian Federalism, and Federalism and the Economic Union — have been blended into one unified research effort. Consequently, the volumes on Federalism and the Economic Union as well as the volume on The North are the results of an inter-disciplinary research effort.

We owe a special debt to the research coordinators. Not only did they organize, assemble and analyze the many research studies and combine their major findings in overviews, but they also made substantial contributions to the Final Report. We wish to thank them for their performance, often under heavy pressure.

Unfortunately, space does not permit us to thank all members of the Commission staff individually. However, we are particularly grateful to the Chairman, The Hon. Donald S. Macdonald; the Commission's Executive Director, J. Gerald Godsoe; and the Director of Policy, Alan Nymark, all of whom were closely involved with the Research Program and played key roles in the contribution of Research to the Final Report. We wish to express our appreciation to the Commission's Administrative Advisor, Harry Stewart, for his guidance and advice, and to the Director of Publishing, Ed Matheson, who managed the research publication process. A special thanks to Jamie Benidickson, Policy Coordinator and Special Assistant to the Chairman, who played a valuable liaison role between Research and the Chairman and Commissioners. We are also grateful to our office administrator, Donna Stebbing, and to our secretarial staff, Monique Carpentier, Barbara Cowtan, Tina DeLuca, Françoise Guilbault and Marilyn Sheldon.

Finally, a well deserved thank you to our closest assistants: Jacques J.M. Shore, *Law and Constitutional Issues*; Cynthia Williams and her successor Karen Jackson, *Politics and Institutions of Government*; and I. Lilla Connidis, *Economics*. We appreciate not only their individual contribution to each research area, but also their cooperative contribution to the research program and the Commission.

IVAN BERNIER
ALAN CAIRNS
DAVID C. SMITH

The Royal Commission's Macroeconomics Research Studies Program was designed to shed light on the macroeconomic evolution of the Canadian economy over the postwar period and particularly over the last two decades, on current macro policy issues, and on overall prospects for the Canadian economy. The results of the research program have provided background for the Commission's Final Report. The individual studies which constituted the research program are contained in volumes 19 to 25 of the Economics Section of the research publication series.

Volume 22 deals with aspects of long-term growth and prospects.

- "The Prospects for Productivity," by Michael Denny, reviews issues in the measurement of productivity and its determinants. The study provides a general survey of what is known about the contribution of various factors to productivity growth in general and to the recent slowdown in, and future prospects for, Canadian productivity growth.
- "Economic Growth and Productivity in Canada: 1955–90," by John Helliwell, Mary E.MacGregor and Tim Padmore, provides empirical estimates of the contribution of various factors to the historical evolution of real income and productivity growth and to growth prospects. Of particular note is the application of the MACE model to the analysis of the contribution of changes in relative energy prices and wages, of profitability, and of the strength of demand to productivity growth and growth prospects.
- "Global Futures and Canadian Prospects: A Review of the Global Modelling Literature," by A.R. Dobell and B.R. Kennedy, provides a general survey of the structure and implications of a series of "global

models," starting with the model underlying the Club of Rome's "Limits to Growth" study. Strengths and weaknesses of the various approaches to global modelling are discussed, and potential implications for the Canadian economy are noted.

- "Savings in Canada: Retrospective and Prospective," by Gregory V. Jump and Thomas A. Wilson, reviews the historical evolution of savings, and prospects for saving, using unadjusted and inflation-adjusted savings data. It provides an analysis of the role and determinants of savings in an open economy, and of particular factors — especially tax factors — that influenced savings behaviour over the past two decades.
- "A Note on Demographic Projections for Canada: Review and Implications," by Douglas Green, Judith Gold, and John Sargent, reviews demographic trends since 1921 and presents a range of demographic projections extending to 2030 and, in one case, to 2100. Studies of the implications of the changing age structure of the Canadian population for the "burden" of social security and other government expenditure programs are surveyed.

Taken together, the studies in this volume do not purport to provide a comprehensive picture of the likely future evolution of the Canadian, or world, economies. They should provide the reader with substantial food for thought on forces which will be important in shaping that future.

JOHN SARGENT

ACKNOWLEDGMENTS

The Commission's Macroeconomics Research Studies Program benefited from the advice and assistance of a great many individuals.

David C. Smith, Research Director of the overall Economics Research Program, had a major role in conceiving the broad outlines of the Macroeconomics Program, and provided invaluable advice throughout.

The members of the Macroeconomics Research Advisory Group gave generously of their time and expertise; their advice made a major contribution to the design of the program, to the development of terms of reference for the individual studies, and to the review of early drafts of the studies. The Research Advisory Group members were John Crow, Senior Deputy Governor, Bank of Canada, Ottawa; Wendy Dobson, Executive Director, C.D. Howe Institute, Toronto; Pierre Fortin, Professor of Economics, Université Laval, Quebec; Charles Freedman, Adviser, Bank of Canada, Ottawa; John Grant, Vice-President and Chief Economist, Wood Gundy, Inc., Toronto; John Helliwell, Professor of Economics, University of British Columbia, Vancouver; David Laidler, Professor of Economics, University of Western Ontario, London, Ont.; Paul-Henri Lapointe, Director, Special Projects and Policy Analysis Division, Department of Finance, Ottawa; John McCallum, Professor of Economics, Université de Québec à Montréal; Sylvia Ostry, Ambassador for Multilateral Trade Negotiations, Department of External Affairs, Ottawa; Ross Preston, Senior Project Director, Economic Council of Canada, Ottawa; Douglas Purvis, Professor of Economics, Queen's University, Kingston; Brian Scarfe, Professor of Economics, University of Alberta, Edmonton; Alasdair Sinclair, Vice-President (Academic), Dalhousie University, Halifax; David Slater, Chairman,

Economic Council of Canada, Ottawa; Gordon Sparks, Professor of Economics, Queen's University, Kingston; William White, Adviser, Bank of Canada, Ottawa; and Thomas Wilson, Professor of Economics, University of Toronto.

Commissioner Clarence L. Barber provided valuable comments on a number of the individual studies.

Craig Riddell, in addition to his responsibilities as Research Coordinator of the Labour Markets and Relations Section of the Economics Research Program, attended several meetings of the Macroeconomics Research Advisory Group and contributed significantly to the overall Macroeconomics Program.

The referees of the individual studies, who were mainly drawn from the Canadian academic community and some of whom were also members of the Research Advisory Group, in all cases made best efforts to assess the studies against the unique requirements of a Royal Commission research program and provided useful suggestions and comments on the individual studies.

The highly competent and energetic assistance of Barbara Cowtan, secretary, and of researchers Judith Gold and Douglas Green was of immense help. The efforts of Lilla Connidis — Assistant Director, Economics Research — and Tina DeLuca, Marilyn Sheldon, and Donna Stebbing of the secretarial staff were also essential to the administration and processing associated with individual studies, and to the organization of symposia and of Research Advisory Group meetings.

Lastly, the authors of the individual studies contributed not only through the quality of their work but through doing their best to shape the coverage of their studies to the suggested specifications — which were always provided but often less than pellucid — to meet deadlines that were tight, and to respond to the multiple and not always consistent suggestions of referees, RAG members, copy editors, and the coordinator.

All the above deserve much credit for whatever of value may have been produced in the course of the Macroeconomics Research Studies Program, but responsibility for any gaps in the program, and for failures to explore particular approaches to the individual topics considered, properly rests with the coordinator.

J.S.

The Prospects for Productivity

MICHAEL DENNY

Productivity growth is not a final objective but a means to either a higher material standard of living, as measured roughly by real income per capita, or the easier attainment of any particular material standard. In the long run, productivity growth is the principal source of gains in real income, the only other source being rents on natural resources. In the short run, increases in real income may have many other causes, but if we are considering the long run, productivity growth must be at the centre of any increase in real income.

In the first section of this paper, I will discuss some conceptual snares surrounding the measurement and interpretation of productivity. The important point is that measured productivity is usually the consequence of a mixture of long-run and short-run forces and that it is often difficult to make accurate separate estimates of these forces.

The most important long-run force behind productivity growth is technical change. Some technological change may originate in Canada, but most of it will be developed elsewhere in the world, although it can still benefit Canadians. The second section stresses the importance of long-run technical change and the difficulties of influencing its rate.

Productivity growth in Canada and the rest of the world has been slower during the last decade than in the two that preceded it, and concern has been expressed that this was an unusual situation, one which could not be adequately explained. In the third section, I will discuss some of the literature dealing with this issue.[1] For our purposes, the important question is simply: How convincing is the evidence that there has been a slowdown in the productivity growth rate? If we were to project a slowdown for the next quarter century, it would imply a lower growth of real income for Canadians.

TABLE 1-1 Growth of Labour Productivity, Canada and the United States (average annual percentage)

Canada		Long Run[a]	United States	
1891–1910	1.07		1889–1909	1.97
1910–26	1.21		1909–29	1.95
1926–56	3.12		1929–57	2.42

| | Medium Run[b] | | | |
| | 1961–73 | | 1973–79 | |
	United States	Canada	United States	Canada
Agriculture	4.6	6.7	3.6	0.7
Mining	2.2	5.0	−5.2	−6.9
Communications	4.6	5.2	5.8	6.7
Manufacturing	2.6	4.6	0.6	2.3

Source: a. M. Denny and M. Fuss, *Productivity: A Selective Survey of Recent Developments and the Canadian Experience* (Toronto: Ontario Economic Council, 1982), Tables 2 and 11.
b. A. Sharpe, "A Comparative Analysis of the Canadian and American Productivity Slowdown" (1983, mimeo.), Table 3.

In the fourth section, I review what little evidence there is and discuss some hypotheses about why some countries have high rates of productivity growth. This discussion will raise issues for future research and, at the same time, provide quandaries for policy makers. The final section makes a few suggestions for policy makers, although it is difficult to give exact advice on ways to improve productivity growth.

Before we begin, a little historical perspective will be useful. Canada has one of the highest per capita incomes in the world, and in general terms, our productivity growth has been adequate, although not spectacular. Tables 1-1 and 1-2 provide some evidence of our long- and medium-run growth in labour productivity and the relative levels of total factor productivity as compared with three other countries.[2] Over long periods of time, our productivity growth has not been substantially worse than that of the United States. The level of our productivity, however, tends to be lower, and, at different times, one country may do better in terms of growth than the other. Meanwhile, the countries with rapidly growing economies, such as Japan and West Germany, have been catching up with North America; the United Kingdom, in contrast, is the prime example of a country that is catching up relatively slowly. Unfortunately, it is extremely difficult to isolate the reasons for the superior productivity of one country compared to another. Our goal should probably be to retain our productivity position in relation to the United States. Any attempt to raise our productivity growth to that of the expanding nations is unlikely to succeed.

TABLE 1-2 Relative Levels of Total Factor Productivity (U.S. = 100.0)

	Canada	United Kingdom	Germany	Japan
1950	82.0	—	46.2	44.9
1955	83.2	66.8	60.9	44.9
1965	85.9	67.7	78.5	60.4
1970	91.4	74.2	90.9	77.8

Source: M. Denny and M. Fuss, *Productivity: A Selective Survey of Recent Developments and the Canadian Experience* (Toronto: Ontario Economic Council, 1982), Tables 2 and 11.

Productivity: Conceptual Snares

It is useful to make a few clarifying remarks about the conceptual snares surrounding the measurement of productivity. Because of the broad and loose manner in which the term productivity is frequently interpreted and used, the result is often confusion and fruitless discussion. In its widest sense, productivity is simply a ratio of aggregate output to aggregate input. This is the form of productivity that is most widely understood. However, it is difficult to link this definition directly to economic theory because, even at this level of generality, the variation in the definitions of output and the list of inputs creates confusion when comparing empirical evidence.

Productivity as a ratio of aggregates is an average concept that tends to upset the economic purist. Although behaviour may be determined by marginal concepts, average concepts are nevertheless important for descriptive purposes. Productivity is often used as a summary scalar measure of our economic ability to turn resources into outputs. The transformation of inputs into outputs can be affected by a wide variety of influences, and although it is convenient to capture the consequences of all these influences within one overall productivity measure, an enormous price may implicitly be paid for the loss of detailed information. For example, overall measures such as temperature, profits and productivity provide useful summaries, but at the expense of disguising the origins of the levels and changes in the observed values. In other words, knowing the level or rate of change of profits (or productivity) does not tell you why the changes occurred; in fact, it is often impossible to sort out the varied influences that alter productivity. Yet that is often what people wish to know, and consequently, there is a tendency to search for simplistic answers.

In attempting to provide a framework in which to interpret productivity, most economists have borrowed heavily from the theory of production. This has been very useful, although it has left certain problems unresolved. Those who have not appealed to production theory have been left with no theory or at best some non-economic index number theory. In my discussion, I will use production theory.

The simplest, most widely used and understood measure of productivity is labour productivity, and an important conceptual issue can be illustrated with this measure. There is no uniform agreement on how labour should be measured: that is, do we want to measure person-years or -hours, worked or paid, quality-adjusted or not? This leads to two difficulties. First, it is often impossible to compare different studies of productivity because they use different units for labour inputs; and second, a productivity change for some researchers is an input change for others. This latter point is important because policy changes that affect one measure of productivity positively will affect another measure negatively. For example, a policy to aid in the training of workers will not increase productivity if labour input is adjusted for skills, but it will increase productivity if no such adjustment is made.

Among academic economists there is considerable consensus that we ought to measure labour as the use of a resource flow. This suggests that hours worked would be preferable to employment or hours paid. We might also like to measure hours worked in some standard unit of effort if it were possible to measure effort. Using time without an adjustment for effort is a crude compromise required by the limitations of our resources and our means of measurement. It is the failure to have a standard procedure that leads to problems, but they are clearly no worse that the problems of, for example, interpreting corporate income statements.

The measurement of the quality of inputs and outputs is more contentious. Although most economists would probably argue for measuring inputs of constant quality, there are at least some exceptions, such as John Kendrick. The general issue is whether we wish to eliminate changes in the quality of inputs from the measurement of productivity change. For example, if the work force has become more highly trained or educated, should this be treated as a quality adjustment? If it is, then productivity will not rise with an improvement in labour quality. Output will of course rise with the improvement in labour quality, but this will be due to "more" labour being used. If the labour input measure is not adjusted for quality, then productivity will rise with an improvement in labour quality. Remember that output *will* be rising in either case, but in one case the increase will be attributed to a productivity increase and in the other to an increase in the use of resources.

There may be no consensus on this issue, although sometimes if we state the purpose for which we are measuring productivity, it can become clearer which is more useful in a particular situation. For our purposes, it is sufficient to remember that differences such as this hinder a clear understanding of what people mean when they talk about productivity. As mentioned above, the result can be serious problems when different studies are being compared. For this reason we can argue that readers and writers must be more careful in defining the productivity measure that they are considering. It can also be argued that there is some appeal to using growth accounting, which clearly indicates what items are being treated as a change in outputs or inputs and what is included as a productivity change.

I have used labour productivity to illustrate a problem that applies to all measures of productivity. Moreover, in discussing the quality issue, the lack of agreement about how to adjust empirically for changes in quality has deliberately been avoided. This difficulty will exist regardless of whether quality adjustments are included in, or excluded from, measured productivity.

Although labour productivity is the most widely used concept, there has been a steady movement toward using Total Factor Productivity (TFP) measures. The trend is widespread at the conceptual level but is hindered in practice by a lack of understanding of the concept by policy makers and perhaps more seriously by the increased need for data to measure TFP. In many cases the data are either not available at all or are slow to be available and may contain errors.

The switch to TFP can be explained simply with reference to labour productivity. Suppose outputs are produced using labour, capital and other purchased inputs, called materials. Labour productivity rises because of increases in TFP and increases in the capital-labour and materials-labour ratios. By switching to TFP, we are concentrating on productivity measures that exclude the growth in factor intensity, for example, the capital-labour ratio, as a source of productivity growth. The choice between the two productivity concepts may be based on the particular purpose in hand.

In discussing TFP, I have implicitly opened up one further conceptual issue — whether output is to be measured as gross or net output. In the example above, we were using gross output. When we are considering the whole economy, however, the usual practice is to measure the output flowing to final demand, i.e., net output. Although there have been many erroneous things said about double counting in the use of gross output, this is not the place to argue the case. Suffice it to say that in almost all situations gross output measures can be justified. The difficulties with net output measures arise from their interpretation in production theory. It is unlikely that the separability requirements for net output measurement are satisfied. In practice, this implies that the net output measures we use are difficult to justify. We will not pursue this question further except to note that the prevalence of different output measures further confounds the attempts to compare empirical estimates.

It may be argued that the discussion of the prospects for productivity does not depend on the resolution of the arcane problems described in this section. But it is my somewhat bitter experience that conceptual confusion about productivity seriously hinders many practical discussions.

Technical Progress

In the long run it is technical progress that drives the improvements in our standard of living. Other reasons for TFP growth may be important in the short or medium run, but they do not seem as important in the long run. If we accept this definition as a useful starting point, what can be said about our future prospects?

Although there have always been those willing to argue that scientific discoveries are facing diminishing returns, these arguments do not seem particularly convincing. I would not rate the likelihood of sharply diminishing returns to scientific endeavours as one of the world's serious problems.[3] Admittedly, we could argue that economists have no special talent for foreseeing the technological future, but the obvious extension is that no group has a monopoly on forecasting the technological future. Nor is there much consensus. We are left, I believe, in the position that we do not know. It is very easy to destroy arguments that attempt to paint a known negative or positive future because so much is uncertain. If we are willing to argue against any bleak forecast, our argument must be based on a combination of this uncertainty and the fact that there are large areas of knowledge in which advances continue to be rapid. That is not to say that the future will be bright: we simply do not know.

We should not conclude that there is nothing to be done. The payoffs for supporting research have been uncertain, and that will continue to be the case. The process of deciding on support for research should remind us of the difficulties inherent in any simple description of our technological future. At any moment there are research directions with very different a priori expected payoffs and of course there is always the possibility of successful gambles. Any simple prediction about the technological future either has to be based on the strategic importance of a few discoveries or must cover a bewildering array of possibilities. But it is very difficult to foresee which discoveries will be of strategic importance. Even with hindsight there are still significant difficulties.

The arguments for a known technological future are further weakened by the range of technological possibilities that may be built on our current scientific knowledge. Moreover, it takes a long time for scientific knowledge to be fully exploited as technology for production. At the same time, engineering advances and their practical applications may carry us a long way even if basic science falters.

We understand very little about the processes by which new knowledge is discovered and put into commercial production and use. There are studies of the diffusion of new technologies and case studies of the development of major techniques, but the diversity of detailed innovations makes it difficult to measure changes and the effects of these changes at the micro level except in case studies. There has been a tendency to use information on patents and R&D expenditure as available indicators of activities associated with technical change. However, it is quite difficult to link these indicators to measures of productivity change, and only limited success has been achieved.

The literature[4] suggests that innovations resulting from R&D can improve productivity but that the exact relationships in the process are not well established. There is some evidence that, in the United States, government-sponsored R&D has a different impact on productivity growth in the private sector than privately funded R&D. Expenditures on R&D are investments in a stock, and the returns to that stock over time are evident although not precisely captured in most of the available statistics.

If there is a battleground for disputes about the future of technology, it is more directly in the applied areas that we should concentrate. Among others, Don Daly in Canada and Bela Gold in the United States have argued that the productivity problems revolve around the development and adoption of successful commercial designs and not basic research. More will be said about this topic in a later section.

For government policies to be effective they will have to continue to support, directly through subsidies and indirectly by fostering private incentives, the range of activities from basic research to commercial production. We must continue to evaluate the social and private returns to continued invention, adaptation and adoption of new techniques because this is the most likely way that productivity can be improved in the long run.

The Great Productivity Slowdown

The fifteen years since 1970 have been bitter times for productivity growth. Around the world and in various countries and industries, productivity growth has been slower than the average experienced before 1970. There is no doubt that the 1970s will be considered years in which most sectors of the world economy did not realize the productivity growth expected at the beginning of the decade. Table 1-3 shows some numerical examples of the decline in the growth of labour productivity in the manufacturing industries in developed countries. Table 1-1 presented evidence for other industries in Canada and the United States.

There have been a number of attempts to assess what went wrong during the slowdown. I have argued elsewhere (Denny and Fuss, 1982) that we do not know why the slowdown occurred,[5] and there is no need in this paper to reconsider the full line of arguments. What is important is to know if the analyses of the slowdown suggests new policies for

TABLE 1-3 Labour Productivity in Manufacturing, 1960–73, 1974–81

	1960–73	1974–81	Change
Japan	10.8	6.8	−4.0
Holland	7.5	5.2	−2.3
Italy	7.0	3.7	−3.3
Sweden	7.0	2.0	−5.0
France	5.8	4.2	−1.6
Germany	5.0	4.0	−1.0
Canada	4.0	1.0	−3.0
United Kingdom	3.8	1.3	−2.5
United States	2.7	1.1	−1.6

Source: OECD, quoted in A. Sharpe, "A Review of the Productivity Slowdown Literature" (1982, mimeo.).

enhancing productivity growth. I believe that these studies do not provide convincing evidence that new policy directions are needed.

Five Studies of the Slowdown

To indicate the variety of arguments about the slowdown, I want briefly to consider five studies. The first two, by Helliwell (1985) and Darby (1984), argue that there was no slowdown with any long-run consequence. The other three, by Nordhaus (1982), Sharpe (1982) and Mohr (1983), argue that there has been a slowdown that might or does have long-run consequences.

In his study for this Royal Commission, which is the second paper in the present volume, Helliwell (1985) has argued that the MACE econometric model suggests that there was no slowdown in productivity, i.e., in labour efficiency. In other words, the observed slowdown in the usual measures of labour productivity did not signal the beginning of a new era of slower productivity growth. Rather, the slowdown can be explained within the model as the result of lower levels of capacity utilization and higher unemployment. The model supports the hypothesis that labour efficiency, which is the concept of interest for the long run, did not fall. There is more limited support for the hypothesis that productivity growth has a component associated with catching up with advanced practices and that this component may have fallen. Although the arguments are developed in a slightly different manner, the results are similar to Helliwell (1983).

Darby (1984) has argued from a very different perspective that the slowdown in U.S. productivity is a statistical illusion. His conclusions are based on the presumed existence of errors in the usual measures of labour input. When these errors are corrected, the slowdown disappears. The errors in the usual labour measures occur because the weights used to aggregate labour of different quality are wrong. The recent slowdown in productivity, as conventionally measured, is also affected by the price control program that occurred under President Nixon, which resulted in an erroneous measurement of output in the mid-1970s. Darby has convinced few economists because his strong assumptions about aggregation weights are not backed up with sufficient research and they conflict with other results based on the mismeasurement of labour. (See, for example, Chinloy, 1980 and 1981; Canada, 1980.)

Nordhaus (1982), in contrast, argued that there had indeed been a slowdown in productivity. Like Darby (1984), he was analyzing the U.S. economy and considering the long-run evidence over most of the 20th century. One interesting hypothesis he investigated was the possibility that, historically, average productivity growth was subject to substantial variation. Since this is true for the United States, then the recent period of low productivity growth is simply a bad draw, but one that should be expected every few decades. I believe that this argument can be supported by evidence from Canada and other countries and deserves further research. As I discussed above, productivity growth, particularly at the aggregate level, is subject to myriad forces and we should expect substantial unexplained variations.

Nordhaus attempts to quantify the causes for the 2.5 percent decline in average productivity growth after 1973, i.e., 1973–80, in relation to the period before 1965. Using relatively simple estimates and borrowing from others, he estimates that 60 percent of the decline in growth can be attributed to specific causes: cyclical (12 percent), slower capital stock growth (12 percent), energy prices (8 percent), regulation (8 percent), decline in R&D (4 percent), demographic shifts in the labour force (4 percent), and sectoral shifts (12 percent). Many of these factors will appear in other estimates, but in all cases there is a significant amount of judgment about the relative importance of different factors. Nordhaus's quantification of the specific factors does not conflict with his earlier point about the long-run variability of productivity growth. Rather, the estimates are an attempt to assess what occurred in this particular slowdown.

Sharpe (1982) and Mohr (1983) are summary articles that survey the estimates and use judgment to estimate the importance of various causes of the slowdown. Their conclusions are presented in Table 1-4. Mohr estimates that 10 to 20 percent of the aggregate slowdown can be attributed to shifts in the relative importance of different industries and the remainder to declines within particular industries. Like Nordhaus, he assigns some importance to regulation and the decline in labour quality. The main source of the slowdown is the decline in output growth, which Mohr associates with macroeconomic policy. The capital growth factor is also related to demand management. Sharpe's judgment about Canada also places heavy emphasis on the decline in output growth and on shifts in the relative importance of different sectors.

**TABLE 1-4 Sources of the Slowdown in Productivity Growth,
Canada and the United States**

	Percentage
United States[a]	
Intrasectoral and intersectoral decomposition	
Declines in productivity growth within sectors	80–90
Changes in the industrial composition of output and labour	10–20
	100
Factor decomposition	
Output growth	40–60
Capital growth	25–35
Labour quality	4–10
Regulation	8–12
Unexplained	20–50
	100
Canada[b]	
Output growth decline	50
Compositional shifts	20
Other significant factors:	
Energy prices	—
Regulation	
Natural resource depletion	
Increased frequency of shocks	

Sources: a. M. Mohr, "Diagnosing the Productivity Problem and Developing an RX for Improving the Prognosis" (Washington, D.C.: U.S. Department of Commerce, 1983, mimeo.), p. 11.
　　　　　b. A. Sharpe, "A Review of the Productivity Slowdown Literature" (1982, mimeo.).

We do not have to agree with any of these studies in detail to find useful material for our purposes. These papers and many others agree that much of the decline in productivity growth is associated with short- or medium-run factors that will probably be reversed as economic growth returns. There are three points that we can usefully draw from these diverse studies.

- A large part of the slowdown can be attributed to short- to medium-run factors associated with the failure of macroeconomic policy or cyclical factors.
- There are no specific long-run factors that have been identified as significant major causes of a long-run productivity slowdown.
- Some unexplained decline in productivity probably remains, but it has been difficult to isolate the many factors that may be the cause. Alternatively, it may be that the 1970s were simply one of the recurring historical periods with low rates of productivity growth.

There are many aspects of the productivity decline that should be addressed directly rather than by considering one study after another. We will consider a variety of these issues below.

Other Aspects of the Slowdown

The growth of labour productivity moves with the business cycle. Changes in input quantities, at least in the form in which we currently measure them, do not move as quickly as output changes. In the very short run, we can assume that sharp movements in productivity are cyclical. In fact, there have been some attempts to explain the slowdown as predominantly a cyclical phenomenon, but as the length of the slowdown grows, this type of explanation becomes more difficult. The continued investigation of the slowdown is driven by the fear that we are embedded in a long-run slowdown that is not associated with any cycle. Unfortunately, the studies that have attempted to separate the cyclical from the non-cyclical components of the slowdown suffer from several problems. There is no easy definition of a standard cycle and, consequently, the method that has been used can be criticized for being relatively arbitrary. Certainly the techniques have not been very robust and there may be no robust techniques available. The results support the importance of cyclical effects in providing a rationale for part of the slowdown. In the few cases in which most of the slowdown has been "explained" by cyclical effects, the results depend on the period selected and the methods used to determine the cyclical component. I think that any consensus that exists would reject the cycle as a satisfactory single explanation of the slowdown. Given our measurement problems, the most that can be said is that an important, if unknown, portion of the measured slowdown is related to cyclical movements in output. If the slowdown is to be completely explained, other factors must be considered.

Even though the cycle cannot eliminate the fear that we face a more permanent reduction in productivity growth, there have been occasional arguments that there has been no slowdown. This assertion can be interpreted in several ways. Sometimes the argument has been about aggregation and sometimes it has involved measurement problems. There is enough evidence at all levels of aggregation in Canada and other countries to eliminate any aggregation arguments, for it is clear that there has been a slowdown in productivity in most industries at all levels of aggregation. Some of the slowdown can be accounted for by shifts of resources between industries, but the available evidence does not support any contention that the slowdown is a reflection of aggregation and the shifting of resources between industries alone. A number of studies[6] suggest that labour productivity at the aggregate level has been significantly diminished by the slow growth in high-productivity sectors in relation to low-productivity sectors. Other studies deny that this is the case. One reason for not placing too much emphasis on this explanation is that in the United States and Canada there is abundant evidence that most industries have suffered from slower labour productivity and probably much slower TFP growth since 1970 (see Denny and Fuss, 1982; Mohr, 1983; and Sharpe, 1982, 1983).

An example of the problems of the research on the slowdown can be illustrated with the first two factors that we have discussed: cyclical and sectoral shifts. The business cycle is almost always investigated as an aggregate effect, and the search for sectoral shifts is a study of aggregation effects. Yet the latter investigation is usually done without first pursuing the disaggregated cyclical effects. We know that this will confuse the shift effects with the cycle since the latter does not have the same timing or magnitude in different industries.

Errors in the measurement of inputs and outputs have often been cited as problems in evaluating the slowdown (Canada, 1980; Mohr, 1983). In general, the arguments have failed as explanations for the slowdown. Although there are plenty of difficulties with the data, in most cases they existed before the slowdown and no adequate arguments have been advanced to demonstrate that data problems created the slowdown. Data problems do make it difficult to evaluate the magnitude of the slowdown in different sectors of the economy. There are many industries in which output measurement is deficient, as in services and construction, and the input data are often unavailable for material inputs and of dubious quality in the case of capital. However, considerable attention has been directed to the role in the slowdown of one material input — energy.

Energy and, in particular, the shocks generated by the sharp energy price movements of the 1970s, have offered an appealing, sometimes tantalizing, explanation for the slowdown. The attempts to make a convincing case for the energy shocks as a major explanation of the slowdown have not succeeded. I believe a consensus could be reached on this point. At the same time, there remain strong beliefs that, while the links have not been pinned down as easily as many had hoped and believed, they still exist and await some judicious revelation.

The worldwide nature of the productivity slowdown and the fact that it apparently began in the 1970s suggested that some shock to the world economy was responsible. The oil problems of the 1970s were certainly a shock, and the timing was apparently correct. But more detailed investigations foundered on two difficulties. The timing simply does not correspond as well as some casual impressions might suggest,[7] and the mechanisms that might cause a productivity slowdown to result from a sharp energy price increase do not seem to be able to provide effects with sufficiently large magnitude.[8] These are microeconomic mechanisms, not macroeconomic phenomena. If the detailed studies of the role of energy have been disappointing, why does there remain a strong residual belief in its importance? It is based on the belief that, although the timing in different industries and countries varies, there remains sufficient correlation to suggest some common worldwide cause. Moreover, few other events have had the high profile of the energy shocks, and thus people are drawn to investigate them further.

Recent Emphasis on Capital

The most recent attempts to link the slowdown with energy have broadened the microeconomic mechanism. New studies (such as Bailey, 1981; Berndt and Fuss, 1981) have concentrated on the effects of energy price increases on the capital stock. Simply put, the argument is that the installed capital has relatively fixed energy consumption characteristics and that the sharp energy price increase reduced the net present value of this stock. But current measurement techniques do not capture this phenomenon. Consequently, the measured stock and/or its cost share is too high, which reduces productivity. This is an ingenious and interesting argument that may advance our understanding, but at present it has been difficult to apply empirically, although some attempts have been made using Tobin's q to revalue the stock.[9] The empirical results that have been obtained provide a partial explanation of the slowdown, but they depend on the validity of the methods used to revalue capital.

The role of capital can be considered further by recalling the relation between labour productivity and TFP. The growth in the capital-labour ratio directly affects the growth of labour productivity. The capital-labour ratio kept growing relatively quickly as output growth slowed down. The slowdown in labour productivity arrived later and, in general, the growth in the capital-labour ratio has not been a predominant source of the slowdown.[10] Some studies give prominence to a slowdown in the capital-labour ratio. These are often studies that adjust capital or labour for cyclical effects, a practice that has been sharply criticized by some. The range of estimates of the importance of the capital-labour ratio is very large. What should be remembered, however, is that TFP growth has slowed down and that slowdown is not due to the capital-labour ratio.

The emphasis on the capital-labour ratio occurs for natural reasons. First, changes in this ratio can be very important in changing labour productivity, if not TFP. Moreover, there have been some interesting patterns in the growth of capital and labour, taken separately at the aggregate level. However, there is very little evidence that the ratio of investment to gross national expenditure (GNE) has been a source of the slowdown; in fact, investment has continued in the face of slow output growth and excess capacity. While this may not be entirely surprising, it does limit the role of capital formation, the pipeline for technical progress, as an explanation of the slowdown. That argument can be partially rescued if the recent investment growth can be linked to "unproductive" investment in anti-pollution equipment. It should be noted, however, that there are only some industries in which a partial role can be assigned to investment generated by environmental regulation. Nevertheless, stories about the slowdown that are based on capital will automatically continue to receive strong interest and support because capital investment is the mechanism through which many technical improvements are put in place. This mechanism is also thought to be amenable to policies fostering savings and investment.

Whereas stories about capital have maintained their fascination, there has probably been a decline in the emphasis on labour tales as the slowdown has persisted. Darby (1984) is the recent exception. In earlier studies, Kendrick, Denison, and Jorgenson and Griliches had made adjustments for labour quality an issue in productivity measurement. That is because the 1970s were characterized by a rapid growth of the labour force, an increase in the proportion of women, and a decline in the workers' average age. If the wage rate is used to weight the labour categories, then these demographic and behavioural trends will tend to reduce productivity growth. The continued growth in the educational levels attained will tend to increase productivity. Although these effects can be measured, they have not played a large part in the slowdown.

This may be an appropriate place to note one problem that has worsened as the number of studies and the length of the slowdown increase. If no one has found convincing evidence for a "single-factor" theory of the slowdown, many studies have been able to attribute part of the slowdown to a few of the wide variety of factors. Once we begin with the hypothesis that the slowdown is multi-faceted, it becomes difficult to judge particular empirical results. There are many studies that concentrate on one or a small number of factors while ignoring other factors that some other people have found important. Basically, this creates problems of potential misspecification and spurious correlation. Given the results to this stage, studies ought to begin by consistently evaluating the joint effects of many factors. Unfortunately, this is not done, and some uneasiness must greet new results on some particular factor when other factors are ignored. Having said this, I will consider briefly below the wide range of factors that have arisen in the debate.

One of the earliest and most extensive studies of the slowdown was by Denison (1979). He not only considered the usual factors but compiled a list of possible reasons for the slowdown which incorporated many reasons expressed in business and the press. Some of these items have been discussed already, but a complete list may be helpful:

- curtailment of expenditures on R&D;
- decline in the opportunity for new advances;
- decline in Yankee ingenuity and the deterioration of U.S. technology;

- increased lag in the application of capital owing to the aging of capital;
- diversion of input to comply with government regulations;
- government-imposed paperwork;
- regulation and taxation — diversion of executives' attention;
- government regulation leading to delay of new projects;
- regulation and taxation — misallocation of resources;
- the effects of high taxes on incentives;
- capital gains provision of the 1969 Revenue Act;
- demise of the work ethic;
- impairment of efficiency by inflation;
- lessening of competitive pressure and changes in the quality of management;
- rise in energy prices;
- shift to services and other structural changes; and
- possible errors in data.

Denison concluded after a brief investigation that there did not seem to be any convincing evidence of a major role for any of these factors. He did, however, urge that a more serious investigation of many of them be undertaken. Unfortunately many of the suggested reasons remain unresearched and the ones that have received more attention have not yielded convincing results.

Summary

What can we learn from these efforts to explain the slowdown? In particular, what can we learn that will help us forecast the future? The points that we made earlier are not altered sharply by our more detailed discussion of the slowdown. First, there remains the possibility that we should expect a slowdown every two or three decades. For example, the 20 years following World War II were decades of extremely rapid productivity growth, but these rates could not be maintained. This type of argument needs further research for many countries. Second, the decline in productivity is not new in kind and therefore policy makers do not need new special policies to cope with it. That is good news, for there are always many difficulties in translating policy suggestions into programs that will increase productivity and new problems are not welcome. While we do not fully understand the productivity growth during the 1970s, there were many factors at work and they do not signal a new dismal epoch. Thus, policy makers can concentrate on the issues surrounding productivity that will be with us, in varying strengths, at all times.

The struggles to understand the slowdown should remind us of the complexity of the phenomena that are being captured in most simple productivity measures. Productivity growth can be altered by a vast range of activities. As Gold (1981) has argued, at the level of the firm, it is enormously handy to compress the consequences of these diverse changes into a simple summary measure, but it is potentially misleading. When we have to untangle the sources of productivity change, we cannot avoid the complexities that we initially side-stepped in creating the measure.

Why Do Some Units Do Better?

This section provides a research agenda for the future and examines some key policy problems. The word "unit" is used here to mean a plant, a firm, an industry, a region or a country. Doing better in this context means that a unit has higher levels and/or rates of growth of productivity, and countries that do better must have plants, firms, industries and regions that do better.

If we begin at the level of the plant or firm, what evidence exists? It is very limited owing to data problems, although several interesting studies are in progress at the moment.[11] The author has taken part in one firm-level study in telecommunications in which large differences do occur, but it is very difficult to obtain information or pin down the underlying processes generating the results. Consider an industry in which there are many firms whose income statements and balance sheets are available. In almost all cases, the profitability in the short and long run between these firms will be quite different. In studying productivity, we are attempting to separate the effects of prices for inputs and outputs from productivity in determining profitability. Since the comparability of products will be a considerable problem in any detailed study, it is perhaps not surprising that data problems and the complexity of the forces affecting productivity have defied a successful explanation of differentials in productivity levels and rates of growth.[12]

It is at this low level of aggregation that certain investigators insist the productivity problem must be attacked. It is tautological that productivity at any level of aggregation depends on the decisions made at the lowest level of disaggregation. Academic, labour, and indigenous observers of business tend to stress problems at this level because it matches their interests. Economists who treat most of the internal operations of the firm as a "black box" will focus at wider industry, regional or country levels. For the policy maker, it is important to know at what level of aggregation policies must be fine-tuned to be effective.

If we move from firms to industries, we are aggregating specific differentials over the firm. There are industry productivity differentials between industries in different regions and countries. An important unanswered question is the following: Are the observed industry differentials between regions (or countries) affected by government policies and, if so, which policies?

The available evidence suggests that there are interregional differences in Canada but, in manufacturing at least, my impression is that they are not increasing significantly and that all regions have benefited from productivity growth.[13] We might add a caution that the data are sufficiently weak that this conclusion could be overthrown with better data. Comparing Canada with the United States, there is substantial evidence that there are level differences between the two countries in many industries, although Canada's position is not consistently inferior (see Frank, 1977; Denny and Fuss, 1982).

The open question regarding the differences in productivity both between regions and between Canada and the United States is whether there are existing government policies that are responsible for the differences or alternative policies that might close the differences in level. The most likely possibilities are trade and competition policies.[14]

At the industry level, it is perhaps more obvious than at the country level that the opportunities for productivity gain in different industries are not the same. Unfortunately, there are few studies that go beyond this level. Information is needed on the sources of the differential opportunities to ensure that what may seem to be obvious is, in fact, true. Since industries have different products, the emphasis should be on identifying the source of the differential productivity gains. At the country level, there have been a large number of attempts to measure the productivity differentials between countries, but for the most part without assigning the differentials to any particular sources.

The cross-sectional measurement of productivity differentials is more difficult in practice than the time-series measurement. In other words, there are more data problems and difficulties with comparability across different units than for the same unit through time. Moreover, it is only recently that the comparison of productivity levels, as opposed to rates of growth, has had a very solid theoretical basis.

In recent decades, Japan and West Germany have often been considered as having faster rates of growth of productivity than other countries. But is their performance simply a matter of catching up with the United States? If so, why were they better able to catch up than other countries, such as Britain and Italy? This type of question often elicits unsatisfactory responses based on "national character." If catching up with the United States is not the answer, then what has led to their improved relative performance? As a first approximation, catching up is obviously important in most industries, but for some Japanese and West German industries the catching up is over. The distinction is important for understanding the possibilities available to Canada.

It is very unlikely that long-run rates of productivity growth of the type generated in Japan or West Germany can be sustained in other than a catch-up phase. That is, these countries will slowly find their spectacular productivity growth rates falling. If this hypothesis is false, then the world is about to experience a productivity boom such as we have never seen before, and that seems unlikely. If it were the case, our problem would be to find a way of catching up.

If Canada looks weak compared to the high flyers that are catching up to Canada and the United States, the policy issues are different. While the U.S./Canadian productivity differentials are not trivial, they are not growing sharply, and I believe they represent a different problem. Canada does not have to catch up with the United States to the degree that either West Germany or Japan has done or to the extent that recent high flyers, such as South Korea, may be doing.

I would suggest two important questions for Canada: first, how do we adapt to the catching up by other countries, and second, how do we maintain our productivity at levels that are within reach of the best performances? The transition to a wider competition may eliminate some rents currently buried in our real incomes,[15] but if the organizational and technical capabilities are assembled at low prices in new industrialized nations, adjustments will continue to be thrust upon us.

D.J. Daly has for many years been in the forefront of those who have argued that productivity requires more direct government attention than it has received. The recent proposal to form a national productivity centre is partially due to Daly's persistent arguments, which are directed toward the question of why some units do better. Daly argues that the basic productivity problem is not the recent slowdown in productivity growth and, moreover, is not the failure of demand management. Rather, he places the problem on the supply side. An inadequate business management operating in an unsuitable government policy environment has combined to produce what Daly calls a high-cost–low productivity result. The basis of his approach is his comparison at the disaggregated firm level, of the differences in productivity between Canadian firms and those in other countries.

The types of questions that Daly raises are very important. He belongs to the free-trade camp in the sense that he believes that any nationalist policy which limits domestic competition (and potentially limits our access to foreign markets) contributes to Canada's low productivity. Canada needs world-class firms able to operate successfully in the international marketplace. Canada's failures are due to a lack of specialization and a slowness to adopt new techniques and the best management and labour practices. In other words, either the protected environment alone or that environment in conjunction with institutional barriers and national character have left Canada in a relatively poor productivity position.

In many ways, Daly can be interpreted as stating that the core of the productivity problem is at the firm level, although that does not imply that it is the firm's fault. The government's role is limited to its ability to create the right environment for the firm. Daly argues that Canadian firms need a commercial policy that fosters competitiveness, and trade and taxation policies that reward innovation; the country does not need a massive industrial strategy or a huge science policy. He is suspicious of the government's ability to pick winners and believes that it is not basic research but the concrete adoption of best practices that is important.

Daly's position has much to recommend it, although it needs much better documentation and research that would establish the importance of this approach compared to others.

Doing Better

Like most observers, I believe that even without any radical change in government policy, our productivity will be higher during the next decade than it was during the last. While we do not have a full or convincing explanation of the slowdown, the evidence seems to preclude a long-run productivity slowdown of several more decades. At the same time, the expected improvement in productivity growth is modest. It will not place us among the world leaders in national productivity growth, and it may not permit a productivity growth rate as high as we achieved from 1948 to 1968.

The early postwar decades, when judged against the historical record, were years of unusually high productivity growth that may not be repeated in the 1980s and 1990s. Thus, we should expect that our productivity performance will be similar to that of the United States but much lower than South Korea or Japan. Within Canada, the individual regions can expect productivity growth that is dependent on their mix of industries. However, there is no evidence that productivity is or will be very different in the various regions of the country.

The world leaders in productivity growth are those countries that are rapidly catching up with the developing countries. The challenge from these countries has several dimensions, which provide opportunities as well as threats. The potential for growth of worldwide productivity will remain substantial; our task is to find ways to participate in this growth with minimal damage. Countries such as Japan and South Korea will provide new low-cost supplies for both our consumers and some of our producers. These countries and others, will force adjustments on Canadian industries that will be painful in some cases. However, there is no sensible long-run way to avoid these adjustments, although we can alter the size and the distribution of the adjustment costs.

The continued growth of new industrial countries will create a more dynamic international market. Canada will benefit through an increased demand for some of our products that will result from higher real world incomes. New knowledge and products will provide both increases in real income and production opportunities for Canadian entrepreneurs. We may find that we will lose some rents in our current incomes. This loss is most likely to be in relative rather than absolute incomes. However, to the extent that sharp shifts in our trade patterns occur, absolute declines are possible, although unlikely, for the population as a whole. The argument may be briefly outlined. Given the legal and cultural restrictions on international migration, workers with the same skills have very different incomes in different countries. These income differentials are predominantly determined by the differences in the skill, capital and resource bases in different countries. As other countries increase their skill and capital bases, the income gap will close between Canada and developing countries. In this process, some of the rents in our income may be eliminated since other countries' capabilities will more closely match our own. But this does not necessarily imply a lower real income for Canadians.

We must pursue a strategy that accepts the continuing adjustment to changing competition on a worldwide scale. I do not have a detailed list of policies that can be strongly recommended, but the following deserve serious consideration.

Macro Management   There is a chicken-and-egg problem with output growth and productivity. Measured productivity growth moves sharply with short-run cycles. As a first approximation, the loss in potential output due to the underuse of resources is partly picked up by the productivity measure. In the long run, productivity advances through technical developments that fuel output growth. It is in the medium run, two to five years, where there is uncertainty about the interaction between output growth and productivity. In addition, there is uncertainty about the influence of cycles on productivity. Do we lose more than the potential output for the cycle period? That is, do we diminish potential output in the future? The mechanisms linking inflation cycles and unemployment to long-run productivity growth are poorly understood. There is some belief that an improved macro performance would enhance our productivity performance, but is this true? How can we improve the macro management? The failure of most countries to reach relatively full resource utilization during the 1970s is a clear weakness that needs to be overcome.

International Trade   A widespread consensus exists among economists that we must continue expanding our efforts to eliminate international trade barriers since trade is our source of the larger markets for specialized products and competition.

Domestic Competition   A country of Canada's size must depend on trade for competition in many areas. However, there are large sectors of the economy in which international trade will play only a small role. In these sectors, we must work to reduce internal trade barriers in an attempt to strengthen competition. The mature industrial economies are becoming service economies, and it is efficiency in these industries that will dominate our long-run prospects. Many of these service industries are more protected and regulated than the non-service industries. The goods sector will be less important except to the extent that the potential for exports can be realized.

Notes

This study was completed in November 1984.

I would like to thank the participants in productivity workshops in Canada and the United States for their comments. Don McFetridge was an able, patient and supportive guide in the creation of the report. The opinions expressed in the paper, however, are my own.

1. A relatively complete catalogue of studies is contained in Sharpe (1982).

2. The exact comparison chosen will tend to give somewhat different results. For example, see Denny and Fuss (1982), Tables 2, 10 and 11.

3. I agree with the critical comments by Mansfield (1983) and Rosenberg and Frischtak (1983) on the recent upsurge of arguments in regard to innovations and long-run savings in economic growth.

4. An overview of this literature can be ascertained by Terleckyi (1980), Griliches (1980), Scherer (1983), Piekarz (1983), and the references they cite.

5. A useful and extensive bibliography of studies, with comments, can be found in Sharpe (1982).

6. Mohr (1983) provides detailed evidence for the United States which allocates 80 percent of the TFP slowdown to declines within industries. Sharpe (1982) summarizes the Canadian estimates. More casual observers such as Thurow have attempted to attribute 40 percent to shifts between industries. In both Canada and the United States the best estimates are 15 to 20 percent.

7. This is true for both the United States (see Mohr, 1983) and Canada (see Denny and Fuss, 1982).

8. The crucial point here is the small proportion of energy in total costs. It does not preclude macroeconomic hypotheses of energy feeding through aggregate demand management.

9. Tobin's $q \times 3$ is the ratio of the market value to the replacement value of the stock. Most empirical work has used the average q value, although theoretically it is the marginal q that is required (but unavailable). The estimation of the replacement value of the stock is subject to substantial difficulty.

10. There is some dispersion across industries and countries. For Canadian manufacturing, see Denny and Fuss (1982). For broader industrial coverage, see Sharpe (1982, 1983) and Mohr (1983).

11. Much of this work is concentrated at, or coordinated by, the Economic Council of Canada.

12. These difficulties are the major limitation on any strategy that suggests that the government can pick winners as an industrial strategy. If the markets for shares are efficient and yet follow a random walk, then it is clear that the best estimate of the value of the firm today is a poor estimate of the value of the firm tomorrow. Governments cannot do better than the market.

13. For some examples, see Denny, Fuss, and May (1981).

14. Daly's submission to the Royal Commission (1985) is an example. Additional studies have been done by Saunders (1981) and Bernhardt (1981).

15. At the moment, this is an unsubstantiated hypothesis. The rents or quasi-rents are easily illustrated in mining. Less obvious may be rents in lawyers' income or wages in general.

Bibliography

Auer, L. 1969. "Canadian Agricultural Productivity." Economic Council of Canada Staff Study 24. Ottawa: Queen's Printer.

_____. 1979. *Regional Disparities of Productivity and Growth in Canada.* Study prepared for the Economic Council of Canada. Ottawa: Minister of Supply and Services Canada.

Bailey, M.N. 1981. "Productivity and the Services of Capital and Labor." *Brookings Papers on Economic Activity* 1: 1–50.

Berndt, E., and M.A. Fuss. 1981. "Productivity Measurement Using Capital Asset Valuation to Adjust for Variations in Utilization." Working Paper 8125. Toronto: University of Toronto, Institute for Policy Analysis.

Berndt, E., and M. Khalad. 1979. "Parametric Productivity Measurement and Choice Among Flexible Functional Forms." *Journal of Political Economy* 87: 1220–45.

Berndt, E., and G.C. Watkins. 1981. "Energy Prices and Productivity Trends in the Canadian Manufacturing Sector, 1957–76: Some Exploratory Results." Ottawa: Economic Council of Canada.

Bernhardt, I. 1981. "Sources of Productivity Differences Among Canadian Manufacturing Industries." *Review of Economics and Statistics* 63: 503–12.

Bernstein, J. 1985. "Research and Development, Patents, and Grant and Tax Policies in Canada." In *Technological Change in Canadian Industry*, volume 3 of the research studies prepared for the Royal Commission on the Economic Union and Development Prospects for Canada. Toronto: University of Toronto Press.

Canada. 1976a. Department of Industry, Trade and Commerce. Office of Policy Analysis. "An Analysis of Regional Productivity Variation in Canadian Manufacturing Industries." Ottawa: The Department, mimeo.

_____. 1976b. Department of Industry, Trade and Commerce. Office of Policy Analysis. "Productivity and Competitiveness in the Canadian Economy." Ottawa: The Department, mimeo.

_____. 1980. Department of Finance. "Recent Changes in Patterns of Productivity Growth in Canada." Ottawa: The Department.

Caves, R.E. 1975. *Diversification, Foreign Investment and Scale in North American Industries.* Study prepared for the Economic Council of Canada. Ottawa: Information Canada.

Caves, D.W., and L. Christensen. 1980. "The Relative Efficiency of Private and Public Firms in a Competitive Environment: The Case of Canadian Railroads." *Journal of Political Economy* 88: 958–76.

Caves, D.W., L. Christensen, and W.E. Diewert. 1982. "Multilateral Comparisons of Output, Input, and Productivity Using Superlative Index Numbers." *Economic Journal* 92: 73–86.

Caves, D.W., L. Christensen, and M. Tretheway. 1981. "U.S. Trunk Air Carriers, 1972–77: A Multilateral Comparison of Total Factor Productivity." In *Productivity Measurement in Regulated Industries*, edited by T.G. Cowing and R.E. Stevenson. New York: Academic Press, pp. 47–76.

Caves, R.E., M.E. Porter, and A.M. Spence, with J.T. Scott. 1980. *Competition in the Open Economy: A Model Applied to Canada.* Cambridge, Mass.: Harvard University Press.

Chinloy, P. 1980. "Sources of Quality Change in Labor Input." *American Economic Review* 70: 108–20.

_____. 1981. *Labour Productivity.* Cambridge, Mass.: Abt Books.

Christensen, L.R., D. Cummings, and D.W. Jorgenson. 1980a. "Economic Growth, 1947–73." In *New Developments in Productivity Measurement and Analysis*, edited by J.W. Kendrick and B. Vaccara. Chicago: University of Chicago Press.

_____. 1980b. "Relative Productivity Levels, 1947–73: An International Comparison." Discussion Paper 773. Cambridge, Mass.: Harvard University.

Clark, P. 1978. "Capital Formation and the Recent Productivity Slowdown." *Journal of Finance* 33: 965–75.

Cowing, T., and R. Stevenson. 1981. *Productivity Measurement in Regulated Industries.* New York: Academic Press.

Daly, D.J. 1985. "Rationalization and Specialization in Canadian Manufacturing." In *Canadian Industry in Transition*, volume 2 of the research studies prepared for the Royal Commission and the Economic Union and Development Prospects for Canada. Toronto: University of Toronto Press.

Daly, D.J., and D. Walters. 1967. "Factors in Canada–U.S. Real Income Differences." *International Review of Income and Wealth* 13 (December): 285–309.

Daly, D.J., B.A. Keys, and E.J. Spence. 1968. *Scale and Specialization in Canadian Manufacturing.* Economic Council of Canada Staff Study 21. Ottawa: Queen's Printer.

Daly, D., ed. 1983. *Research on Productivity of Relevance to Canada.* Ottawa: Social Science Federation of Canada.

Darby, M. 1984. "The U.S. Productivity Slowdown." *American Economic Review* 74: 301–23.

Denison, E.F. 1962. *The Source of Economic Growth and the Alternatives Before Us.* Supplementary Paper 12. New York: Committee for Economic Development.

_____. 1967. *Why Growth Rates Differ: Postwar Experience in Nine Western Countries.* Washington, D.C.: Brookings Institution.

_____. 1974. *Accounting for U.S. Economic Growth 1929–69.* Washington, D.C.: Brookings Institution.

_____. 1979. *Accounting for Slower Economic Growth: The United States in the 1970's.* Washington, D.C.: Brookings Institution.

Denny, M. 1980. "New Techniques and Recent Evidence on the Levels and Growth of Regional Labour Productivity in Canadian Manufacturing." *Economic Policy Review* 2, PEAP. Toronto: University of Toronto, Institute for Policy Analysis.

Denny, M., A. de Fontenay, and M. Werner. 1982. "Comparing the Efficiency of Firms: Canadian Telecommunications Companies." Working Paper 8204. Toronto: University of Toronto, Institute for Policy Analysis.

Denny, M., and M. Fuss. 1980. "Intertemporal and Interspatial Comparisons of Cost Efficiency and Productivity." Working Paper 8018. Toronto: University of Toronto, Institute for Policy Analysis.

_____. 1982. *Productivity: A Selective Survey of Recent Developments and the Canadian Experience.* Toronto: Ontario Economic Council.

_____. 1983a. "Intertemporal Changes in the Levels of Regional Labour Productivity in Canadian Manufacturing." In *Developments in Econometric Analysis of Productivity*, edited by A. Dogramaci. Boston: Kluwer-Nijhoff.

_____. 1983b. "A General Approach to Intertemporal and Interspatial Productivity Comparisons." *Journal of Econometrics* 23: 315–30.

Denny, M., M. Fuss, C. Everson, and L. Waverman. 1981. "Estimating the Effects of Diffusion of Technological Innovations in Telecommunications: The Production Structure of Bell Canada." *Canadian Journal of Economics* 14: 24–43.

Denny, M., M. Fuss, and C.D. May. 1981. "Intertemporal Changes in Regional Productivity in Canadian Manufacturing." *Canadian Journal of Economics* 14: 390–408.

Denny, M., M. Fuss, and L. Waverman. 1979. *Energy and the Cost Structure of Canadian Manufacturing Industries.* Technical Paper 12. Toronto: University of Toronto, Institute for Policy Analysis.

_____. 1981. "The Measurement and Interpretation of Total Factor Productivity in Regulated Industries, with an Application to Canadian Telecommunications." In *Productivity Measurement in Regulated Industries*, edited by T.G. Cowing and R.E. Stevenson. New York: Academic Press, pp. 179–218.

Denny, M., and J.D. May. 1980. "Regional Productivity in Canadian Breweries." *Canadian Journal of Regional Science* 3: 209–26.

Diewert, W.E. 1976. "Exact and Superlative Index Numbers." *Journal of Econometrics* 4: 115–46.

_____. 1980. "Aggregation Problems in the Measurement of Capital." In *The Measurement of Capital*, edited by D. Usher. Studies in Income and Wealth 45. Chicago: University of Chicago Press, pp. 433–528.

Eastman, H.C., and S. Stykolt. 1967. *The Tariff and Competition in Canada*. Toronto: University of Toronto Press.

Economic Council of Canada. 1975. *Looking Outward: A New Trade Strategy for Canada*. Ottawa: Information Canada.

_____. 1977. *Living Together: A Study of Regional Disparities*. Ottawa: Minister of Supply and Services Canada.

Fowler, D.J. 1976. "A Comparison of the Performance of Canadian and U.S. Manufacturing and Mining Industries." Ph.D. dissertation, University of Toronto.

Frank, J.G. 1977. *Assessing Trends in Canada's Competitive Position*. Ottawa: Conference Board of Canada.

Fraumeni, B. and D. Jorgenson. 1981. "Capital Formation and U.S. Productivity Growth." In *Productivity Analysis: A Range of Perspectives*, edited by A. Dogramaci. Boston: M. Nijhoff Publishing.

Fuss, M. 1980. "Modelling the Cost and Production Structures of Manufacturing Industries." *Economic Policy Review* 2, PEAP. Toronto: University of Toronto, Institute for Policy Analysis.

Gilbert, M. and Associates. 1958. *Comparative National Products and Price Levels*. Paris: Organisation for Economic Co-operation and Development.

Gilbert, M., and I. Kravis. 1954. *An International Comparison of National Products and the Purchasing Power of Currencies*. Paris: Organisation for Economic Co-operation and Development.

Gold, B. 1981. "Improving Industrial Productivity and Technological Capabilities." In *Productivity Analysis: A Range of Perspectives*, edited by A. Dogramaci. Boston: M. Nijhoff Publishing.

Gollop, F.M., and D.W. Jorgenson. 1980. "U.S. Productivity Growth by Industry, 1947–73." In *New Developments in Productivity Measurement and Analysis*, edited by J.W. Kendrick and B. Vaccara, pp. 17–124. Studies in Income and Wealth 44. Chicago: University of Chicago Press.

Griliches, Z. 1980. "R&D and the Productivity Slowdown." *American Economic Review* 70: 343–48.

Heath, J.B. 1957. "British-Canadian Industrial Productivity." *Economic Journal* 67 (March): 665–91.

Helliwell, J. 1983. "Stagflation and Productivity Decline in Canada, 1974–82" Working Paper 1185. Cambridge, Mass.: National Bureau of Economic Research.

Helliwell, J., Mary E. MacGregor, and Tim Padmore. 1985. "Economic Growth and Productivity in Canada, 1955 to 1990." In *Economic Growth: Prospects and Determinants*, volume 22 of the research studies prepared for the Royal Commission on the Economic Union and Development Prospects for Canada. Toronto: University of Toronto Press.

Hulten, C.R. 1975. "Technical Change and the Reproducibility of Capital." *American Economic Review* 65: 956–65.

_____. 1979. "On the Importance of Productivity Changes." *American Economic Review* 69: 126–36.

Jorgenson, D., and Z. Griliches. 1967. "The Explanation of Productivity Change." *Review of Economic Studies* 34: 249–83.

Jorgenson, D.W., and B. Fraumeni. 1981. "Substitution and Technical Change in Production." In *Modelling and Measuring Natural Resource Substitution*, edited by E. Berndt and B. Fields. Cambridge, Mass.: M.I.T. Press.

Jorgenson, D.W., and M. Nishimizu. 1978. "U.S. and Japanese Economic Growth, 1952–74: An International Comparison." *Economic Journal* 86: 1–44.

Kendrick, J. 1961. *Productivity Trends in the U.S.* Princeton: Princeton University Press.

————. 1973. *Postwar Productivity Trends in the U.S., 1948–69.* New York: National Bureau of Economic Research.

————. 1980a. "Productivity Trends in the United States." In *Lagging Productivity Growth: Causes and Remedies*, edited by S. Maital and N. Meltz. Cambridge, Mass.: Ballinger.

————. 1980b. "Remedies for the Productivity Slowdown in the United States." In *Lagging Productivity Growth: Causes and Remedies*, edited by S. Maital and N. Meltz. Cambridge, Mass.: Ballinger.

Kendrick, J.W., and B. Vaccara, eds. 1980. *New Developments in Productivity and Measurement and Analysis.* Studies in Income and Wealth 44. Chicago: University of Chicago Press.

Kim, M. 1982. "The Structure of Technology of the Canadian Trucking Industry." Ph.D. dissertation, University of Toronto.

Kravis, I. 1976. "A Survey of International Comparisons of Productivity." *Economic Journal* 86: 1–44.

Kravis, I., A. Heston, and R. Summers. 1978a. *United National International Comparison Project: Phase II International Comparison of Real Product and Purchasing Power.* Baltimore: Johns Hopkins Press.

————. 1978b. "Real GDP Per Capita for More Than One Hundred Countries." *Economic Journal* 88: 215–42.

Kravis, I., A. Kennessey, A. Heston, and R. Summers. 1975. *A System of International Comparisons of Gross Products and Purchasing Power.* Baltimore: Johns Hopkins Press.

Lithwick, N.H. 1970. *Economic Growth in Canada.* 2d ed. Toronto: University of Toronto Press.

Maital, S., and N. Meltz, eds. 1980. *Lagging Productivity Growth: Causes and Remedies.* Cambridge, Mass.: Ballinger.

Maizels, A. 1958. "Comparative Productivity in Manufacturing Industry: A Case Study of Australia and Canada." *Economic Record* 34: 67–89.

Mansfield, E. 1983. "Long Waves and Technological Innovation." *American Economic Review* 73: 141–45.

May, J.D., and M. Denny. 1979. "Post-War Productivity in Canadian Manufacturing." *Canadian Journal of Economics* 21: 29–41.

Mohr, M. 1981. "Concepts in the Theory and Measurement of Productivity." mimeo.

————. 1983. "Diagnosing the Productivity Problem and Developing an RX for Improving the Prognosis." Washington, D.C.: U.S. Department of Commerce, mimeo.

Nadiri, M.I. 1970. "Some Approaches to the Theory and Measurement of Total Factor Productivity: A Survey." *Journal of Economic Literature* 8: 1137–77.

————. 1972. "International Studies of Factor Inputs and Total Factor Productivity, A Brief Survey." *Review of Income and Wealth* 18: 129–54.

————. 1980. "Sectoral Productivity Slowdown." *American Economic Review* 70: 349–52.

Nishimizu, M., and J.M. Page. 1981. "Total Factor Productivity Growth, Technical Progress and Technical Efficiency Change: Dimensions of Productivity Change in Yugoslavia, 1965–78." Washington, D.C.: Development Economics Branch, World Bank, mimeo.

Nordhaus, W.D. 1972. "The Recent Productivity Slowdown." *Brookings Papers on Economic Activity* 3: 493–536.

————. 1982. "Economic Policy in the Face of Declining Productivity Growth." *European Economic Review* 18: 131–47.

Norsworthy, J.R., M. Harper, and K. Kunze. 1979. "The Slowdown in Productivity Growth: Analysis of Some Contributing Factors." *Brookings Papers on Economic Activity* 2: 136–71.

Norsworthy, J.R., and D. Malmquist. 1983. "Input Measurement and Productivity Growth in Japanese and U.S. Manufacturing." *American Economic Review* 73: 947–68.

Ostry, S., and P. Rao. 1979. "Productivity Trends in Canada." In *Lagging Productivity Growth: Causes and Remedies*, edited by S. Maital and N. Meltz. Cambridge, Mass.: Ballinger.

Perry, G.L. 1970. "Changing Labor Markets and Inflation." *Brookings Papers on Economic Activity* 3: 411–41.

—————. 1971. "Labor Force Structure, Potential Output and Productivity." *Brookings Papers on Economic Activity* 3: 533–65.

Piekarz, R. 1983. "R&D and Productivity Growth: Policy Studies and Issues." *American Economic Review* 73: 210–14.

Posner, H. 1971. "An Analysis of Canadian Manufacturing Productivity." Economic Council of Canada Staff Study 31. Ottawa: Information Canada.

Rao, P.S., and R. Preston. 1983. "Inter-Factor Substitution and Total Factor Productivity Growth." Ottawa: Economic Council of Canada.

Rosenberg, N., and C. Frischtak. 1983. "Long Waves and Economic Growth: A Critical Appraisal." *American Economic Review* 73: 146–51.

Saunders, R. 1981. "The Determinants of Productivity in Canadian Manufacturing Industries." *Journal of Industrial Economics* 29: 167–84.

Scherer, F.M. 1983. "R&D and Declining Productivity Growth." *American Economic Review* 73: 215–19.

Sharpe, A. 1982. "A Review of the Productivity Slowdown Literature." mimeo.

—————. 1983. "A Comparative Analysis of the Canadian and American Productivity Slowdown." mimeo.

Summers, R., I.B. Kravis, and A. Heston. 1980. "International and Comparison of Real Product and Its Comparison: 1950–77." *Review of Income and Wealth* 26: 19–26.

Terleckyi, N. 1980. "What Do R&D Numbers Tell Us About Technological Change." *American Economic Review* 70: 55–61.

Walter, D. 1968. *Canadian Income Levels and Growth: An International Perspective*. Economic Council of Canada Staff Study 23. Ottawa: Queen's Printer.

—————. 1970. *Canadian Growth Revisited, 1950–67*. Economic Council of Canada Staff Study 28. Ottawa: Queen's Printer.

Waverman, L. 1980. "Energy and Canadian Manufacturing: A Tale of One Input." *Economic Policy Review* 2, PEAP. Toronto: University of Toronto, Institute for Policy Analysis.

West, E.C. 1971. *Canada-United States Price and Productivity Differences in Manufacturing Industries, 1963*. Economic Council of Canada Staff Study 32. Ottawa: Information Canada.

2

Economic Growth and Productivity in Canada, 1955–90

JOHN F. HELLIWELL
MARY E. MACGREGOR
TIM PADMORE

This paper combines history, economic modelling and forecasting to examine the main factors underlying Canadian economic growth between 1955 and 1990. Between 1955 and 1973 per capita real incomes grew on average by 3.1 percent per annum, while between 1973 and 1982 the average growth rate was less than 0.8 percent. What happened, and what does it mean for the future? Any study of Canada's future economic prospects must first explain why this dramatic slowdown in growth took place, and then draw implications for future economic performance. This paper attempts to disentangle some of the main factors contributing to the slowdown, and to make some comparable projections to 1990, making use of the MACE model of the Canadian economy.

In the first section of the paper, past and future changes of real income per capita are separated into what we describe as the seven great ratios of macroeconomic growth in an open economy.[1] We then dig further and present research results suggesting why those ratios have fluctuated and how they are likely to move in the future.

The second section of the paper deals with changes in the level of output per employee, a commonly used measure of labour productivity. Our recent modelling, based on data from 1952 to 1982 and reported in the appendix and in more detail in the appendices to Helliwell, Mac-Gregor and Padmore (1984), supports our earlier conclusion (reported in Helliwell, 1984) that the 1970s slowdown in productivity growth was neither inexplicable nor irreversible. All of the three factors chiefly responsible for the slowdown — unexpectedly low sales, abnormally low profitability and the substitution of labour for energy and capital — are expected to be reversed or to become less important, barring major unpleasant surprises, during the rest of the 1980s.

In the first two sections of the paper our analysis of past and future productivity growth is based on the hypothesis that the underlying rate of growth of labour efficiency is constant. In the third section we report the results of tests of this hypothesis against several alternatives, most of which involve some permanent slowdown of productivity growth in the 1970s. All of the alternatives tested are found to be empirically inferior to the assumption of a constant growth in efficiency, which is therefore maintained in the main version of the model. Since there is some international evidence (Helliwell, Sturm and Salou, 1985) in favour of one of the slowdown hypotheses (involving convergence to U.S. rates of efficiency growth, as discussed in the fourth section), and since it is empirically the strongest of the alternatives tested thus far, we have prepared an alternative version of MACE based on this hypothesis. The forecasts and features of this alternative version, which we refer to as the "catch-up" model, are discussed in the third section and documented partly in the appendix and fully in the appendices to Helliwell, Mac-Gregor and Padmore (1984). In the fourth section we suggest ways of placing the Canadian experience in an international context to permit a better evaluation of past Canadian performance and to provide some cross-checks on our alternative projections of future growth of actual and potential output. The concluding section summarizes our results and traces some of their implications for economic policy.

Seven Ratios of Growth in an Open Economy

We start with the goal of explaining changes in per capita real income, which we define as nominal GNP divided by the price of final expenditure and divided again by the total population.[2] Figure 2-1 shows the average annual changes in this ratio, and of each of its seven component ratios, over each of the three main periods covered by our study: 1955–73, 1973–82, and 1982–90. The first panel of Figure 2-2 shows the year-by-year changes in this ratio from 1955 to 1990. The subsequent panels decompose the changes in real income per capita into changes in the seven key ratios, which can be multiplied together to give real income per capita:
1. relative prices (determined chiefly by the terms of trade);
2. national income relative to domestic output;
3. utilization rates;
4. normal output per employee;
5. employment as a fraction of the labour force;
6. labour force participation rate; and
7. population aged 15 years and over as a share of the total population.
The ratios for 1955 to 1982 are based on actual data. From 1983 to 1990 the figures are derived from the mid-1984 version of the MACE model, for which the equations and forecasts are presented in the appendices to

FIGURE 2-1 Factors Contributing to the Growth of Real Income per Capita in Canada, 1955–73, 1973–82, and 1982–90

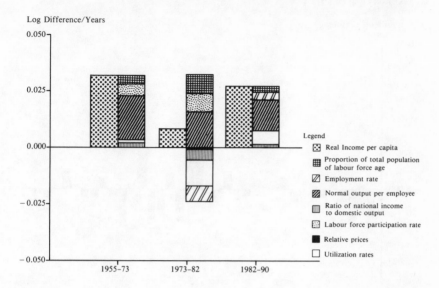

FIGURE 2-2 Factors Contributing to the Annual Growth of Real Income per Capita in Canada, 1955–90

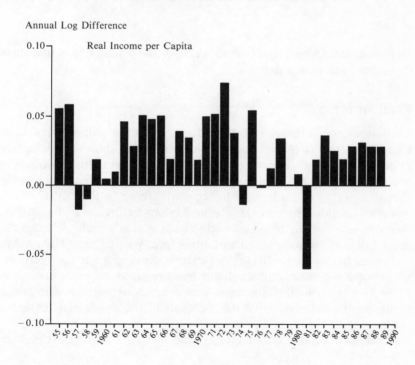

FIGURE 2-2 (cont'd)

1: Relative Prices

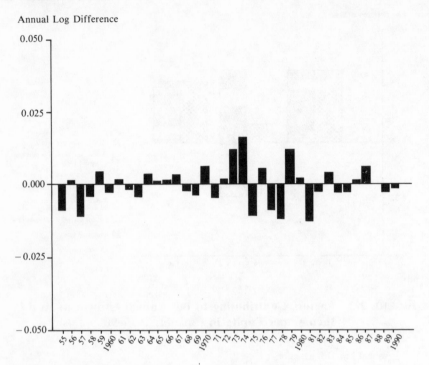

Annual Log Difference

Helliwell, MacGregor and Padmore (1984). We will now look at each of these ratios in closer detail.

Relative Prices

The numerator of this ratio is the price of output produced and sold by Canadians (the GNP deflator); the denominator shows the weighted price of goods and services purchased by Canadians (the spending or absorption price).[3] An increase in the ratio marks an improvement in Canada's terms of trade, and hence an increase in the real spending power of Canadian incomes. Over the 20 years before the mid-1970s, the cumulative effect of terms-of-trade changes was small, although the annual data show substantial variations from year to year. Most industrial countries of the OECD are net energy importers, and their terms of trade were worsened substantially by the world oil price shocks of 1973–74 and 1979–80. Canada, as a net energy exporter, had improvements in the relative price during each of the years of substantial increase in world energy prices.

However, the general weakening of the external value of the Canadian

FIGURE 2-2 (cont'd)

2: National Income to Domestic Output

Annual Log Difference

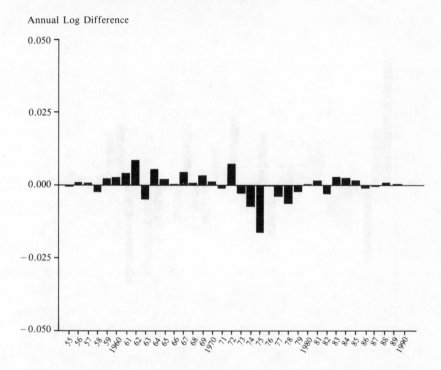

dollar (in real terms after adjusting for differences in inflation rates) over the 1976–78 period was associated with a worsening of the terms of trade. Putting all the factors together, there was a slight net worsening in the terms of trade, and hence in the relative price ratio, over the 1973–82 period.

Ratio of National Income to Domestic Output

Changes in this ratio are especially important for an open economy, like Canada's, which uses a lot of foreign capital in production. National income (real GNP) measures the income accruing to Canadian-owned labour and capital, while domestic output (gross domestic product is the usual aggregate) measures output produced in Canada. Thus, an increase in the use of foreign capital will cause an increase in domestic output in relation to national income, and hence lead to a drop in the ratio. The overall effects of net foreign capital inflows on per capita national income depend on the balance between the payments to foreign capital and the increases in normal output due to the larger capital stock. It is hazardous to attempt to measure this balance at the aggregate level,

FIGURE 2-2 (cont'd)

3: Utilization Rates

Annual Log Difference

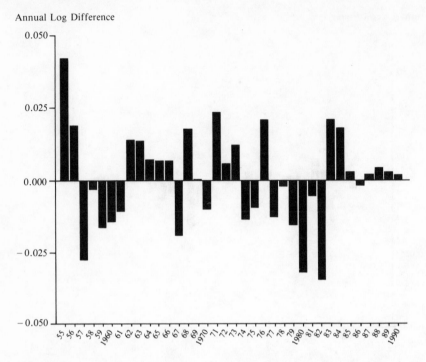

especially as the national accounts understate the costs of foreign equity capital (by using only dividends rather than profits) and overstate the cost of foreign debt (since the nominal interest on foreign debt includes an element of debt repayment if there is any inflation).

In our accounting, we define domestic output at factor cost, where the factors are the capital, labour and energy used everywhere except in the energy-producing sector. Output defined in this way is equal to real GDP less net energy exports, the gross output of the energy-using sector. The ratio of national income to domestic output can therefore rise if there are increases in net energy exports as well as if there are decreases in the use of foreign capital. Over the 1955–73 period Canada shifted from being a net importer of energy to a net exporter, which led to an increase in the ratio of national income to domestic output (as defined in MACE), despite a slight increase in the use of foreign capital. From 1973 to 1982 the ratio declined because of decreasing net energy exports and increasing use of foreign capital. The ratio is projected to increase slightly from 1982 to 1990.

Intensity of Factor Utilization

This ratio is defined as actual output divided by the level of output that would be produced if the quantities of capital, labour and energy now being used were used at average utilization rates. It differs from usual measures of total factor productivity in that it excludes long-run or "normal" increases in labour efficiency. An index of normal efficiency gains is used to convert the labour input into "efficiency units," and thus contributes to the growth of the normal output series.

Figure 2-1 shows that, on average, changes in utilization were close to zero between 1955 and 1973, were very negative between 1973 and 1982 (by more than −1.1 percent a year on average), and are expected to be about 0.6 percent a year between 1982 and 1990, as more normal utilization rates are re-established. Changes in capacity utilization were the single biggest factor underlying the drop in per capita income growth between 1973 and 1982, and of the subsequent increase in per capita growth rates between 1982 and 1990. This factor would have a lesser relative importance if the subperiods were split anywhere else than 1982, since utilization in that year was lower than in any other year.

The proximate causes of the changes in utilization will be discussed in more detail in the next section, which deals with growth of output per worker, decomposed into the utilization rate times the next of the great ratios, normal output per employee.

FIGURE 2-2 (cont'd)

4: Normal Output per Employee

Annual Log Difference

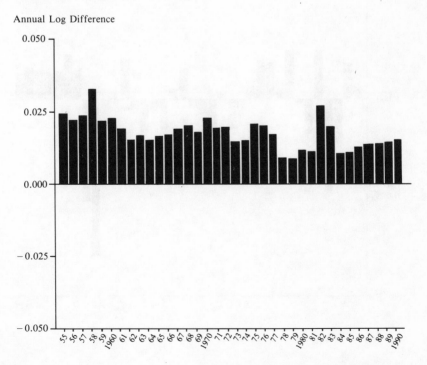

Normal Output per Employee

This ratio measures the amount of output per employee when the utilization rate is at its average value. It rises if capital or energy is substituted for labour or if there is an increase in the efficiency index. Figures 2-1 and 2-2 show that increases in normal output per employee have been the largest contributor to increase in per capita income in each of the three subperiods. As will be shown in the next section, the main factor underlying these increases was the trend increase in labour efficiency. In the 1955–73 period, this was augmented by the substitution of energy for labour, because the relative price of energy had been falling steadily over the 20 years up to 1973. After 1973, of course, that substitution process was reversed as energy rose in relative price and by 1982 became as expensive (in relation to the price of output) as it had been in the mid-1950s. Over the forecast period, normal output per employee is expected to rise less quickly than in either of the preceding periods, but it is still expected to be the largest single factor contributing to the growth in per capita income.

FIGURE 2-2   (cont'd)

5:   Employment Rate

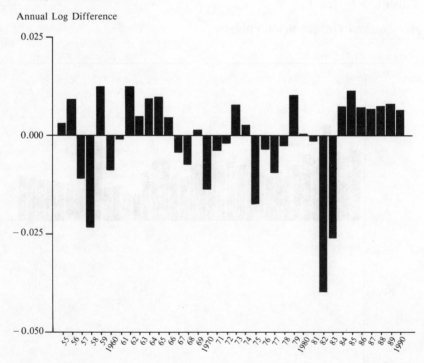

Annual Log Difference

Employment Rate

This is the ratio of total employment, excluding the energy-producing sector, to the labour force. It decreases with increases in the unemployment rate and with increases in direct employment in energy production. Direct employment in the energy-producing sector is small, but it rose substantially during the 1970s. It averaged 1.73 percent of the labour force, without any significant trend, before the early 1970s. From 1973 to 1982 it grew on average at an annual rate of 0.04 percent of the labour force, thereby contributing a roughly equivalent amount to the decline of real income per capita over the same period. To the extent that additional energy employment creates additional energy output, it will provide offsetting increases in real income per capita by increasing the second ratio — national income divided by output — which rises with any increase in net energy exports.

From 1955 to 1973 there was no significant trend in the employment rate; from 1973 to 1982 there was an average annual reduction of 0.7 percent, while an average annual increase of 0.3 percent is forecast from 1982 to 1990. In the second and third periods, changes in the rate of growth of employment are the primary reason for changes in the employment ratio.

Participation Rate

This is the usual measure of labour force participation — the labour force divided by the population aged 15 and over. There have been substantial increases in this ratio during each of the historical periods, especially because of increases in female participation rates. These increases are projected to slow down as the female participation rate approaches the male rate. Over the rest of the 1980s, the increased participation rate of women is expected to be roughly offset by the increase in the proportion of the population over 65 years of age. Those over 65 are more likely to be retired than in the labour force, so that an increase in their population share is accompanied by a reduction in the participation rate. In our control solution, the unemployment rate is projected to remain high for much of the decade, so that "discouraged worker" effects continue to provide a downward pressure on the labour force participation rate.

Proportion of Population Aged 15 and Over

This is the usual measure of the fraction of the population from which the labour force is drawn. It and the participation rate are the only two of the seven ratios that increased more between 1973 and 1982 than during the

FIGURE 2-2 (cont'd)

6: Labour Force Participation Rate

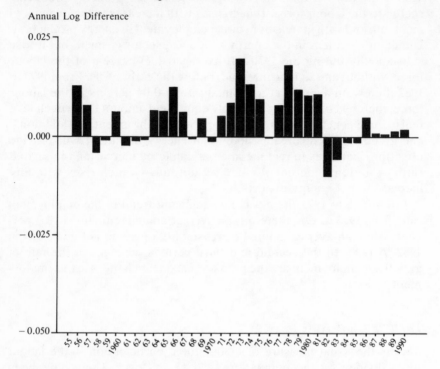

Annual Log Difference

preceding or subsequent periods. The ratio is now historically high, reflecting low birth rates over the past 15 years, and is forecast to show a slight further increase over the rest of the decade.

The product of the seven ratios is equal to per capita real income. Changes in the seven ratios fully determine changes in per capita real income, and hence in the economic prospects for Canadians.

What can be said, by way of summary, about the relative contributions of the seven ratios in explaining Canadian growth from 1955 to 1990? Figure 2-1 summarizes the changes in the rate of growth of real income per capita, and of each of the seven component ratios, during three major subperiods: 1955–73, 1973–82, and 1982–90. The figure shows clearly that the structure of economic growth was very different during each of the two historical periods and is likely to have yet another set of special characteristics over the rest of the decade. Over the 1955–73 period the 3.1 percent average annual rate of growth in per capita incomes came mainly from increases in normal output per employee (1.95 percent per year), in the labour force participation rate (0.5 percent per year), and in the share of the population 15 years of age and over (0.4 percent per year), with very little net change in the other four ratios. From 1973 to

FIGURE 2-2 (cont'd)

7: Proportion of Population of Labour Force Age

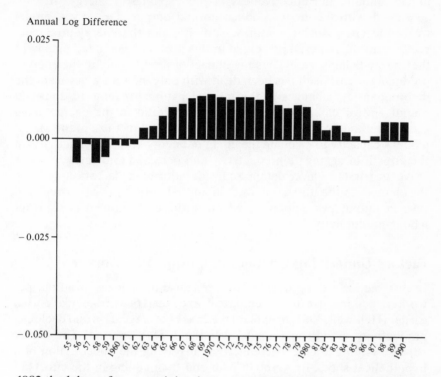

Annual Log Difference

1982 the labour force participation rate and the share of population over 15 years of age increased even faster (at average annual rates of 0.8 percent and 0.85 percent, respectively), while normal output per employee grew less quickly than before (at about 1.5 percent per year); there were substantial negative contributions from changes in the utilization rate (−1.1 percent per year), the employment rate (−0.7 percent per year), and the ratio of national income to output (−0.4 percent per year), bringing the average annual increase in real income per capita down to less than 0.8 percent.

From 1982 to 1990 real income per capita is projected to grow at 2.6 percent per year, mainly as a result of increases in normal output per employee (+1.35 percent per year) supplemented by smaller positive contributions from utilization rates, the employment ratio, and the share of population 15 years and over (0.6 percent, 0.34 percent and 0.26 percent, respectively).

Over the longer term, increases in real income per capita must come from increases in normal output per employee, since all of the other ratios are generally unchanging in an environment of steady growth and stable demography.[4] Increases in normal output per employee, as we shall see in the next section, depend primarily on increases in labour efficiency (including all forms of education and technical progress) and in the amount and effectiveness of the capital and energy that are combined with labour to produce normal output. The MACE model treats the energy-using sector separately from the energy-producing sector, and the material presented in this section has related mainly to the energy-using sector. Thus the impact of productivity in the energy-producing sector itself has been dealt with only indirectly, as one of the determinants of changes in the ratio of national income to domestic output and of changes in the employment ratio in the energy-using sector. In the third section we shall make more direct use of the MACE model's capacity to evaluate the effect of energy sector productivity on the growth of aggregate productivity and per capita incomes.

We turn first to a more detailed consideration of the factors underlying the changes in the utilization rate, in normal output per employee, and thus in output per employee, which is the conventional measure of labour productivity.

Factors Underlying Changes in Output Per Worker

In this section we dig deeper into the cause of changes in output per worker, making use of an empirical and analytical framework used earlier (Helliwell, 1984) to explain the causes of stagflation and declining productivity growth in Canada over the 1974–82 period. The earlier paper was an exercise in cliometrics, involving the construction of a hypothetical shock-free growth path and then adding in the effects of external and internal shocks and policies to find their separate and collective effects on the Canadian economy. In this paper, our aim is less to explain the 1974–82 history in detail than to put that period into a long-term context of Canadian economic growth, spanning most of the second half of the twentieth century.

Figure 2-3 shows the changes in output per employee in the three periods discussed in the previous section. It is thus a repetition of ratios (3) and (4) of the previous section along with their product, which is changes in output per employee. Figure 2-4 then shows the proximate causes of the changes in the utilization rate from the beginning to the end of each period, and Figure 2-5 does the same for the factors determining changes in normal output per employee.

What are the main features of the results? Figure 2-3 shows the dominance of cyclical factors in explaining the drop in the growth of output per employee in the 1970s and hence in explaining the abnormally high increases in the years following the recession trough in 1982.[5] Figure 2-4 shows that in all periods unexpected sales and profitability changes (measured by unit costs relative to the price of output) were the main sources of the changes in the level of output in relation to the normal level. In the 1955–73 period the average change in the utilization

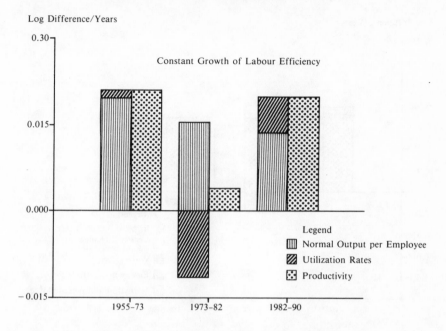

FIGURE 2-3 Changes in Productivity, Normal Output per Employee and Utilization Rates

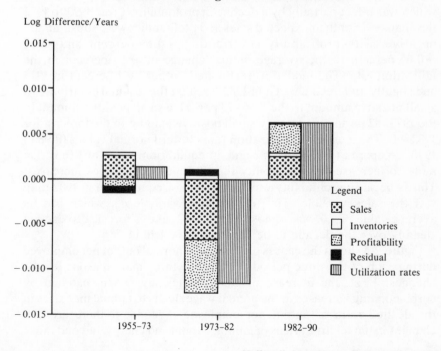

FIGURE 2-4 Contribution of Sales, Inventories, and Relative Unit Costs to Changes in Utilization Rates

FIGURE 2-5 Factors Contributing to the Growth of Normal Output per Employee

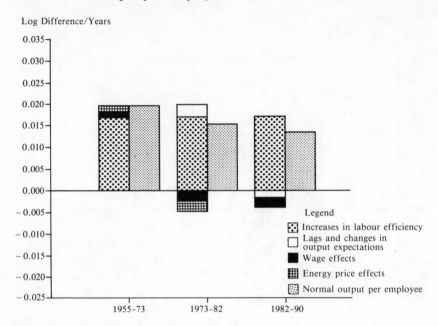

Log Difference/Years

Legend

▦ Increases in labour efficiency
☐ Lags and changes in output expectations
■ Wage effects
⊞ Energy price effects
▨ Normal output per employee

rate was positive (since the ratio of output to normal output was 1.01 in 1955 and 1.04 in 1973), driven by a positive effect from unexpected sales which was offset partially by a decline in profitability. From 1973 to 1982 the changes in both unexpected sales and profitability were substantially negative, with profitability contributing -0.59 percent and sales -0.66 percent to the average annual change of -1.1 percent in the utilization rate. The model overestimated output by 1 percent in 1973 and slightly underestimated it in 1982,[6] so that the residual contributes a small negative amount to the 1955–73 period, a small positive amount to the 1973–82 period, and a very small positive amount to the forecast for 1982–90. The increase in utilization rates toward normal values (0.98 in 1990, compared to 0.94 in 1982 and an equilibrium value of 1.0) is due more to increases in profitability than to unexpected sales increases. This is because profitability was further below equilibrium in 1982 than was the sales variable. The relative cost variable c_q, which has an average value of 1.0, was almost 1.21 in 1982, and is forecast to decline steadily over the decade to be slightly below 1.10 in 1990.

Figure 2-5 shows the causes of changes in normal output per employee during each of the three periods. There are three main reasons for the changes. First, the increase in labour efficiency, when matched by corresponding increases in the annual wage, leads to annual increases in the desired ratio of output per employee. Second, if there are any changes in the relative prices of labour, capital and energy, beyond those wage increases that match the increases in labour efficiency, then firms will attempt to keep their total costs down by changing the proportions in which the three factors are combined. Finally, there are lags in adjusting actual to desired levels of employment, capital and energy use.

How do lags affect normal output per employee? Normal output is defined by a bundle of employment, capital and energy. In the MACE equations for factor demands, employment responds faster than capital and energy to changes in the desired level of output. When anything happens to change desired output, it usually pushes all factor inputs in the same direction, but at different speeds. Since employment adjusts faster than capital and energy, normal output per employee falls when desired output rises, and vice versa. Thus, when desired output is below normal output, as happened in 1982 for example, normal output per employee will be above its long-run cost-minimizing value, since actual employment responds more quickly than normal output to unexpected changes in demand or profitability.

Lags also affect the adjustment of factor proportions to changes in relative prices. There are three prices that determine the desired factor mix in the MACE model: the efficiency wage, the price of energy (including all taxes and distribution charges), and the price of capital goods. For the preparation of Figure 2-5, we have represented relative price changes by measuring changes in the efficiency wage (which is the annual wage divided by the index of labour efficiency) relative to the absorption price (which we use to represent the price of final purchases in general, including capital goods), and likewise measuring changes in the price of energy relative to the absorption price. Thus the change in the desired labour intensity of production, and hence the desired ratio of potential output per employee, is entirely determined by the change in the labour efficiency index and the two relative prices.

Figure 2-5 shows that from 1955 to 1973 all three effects worked to decrease the desired labour intensity of production, and hence to increase the rate of growth of output per worker. The wage per efficiency unit of labour rose faster than the price of capital services, and the price of energy rose more slowly. Both changes increased the price of labour relative to that of the bundle of capital plus energy, and therefore encouraged firms to use less labour relative to the other factors. Over the 1973–82 period both of these relative price changes were reversed, as the wage per efficiency unit of labour rose slightly less quickly than the price of capital services and the price of energy rose much more rapidly. Both of these price changes led to increases in the desired use of labour relative to the bundle of capital plus energy, and hence to a lower growth rate for normal output per employee. These desired changes in relative factor proportions were not fully implemented by 1982, so that the positive contribution from the lag component is partly due to lags in the adjustment to pre-1982 changes in relative prices.

Over the 1982–90 period the increase in normal output per worker is driven chiefly by the increase in labour efficiency. This growth is offset by desired substitution of labour for the other factors, since the wage rate, which is determined by the unemployment rate as well as by the increase in labour efficiency, rises more slowly than the price of capital services. In addition, the 1982–90 period also sees the completion of the adjustment processes that were in train but incomplete in 1982. This is shown by the "expectations and lags" segment in Figure 2-5, which is negative for 1982–90 after being positive for the 1973–82 period.

The contribution of increases in labour efficiency is the same in each of the periods, adding 1.7 percent annually to the increase in normal output per employee. This constant contribution reflects the assumption built into MACE that there was no drop during the 1970s in the underlying rate of labour-embodied technical progress, and that there is therefore no reason to build such a decline into the main projections. Since this is an important assumption, and one which has been rejected by some students of productivity change, we subjected it to some tests against alternatives. We turn now to a discussion of those tests, and to the presentation of another set of projections based on one of the alternatives.

Alternative Models of Long-Term Productivity Growth

The results reported above differ from many current estimates of the rate of growth of productivity over the mid-1980s. For example, the Department of Finance (Canada, 1984, p. 24) forecasts annual growth of real GNP per employee averaging 1.3 percent from 1983 to 1988, whereas results from our MACE model with a constant rate of growth of labour efficiency suggest that economic recovery of the sort envisaged by the Department of Finance and by our projections will push the 1983–88 rate of growth of output per employee to about 2 percent.

In this section we present some evidence from tests of alternative versions of MACE that assume some fundamental slowdown of the long-term rate of productivity increase, and hence that produce lower estimates of future productivity growth. Our preferred procedure for testing different models is to derive the production structure that is consistent with that alternative model, and then estimate the corresponding production equation. In this way we allow the model of underlying increases in labour efficiency to be tested simultaneously and consistently with the model of the determinants of the short-term production decision.

It is important to estimate both the cyclical effects and the hypothesis about long-term productivity increases at the same time, since otherwise there will be a tendency for the part of the model estimated first to take on too much of the explanatory power. This is because most of the models of non-constant increases in labour efficiency involve some slowdown in efficiency increases at the end of the sample period, which terminates in 1982. Since the cyclical position was also unusually bad in

1982, the two sets of influences are correlated. If the model of technological change is estimated first, without allowance for cyclical factors, it is likely to overestimate the extent of the long-term slowdown.

On the basis of recent research using comparable output and productivity data for the seven largest OECD economies, we have found evidence that suggests one alternative hypothesis to test against our assumption that the long-run trend rate of increase in labour efficiency is a constant. The international evidence (which is described briefly in the fourth section) shows that the United States has a lower average trend rate of productivity increase than all of the other countries (except the United Kingdom) and that the other countries' rates were tending to converge toward the U.S. rate. When this model is applied to the Canadian case, it suggests that the process of catch-up was substantially completed by the latter half of the 1970s, and hence that future trend productivity growth for Canada is likely to be of the same magnitude as in the United States.

Table 2-1 shows the direct estimates of the catch-up hypothesis, as well as the key features of the derived equation for the level of production. The corresponding features of the constant growth model are shown above the catch-up results, and four more alternatives are shown below: a quadratic time trend for the labour efficiency index and three models involving post-1973 and post-1979 drops in the underlying rate of technical progress.

We used several types of evidence to test the hypothesis of constant growth of labour efficiency against the alternative models involving some slowdown of long-run productivity growth. The primary evidence is provided by the standard error of the derived production equation, as shown in the right-hand columns of Table 2-1. All of the alternative models have higher standard errors of estimate than does the main model, and some are significantly worse.[7]

Another test of the hypothesis of post-1973 and post-1979 breaks in productivity increase can be made by adding these variables directly to the output equation for the main model. If there had been a reduction of long-run productivity growth starting in 1974, 1980, or in some nearby year, then one or the other of the two variables would obtain a significant coefficient in the output equation. Neither does. In fact, adding either or both of these variables to the output equation raises the standard error of the estimate.

Another check on the validity of the constant-growth assumption is provided by stability tests on the output equation. Tests were performed for every possible breaking year, and in no case was there evidence of instability in the output equation of the main model, although there was some evidence of instability for the alternative models, as shown in Appendix Table II.2 of Helliwell, MacGregor and Padmore (1984).

Finally, it is possible to test the alternative models of long-run productiv-

TABLE 2-1 Alternative Models of Labour Efficiency Growth

Model	Intermediate Equation for the Rate of Technical Progress	Values for Derived q equation		
		Implied τ	F-Test	s.e.e.
1. Constant growth rate	$\ln [\mu^{\tau/(\tau-1)}\Pi] = 0.017003t + 1.6218$ $\quad\quad\quad\quad (21.99)\quad\quad (31.05)$ OLS 1952–82; s.e.e. $= 0.00385$; $\bar{R}^2 = 0.9415$; $DW = 0.63$,	0.53	0.38	0.005826
2. Catch-up hypothesis				
(a) Coefficients on lagged dependent and U.S. variables constrained to sum to 1	$\ln [\mu^{\tau/(\tau-1)}\Pi] = 0.85438 \ln [\mu^{\tau/(\tau-1)}\Pi]_{-1} + 0.14562 \ln (\Pi_{us}) + 0.47506$ $\quad\quad\quad (9.24)\quad\quad\quad\quad\quad (1.57)\quad\quad\quad\quad (1.62)$ OLS 1952–82; s.e.e. $= 0.0296$; $\bar{R}^2 = 0.9637$; $D-H = 0.57$, F-test $= 0.32$	0.66	1.78	0.006407
(b) (a) and U.S. Coefficient $= 0.12$	$\ln [\mu^{\tau/(\tau-1)}\Pi] = 0.88 \ln [\mu^{\tau/(\tau-1)}\Pi]_{-1} + 0.12 \ln (\Pi_{us}) + 0.39380$ $\quad\quad\quad\quad\quad\quad\quad\quad\quad\quad\quad\quad\quad\quad\quad\quad\quad\quad (73.97)$ OLS 1953–82; s.e.e. $= 0.0292$; $\bar{R}^2 = 0.9648$; $D-H = 0.57$, F-test $= 0.32$	0.66	1.89	0.006412
(c) (a) and U.S. Coefficient $= 0.18$	$\ln [\mu^{\tau/(\tau-1)}\Pi] = 0.82 \ln [\mu^{\tau/(\tau-1)}\Pi]_{-1} + 0.18 \ln (\Pi_{us}) + 0.58409$ $\quad\quad\quad\quad\quad\quad\quad\quad\quad\quad\quad\quad\quad\quad\quad\quad\quad\quad (109.6)$ OLS 1953–82; s.e.e. $= 0.0292$; $\bar{R}^2 = 0.9647$; $D-H = 0.25$, F-test $= 0.23$	0.66	1.75	0.006402
(d) (a) and U.S. Coefficient $= 0.20$	$\ln [\mu^{\tau/(\tau-1)}\Pi] = 0.80 \ln [\mu^{\tau/(\tau-1)}\Pi]_{-1} + 0.20 \ln (\Pi_{us}) + 0.65752$ $\quad\quad\quad\quad\quad\quad\quad\quad\quad\quad\quad\quad\quad\quad\quad\quad\quad\quad (121.1)$ OLS 1953–82; s.e.e. $= 0.0293$; $\bar{R}^2 = 0.9645$; $D-H = 0.82$, F-test $= 0.33$	0.66	1.78	0.006399

3. Quadratic	$\ln\left[\mu^{\tau/(\tau-1)}II\right] = 0.030758t - 0.00010271t^2 + 1.0927$ $\quad\quad\quad\quad\quad\quad\quad (2.38)\quad\quad\quad (1.06)\quad\quad (2.55)$ OLS 1953–82; s.e. = 0.0384; $\bar{R}^2 = 0.9418$; $DW = 0.65$	0.49	0.38	0.006461
4. Breaks in time trend after 1973 and 1979 restricted	$\ln\left[\mu^{\tau/(\tau-1)}II\right] = 0.018729t - 0.007t_{74} - 0.005t_{80} + 1.4063$ $\quad\quad\quad\quad\quad\quad\quad (24.47)\quad\quad\quad\quad\quad\quad\quad\quad (31.62)$ OLS 1952–82; s.e. = 0.0328; $\bar{R}^2 = 0.9576$; $DW = 0.80$. F-test = 4.76	0.47	1.60	0.007964
5. Break in time trend after 1973	$\ln\left[\mu^{\tau/(\tau-1)}II\right] = 0.019287t - 0.010279t_{74} + 1.3566$ $\quad\quad\quad\quad\quad\quad\quad (18.52)\quad\quad (2.94)\quad\quad (20.46)$ OLS 1952–82; s.e. = 0.0342; $\bar{R}^2 = 0.9538$; $DW = 0.77$	0.46	2.55	0.009083
6. Breaks after 1973 and after 1979 unrestricted	$\ln\left[\mu^{\tau/(\tau-1)}II\right] = 0.018535t + 0.000114971t_{74} - 0.045183t_{80} + 1.4509$ $\quad\quad\quad\quad\quad\quad\quad (20.2)\quad\quad (0.27)\quad\quad\quad\quad\quad (3.38)\quad\quad (24.94)$ OLS 1952–82; s.e. = 0.0292; $\bar{R}^2 = 0.9663$; $DW = 1.02$	0.49	6.65	0.009252

ity increase by examining the fit and properties of the other equations in which the efficiency index plays an important role. The MACE equations most affected by the productivity index are those for investment, employment and wages. Table 2-A1 (see appendix) compares those equations and the output equation for the main model, the catch-up model, and the model with constrained post-1973 and post-1979 drops in productivity growth. The estimated parameters are similar for the three models, but in all cases the constant-growth hypothesis used in the main model provides better fitting equations than either of the alternatives.

All of the above tests support the main model against the alternatives examined, although the evidence against the catch-up model is less strong than against the other alternatives. We therefore decided to assemble the complete catch-up model and to test its macroeconomic implications.

Figure 2-6 shows the catch-up model's analysis of the size of and reasons for the changes in normal output per worker. It shows averages for each of the three periods and is directly comparable to Figure 2-5. Figure 2-7 shows the seven great ratios for the catch-up model, and should be compared to Figure 2-1. For the historical period, the catch-up model shows a bigger post-1973 decline in the rate of growth of normal output per employee offset by a smaller decline in the rate of utilization. For the forecast period, there is a striking similarity in the two models' forecast rates of growth of real income per capita. How is this possible, when the underlying rate of technical progress in the catch-up model is less by about 0.4 percent a year? The reason is that wages are correspondingly less, at any given rate of unemployment, and the demand for labour correspondingly higher. Since the control solution involves high rates of unemployment, the higher labour requirements can be translated into higher rates of employment for several years before inflationary pressures become very serious.

By the end of the decade, it becomes less and less easy to use more workers to substitute for the lower level of efficiency. By 1990 the labour efficiency index, which is 1.0 in 1971 in both models, is 1.26 in the catch-up model, 9 percent less than the 1.38 value in the main model. The inflationary pressures are starting to show up: the utilization rate is 1.03 in the catch-up model compared to 0.98 in the main control solution, and the unemployment rate is 5.5 percent compared to 8.5 percent in the control solution. As a consequence, the aggregate 1990 inflation rate is 6.5 percent in the catch-up model compared to 4 percent in the control solution. By the end of the decade these pressures on labour supply are starting to be translated into lower growth of real output, as real GNP grows by 3.3 percent in 1990 in the catch-up model compared to 3.6 percent in the control solution.

A comparison of the macroeconomic consequences of the two alternative models of technical progress suggests that their implications for

FIGURE 2-6   Factors Contributing to the Growth of Normal
             Output per Employee: Catch-up Hypothesis

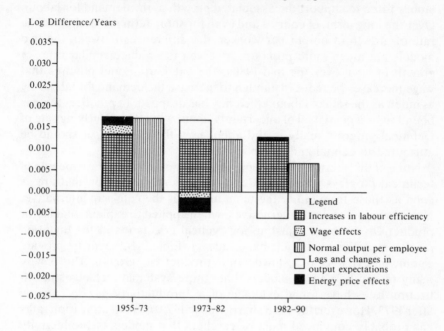

FIGURE 2-7   Factors Contributing to the Growth of Real Income
             per Capita in Canada, 1955–90: Catch-up Hypothesis

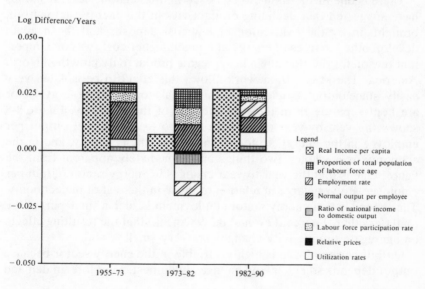

real GNP growth during the middle of the 1980s are not very great, since even with lower productivity growth there has been enough growth of the labour force to support the associated growth in the demand for labour. Over the long term, of course, and even for short-term projections of the rate of growth of output per worker, the differences between the two models are much more pronounced. Even to produce similar rates of growth of GNP over the mid-1980s, the catch-up model requires that wage increases be reduced enough to increase the demand for labour by as much as the rate of labour efficiency has dropped. In practice, there is bound to be a great deal of uncertainty about what the underlying rate of technical progress really is and about how the credit for it should be attributed to capital and to labour.[8]

None of the alternatives with post-1973 or post-1979 splits in the rate of technical progress give overall explanations of production that are as good as those from either the main model or the catch-up alternative. Note that most of these alternatives, when applied to explain total factor productivity without adjusting for cyclical effects (as in the equation results reported at the left-hand side of Table 2-1), seem to provide significant evidence of a slowdown in productivity growth. This is why many researchers using models that ignore systematic changes in utilization rates have found evidence of a "productivity puzzle" arising after 1973. However, the even sharper post-1979 break in utilization rates has probably convinced most researchers that models of productivity slowdown must be estimated in a manner that is consistent with changes in the utilization rate and that changes in utilization rates have played a large part in the productivity performance of the 1970s, and are likely to do so in the 1980s.

There is one further issue to be raised in this section. Several studies have suggested that declining productivity in the energy sector itself, brought on by the exhaustion of low-cost deposits and the need to develop other sources of energy at a much higher cost, was one important reason for the slowdown in aggregate productivity growth in North America. The MACE framework allows this effect to be isolated very easily, since output, employment and capital stock for the energy sector are kept separate from those of the rest of the economy. Figure 2-8 shows the year-by-year changes from 1955 to 1982 in net output per employee in the energy sector, in the rest of the economy, and in the economy as a whole. Two things are immediately apparent from the figure. One is that the year-to-year changes in energy sector output per employee are very large in relation to those in the rest of the economy. The second is that energy sector employment is such a small part of the total (less than 2 percent even at its 1982 peak) that the resulting effects on aggregate productivity changes are very small.

Output per employee is highly variable in the energy sector because output depends so heavily on changes in domestic and foreign demand

FIGURE 2-8   Output per Employee by Sector, 1955–82

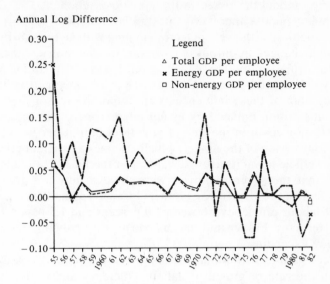

Annual Log Difference

Legend

△ Total GDP per employee
✗ Energy GDP per employee
□ Non-energy GDP per employee

for output (e.g., hydro-electricity, or natural gas or crude oil from connected wells) that do not entail any corresponding changes in employment. The ratio is also subject to changes when large new projects come on stream, such as when western Canadian oil and natural gas started to flow through their pipelines, and when major new electricity projects start generating. These effects are greater for Canada than for many other countries, since there has more frequently been an energy export or import that could be adjusted in response to the change in output, thus permitting a much faster build-up of output from new energy projects than would be possible if domestic energy supply and demand were always in balance. Given the reasons for these larger swings in output per employee in the energy sector, and in light of the large swings in Canada's energy trade during the 1970s and the long lead times for new projects, it would be a mistake to use the year-to-year changes in output per employee as any guide to the future productivity and costs of Canada's energy supply industries.

International Comparisons

How do Canadian productivity performance and prospects compare with those in other countries? The MACE supply-side modelling has been applied on a comparable basis to the seven largest OECD economies, thus permitting international comparisons to be made systematically. Two versions of the model were estimated (as reported in Helliwell, Sturm and Salou, 1984), one assuming a constant rate of labour-augmenting technical progress, and the other applying the "catch-up" model discussed in the previous section.

In both versions, there was substantial empirical support for the MACE structure, with cyclical factors joining with factor substitution in explaining changes in output per worker. In all countries, the ratio of actual to normal production (which we refer to as the utilization rate) was strongly influenced by profitability as well as by unexpected changes in demand. Both of these influences were important reasons, along with factor substitution induced by higher energy prices, for the pervasive post-1973 slowdown in the rate of growth of output per worker.

The first version of the model, which assumes a constant growth rate of labour efficiency at its average value over the 1962–82 sample period, showed that the seven countries were divided into two groups. The United States, the United Kingdom and Canada all had average growth rates of labour efficiency between 1.0 percent and 1.5 percent,[9] while Japan, Germany, France and Italy all had average growth rates of labour efficiency exceeding 3 percent.[10]

The constant-growth model makes no allowance for a possible slowdown in the rate of growth of labour efficiency and is thus likely to overstate the possibilities for future growth in the countries that were opening up, and catching up, to world productivity during the 1960s. The catch-up model was estimated directly, without adjusting for cyclical factors, and is therefore likely to overstate the extent of the 1970s slowdown in the long-term rate of productivity growth.

How is future productivity growth in Canada likely to compare with that in other countries? The constant growth rate model is probably suitable for Canada, the United States and the United Kingdom, but is likely to overstate future productivity growth for the other four countries. The results of the current version of the catch-up model, applied to those four countries, suggest that all four have reached or will soon approach the U.S. rate of efficiency growth, despite having had much higher rates during the 1960s. In all four cases (as shown in Figure 6 of Helliwell, Sturm and Salou, 1985), this implies a convergence of growth rates well before the U.S. efficiency levels have been reached. Those results almost surely understate future productivity prospects for the four countries, especially for Japan. The most likely prospects for those four countries therefore fall between those of the two models presented in the Helliwell, Sturm and Salou paper.

The prospects for future productivity growth in Canada appear to be as good as for the other industrial countries, although it is to be expected that countries with lower productivity levels than those of Canada or the United States will continue to close the gap. The remaining differences in productivity levels are then likely to reflect differences in unmeasured factors of production, such as natural resource endowments, education and skill levels, and the degree to which social and industrial structures are able to treat adjustment to continual change as challenges rather than threats.

Summary and Implications

In the mid-1950s Hood and Scott (1957) produced an important study for the Gordon Commission, drawing together the available data and theoretical models useful for explaining past and likely future growth of Canadian real output and productivity. One feature of the growth in output and productivity that they correctly foresaw would take place between then and 1980 has been a large increase in the availability and use of the kind of data they prepared and an even greater increase in the capacity to apply and test the implications of quantitative models of economic growth and productivity. It has thus been much easier for us to pull together the key elements of the historical record, to trace the likely sources of changes in the key variables and to make projections in a way that is theoretically coherent, based empirically on previous experience, and yet responsive both to the unusual circumstances at the beginning of the projection period and to likely future changes in demography and external circumstances.

What have been the main results of our analysis? The most striking feature of our interpretation, compared to most analyses of the 1970s, is that the sharp decline in the rate of productivity increase is well explained by changes in relative prices and by cyclical factors, and that the rises in the world oil price and the associated world recession were the primary causes of the changes in Canadian output, employment and productivity during the 1970s. This result has important consequences for any analysis of Canada's prospects for future economic development, since a return to more normal utilization rates during the 1980s would imply that positive cyclical effects will combine with continuing growth of normal labour efficiency and relatively constant factor costs to give unusually large increases in output per employee.

It might be tempting to conclude that the strong role we have found for profitability and final demand in explaining output, and output per employee, means that productivity is likely to be improved by any policies that stimulate final demand or increase profitability. Our research does not support this conclusion, since in our model the long-run rate of increase in output per employee is independent of the size and rate of growth of final demand. It is true that any temporary or unexpected increase in final demand will increase output per employee in the short run, but this is just a feature of the adjustment process, and not something that can exploited over the longer run, when all output must be based on factor inputs.

Our international comparisons suggest that broadly the same factors that were responsible for the post-1973 slowdown in Canada also helped to produce the post-1973 slowdown in the other large OECD economies. The 1982 recession was more severe in North America than elsewhere in the OECD with correspondingly slower growth of output per worker in that year, and faster growth thereafter.

Why do our results differ from those of others? We suspect the main reason is that most forecasters tend to extrapolate future productivity growth on the basis of recent past experience. For those who are used to making projections in this way, it would seem very brave, if not foolhardy, to forecast that output per worker will grow almost as fast in the 1980s and 1990s as it did in the 1950s and 1960s, given that the experience of the 1970s was materially worse. In the context of a modelling framework like ours, which treats cyclical and long-term influences on productivity in an integrated way, it is quite natural to produce forecasts that reverse recent past experience to the extent that it was due to cyclical factors that are likely to return to more normal values.

Our analysis also makes it clear that a substantial part of the drop in output per worker was the result of intentional substitution of labour for high-priced energy. This type of "productivity fall" is not really that at all, but is a justified and income-improving response to changes in relative factor costs. A model like ours that allows these effects to be disentangled from the rest provides a better basis for forecasting into a period of more stable energy prices, and permits a more accurate measurement of the size of the cyclical and long-term trends.

We are continuing our efforts to clarify and extend our analysis of the cyclical and long-term forces acting on Canadian economic growth and productivity, using evidence from other countries to provide cross-checks and comparisons with our explanation of Canadian experience. Our results so far tend to confirm our analysis of the Canadian situation and to suggest that similar explanations underlie the 1970s experience, and hence the future prospects, of the other major OECD countries.

Appendix

MACE Supply Structure
Constant Growth of Labour Efficiency

List of Variables
Conventions

* denotes desired value, e.g., k^*_{inv}

~ denotes quantity given by a CES bundle, e.g., $\tilde{k}_{ev}$

– denotes a two period average, e.g.,
$$\bar{k}_{ne} = \frac{1}{2}(k_{ne} + k_{ne\text{-}1})$$

–t denotes a lag of t years, e.g., q_{-1}

^ denotes equilibrium value at normal capacity utilization after lags are worked out, e.g., $\hat{m}_{ne}$

• denotes one-period proportionate change, e.g.,
$$\dot{p}_a = (p_a - p_{a\text{-}1})/p_{a\text{-}1}$$

<> denotes a sample average, e.g., the sample average of r_{nu} for the period 1952–82 (31 observations) is:
$$<r_{nu}> = (r_{nu}{}^{52} + r_{nu}{}^{53} \ldots + r_{nu}{}^{82})/31$$

Variable	Equation No.	Description
a	2.3	Real absorption, billion 1971 $
a_2	Exog	Real U.S. absorption, billion 1972 $ U.S.
c_q	1.10	Production costs relative to the output price for q
D_{aib}		Dummy variable in labour force equation, equal to 1 in 1976 and -1 in 1978, to account for the effects of anti-inflation board policies
e	1.8	Energy expenditure, billion 1971 $
e_v	1.4	Vintage-based energy requirement, billion 1971 $

Variable	Equation No.	Description
i_{gap}	See below 1.11	Ratio of desired to lagged inventories
i_{inv}	1.13	Value of physical change in inventories, billion 1971 \$
i_{ne}	1.1	Business fixed investment (excluding energy investment), billion 1971 \$
i_{new}	See below 1.3	Re-investment with energy use malleable in the current year, billion 1971 \$
k^*	1.9	Optimal capital stock
k_e^*	See below 1.6	Optimal bundle of capital and energy services
$\tilde{k}_{ev}$	1.3	Vintage measure of capital and energy, billion 1971 \$
k_{inv}	1.14	Stock of inventories, billion 1971 \$
k_{ne}	1.2	Business fixed capital stock (excluding energy), billion 1971 \$
m_{car2}	See below 1.12	Imports of cars from the U.S.
m_{ne}	1.12	Imports of goods and services (excluding energy, interest, and dividends), billion 1971 \$
N_e	Exogenous	Total employed in energy sector, millions of persons
N_{ne}^*	See below 1.6	The desired future level of employment in the non-energy sector.
N_{ne}	1.6	Total employed in non-energy sector (excluding armed forces), millions of persons
N_l	1.5	Total civilian labour force, millions of persons

Variable	Equation No.	Description
N_{pl}	Exogenous	Population of labour force age, millions of persons
p_a	3.4	Implicit price of absorption, 1971 = 1.0
p_e	Link	Price of energy to final users, 1971 = 1.0
p_k	See below 1.3	Price of capital services
p_{ke}	See below 1.9	Price of the capital-energy bundle
p_{mne}	3.5	Price of imports of goods and services (excluding energy), 1971 = 1.0
p_q	3.2	Implicit price for gross domestic output including imported energy, 1971 = 1.0
q	1.11	Gross output (at factor cost) of the non-energy sector, billion 1971 $. (Equals real GDP plus net energy imports minus non-energy indirect taxes)
q_a	1.15	Aggregate demand (output less unintended inventory accumulation), billion 1971 $
q^*	1.16	Desired level of profitable future output for factor demands, billion 1971 $
q_{sv}	1.17	Vintage-based synthetic supply, billion 1971 $
r_1	5.7	Average yield on Government of Canada bonds, 10 years and over, percentage
r_{nat}	Exogenous	Natural rate of unemployment. Assumed to continue at the 1982 level of 6 percent after 1982
r_{nu}	1.7	Unemployment rate, percentage
r_s	5.5	Average yield on Government of Canada bonds, 1–3 years, percentage

Variable	Equation No.	Description
t	Exogenous	Time. 1952 = 1, 1953 = 2, etc.
T_i	5.1	Indirect taxes, less subsidies, billion $
T_{ie}	Link	Indirect taxes, less subsidies, on energy billion $
W_e	Exogenous	Wage rate in the energy sector, thousands of dollars per year per employed person
W_{ne}	3.1	Wage rate in the non-energy sector, thousands of dollars per year per employed person
W_{um}	Exogenous	Maximum unemployment benefits, thousands of dollars per year per unemployed person
y	3.6	Real gross national product, billion 1971 $
y_{res}	Exogenous	Residual error of estimate, billion 1971 $
δ_1	Estimated parameter	Annual rate at which energy/capital proportions become malleable in k_{ev}. $\delta_1 = 0.18$
δ_2	Exogenous	Depreciation of rate for non-energy capital stock (including housing). Sample average = 0.045419
Π	Exogenous	Labour productivity index for Harrod-neutral technical progress in CES function for q. The annual growth rate for the forecast period is assumed to continue at the historical estimated rate of 1.70 percent
Π_{us}	Exogenous	U.S. labour productivity index
ρ_r	Estimated parameter	Real supply price of capital, percent $\rho_r = 9.6610$

Variable	Equation No.	Description
$\beta, \gamma, \mu,$ ν, σ, τ	Estimated parameters	Parameters for nested production functions. $\beta = 0.74175; \gamma = 0.15943; \mu = 0.0813723;$ $\nu = 0.655263; \sigma = 0.8700; \tau = 0.53;$

Note: More detail on the derivation of these parameters is available from Helliwell, MacGregor and Padmore, 1984.

Values of Sample Averages:

Variable	Equation	Value
$<\delta_2>$	1.3	0.045419
$<W/p_a>$	1.5	7.1563
$<k_{inv-1}/q_{sv}>$	1.11	0.23365
$<(a+x_{ne})/q_{sv}>$	1.11	1.33966

Supply Equations

Business fixed investment:

$$i_{ne}/\overline{k}_{ne} = \underset{(3.32)}{0.39968} \ i_{ne-1}/\overline{k}_{ne-1}$$

$$+ \ \underset{(6.50)}{0.062981} \ (k^* - \overline{k}_{ne})/\overline{k}_{ne}$$

$$\underset{(4.84)}{-0.048005} \ c_q + \underset{(6.31)}{0.094898} \tag{1.1}$$

2SLS 1954–82 ; s.e.e. = .00329 ; $\overline{R}^2$ = 0.8175 ; $D-H$ = 1.54

Business fixed capital stock:

$$k_{ne} = (1 - \delta_2) \ k_{ne-1} + i_{ne} \tag{1.2}$$

Vintage bundle of capital and energy:

$$\bar{k}_{ev} = (1 - \delta_1 - \delta_2)\tilde{k}_{ev-1} +$$
$$i_{new} \ \{\beta + \gamma[(\gamma p_k)/(\beta p_e)]^{\sigma-1}\}^{\sigma/(\sigma-1)} \tag{1.3}$$

where

$$i_{new} = i_{ne} + \delta_1 k_{ne-1}$$

is re-investment with energy use malleable in the current year, and *where*

$$p_k = (<\delta_2> + 0.01\rho_r)p_a$$

is the price of capital services *and*

$$\rho_r = 100 < 1 - (W_{ne}N_{ne} + ep_e + <\delta_2>\overline{k}_{ne}p_a)/(qp_q)>$$
$$/<(\overline{k}_{ne}p_a)/(qp_q)>$$

so that the ratio of factor costs to revenues is unity, on average.

Vintage-based energy requirement:

$$e_v = (1 - \delta_1 - \delta_2)e_{v-1} + \{(\gamma\ p_k)/(\beta p_e)\}^\sigma i_{new} \qquad (1.4)$$

Labour force:

$$(\dot{N_l}/ N_{pl}) = 0.099471(\overline{q/ q_{sv}}) + 0.0077596(r_{nat}/r_{nu})$$
$$(3.38) \qquad\qquad\qquad (2.06)$$

$$+ 0.0076482\ sech^2[(t - 31)/16]$$
$$(4.79)$$

$$- 0.0080681\ W/(<W/p_a> p_a)$$
$$(2.40)$$

$$+ 0.0058381\ D_{aib} - 0.099163 \qquad\qquad (1.5)$$
$$(2.97) \qquad\qquad (3.57)$$

2SLS 1956–82 ; s.e.e. = 0.00276 ; $\overline{R}^2$ = 0.5714 ; DW = 1.62

F-test on constraint that constant plus coefficients on the 1st, 2nd and 4th terms sum to zero = 4.3, and *where*

$$W = (W_{ne}\dot{N}_{ne} + W_e N_e)/(N_{ne} + N_e)$$

Employment in the non-energy sector:

$$\ln N_{ne} = \ln N_{ne-1} + 0.23819 \ln (N^*_{ne}/N_{ne-1}) \qquad (1.6)$$
$$(17.82)$$

2SLS 1955–82 ; s.e.e. = 0.00847 ; $\overline{R}^2$ = 0.7322 ; DW = 1.30

F-test on the constraint on intercept = 0.185,
where the desired future level of non-energy sector employment is

$$N^*_{ne} = (1/\Pi)[q^{*(\tau-1)/\tau} - vk_e^{*(\tau-1)/\tau}/\mu]^{\tau/(\tau-1)}$$

and where

$$k_e^* = [1 + (v/\mu)^\tau(\Pi p_{ke}/W_{ne})^{\tau-1}]^{\tau/(1-\tau)}q^*$$

Unemployment rate:

$$r_{nu} = 100[N_1 - N_{ne} - N_e]/N_1]$$ (1.7)

Energy demand:

$$\ln e = \ln e_v + 0.019554$$ (1.8)
$$(4.00)$$

2SLS 1955–82 ; s.e.e. = 0.0231 ; $\bar{R}^2 = 0.9977$; $DW = 0.68$

F-test on constraint = 0.42 .

Optimal capital stock:

$$k^* = \beta^{\sigma/(1-\sigma)}[1 + (\gamma/\beta)^\sigma (p_k/p_e)^{\sigma-1}]^{\sigma/(1-\sigma)}$$
$$[1 + (\nu/\mu)^\tau (\Pi p_{ke}/W_{ne})^{\tau-1}]^{\tau/(1-\tau)} q^*$$ (1.9)

where the price of the capital-energy bundle is

$$p_{ke} = (\beta^\sigma p_k^{1-\sigma} + \gamma^\sigma p_e^{1-\sigma})^{1/(1-\sigma)}$$

Average unit cost, relative to output price, for producing gross output of the non-energy sector:

$$c_q = [ep_e + \bar{k}_{ne}(<\delta_2> + .01\rho_r' + 0.0071r_1)p_a$$
$$+ W_{ne}N_{ne}]/(qp_q)$$ (1.10)

and

$$\rho_r' = 100 < 1 - [W_{ne}N_{ne} + ep_e + (<\delta_2> + 0.0071r_1)\bar{k}_{ne}p_a]$$
$$/(qp_q)>/<(\bar{k}_{ne}p_a)/(qp_q)>$$

so that c_q equals unity, on average.

Output equation:

$$\ln q = \ln q_{sv} - 0.25340 \ln c_q$$
$$(11.20)$$

$$+ 0.55404 \ln s_{gap} + 0.093749 \ln i_{gap}$$ (1.11)
$$(18.84) \qquad\qquad (2.93)$$

2SLS 1954–82 ; s.e.e. = 0.00583 ; $\bar{R}^2 = 0.9998$; $DW = 1.21$

F-test for constraints on q_{sv} and intercept = 0.38

where

$$s_{gap} = [(a + x_{ne})/q_{sv}]/<(a + x_{ne})/q_{sv}>$$

and where

$$i_{gap} = <k_{inv-1}/q_{sv}>q_{sv}/k_{inv-1}$$

Non-energy imports:

$$\ln (m_{ne} - m_{car2}) = \begin{array}{c} -1.5729 \\ (93.32) \end{array} + \ln q_{sv}$$

$$\begin{array}{c} -1.3067 \\ (5.79) \end{array} \ln(1/3 \sum_{i=0}^{2} p_{mne-i}/p_{q-i}) \quad (1.12)$$

2SLS $1955-82$; s.e.e. $= 0.0638$; $\bar{R}^2 = 0.9787$; $DW = 0.92$

F-test on constraint $= 1.635$,

where imports of cars from the United States is given by

$$\ln m_{car2} = \begin{array}{c} -6.5938 \\ (9.48) \end{array} - \begin{array}{c} 1.5703 \\ (2.43) \end{array} \ln(p_{mne}/p_q)$$

$$+ \begin{array}{c} 1.1492 \\ (11.70) \end{array} \ln [(0.96756\, a_2 + a)\, tanh\, (t-12)/5]$$

OLS 1966–82 ; s.e.e. $= 0.116$; $\bar{R}^2 = 0.910$; $DW = 1.03$

Change in business inventories:

$$i_{inv} = q + (T_i - T_{ie})/p_a - a - x_{ne}$$
$$+ x_{id}/p_{xne} + m_{ne} - y_{res} \quad (1.13)$$

Stock of non-farm business inventories:

$$k_{inv} = k_{inv-1} + i_{inv} \quad (1.14)$$

Aggregate demand:

$$q_a = q - [i_{inv} - q(i_{gap}^{0.093749} - 1)] \quad (1.15)$$

where the exponent on i_{gap} is the coefficient on inventories from the output equation (1.11).

Desired level of future output for factor demands:

$$q^* = q_a[1 + 1.7(m_{ne} - \hat{m}_{ne})/q](q/q_{-2}) \tag{1.16}$$

where $\hat{m}_{ne}$ is the equilibrium level of imports at normal utilization rates with lags worked out:

$$\ln(\hat{m}_{ne} - m_{car2}) = -1.5729 + \ln q_{sv}$$
$$- 1.3067 \ln(p_{mne}/p_q)$$

Vintage based synthetic supply:

$$q_{sv} = [\mu(\Pi N_{ne})^{(\tau-1)/\tau} + \nu \, \tilde{k}_{ev}{}^{(\tau-1)/\tau}]^{\tau/(\tau-1)} \tag{1.17}$$

TABLE 2-A1 A Comparison of Key MACE Equations Under Differing Labour Efficiency Growth Assumptions

Equation	Constant	Catch-up	Model with Post-1973 and Post-1979 Drops in Productivity
(1.11) $\ln q$			
$\ln q_{sv}$	1.0	1.0	1.0
$\ln c_q$	-0.25340	-0.13741	-0.19523
	(11.20)	(5.53)	(6.4633)
$\ln s_{gap}$	0.55404	0.68035	0.49905
	(18.84)	(23.61)	(11.30)
$\ln i_{gap}$	0.093749	0.13429	0.07829
	(2.93)	(3.53)	(1.79)
s.e.e.	0.00583	0.00641	0.007964
$\overline{R}^2$	0.9998	0.9997	0.9996
$D-W$	1.21	1.02	0.8433
F-test on constraints on q_{sv} and intercept	0.38	1.78	1.596
2SLS 1954–82			
(1.1) $i_{ne}/\overline{k}_{ne}$			
$i_{ne-1}/\overline{k}_{ne-1}$	0.39968	0.53552	0.44769
	(3.32)	(4.02)	(3.20)
$(k^* - \overline{k}_{ne})/\overline{k}_{ne}$	0.062981	0.046483	0.060514
	(6.50)	(4.81)	(4.94)
c_q	-0.048005	-0.058808	-0.049911
	(4.84)	(5.46)	(4.85)

TABLE 2-A1 (cont'd)

Equation	Constant	Catch-up	Model with Post-1973 and Post-1979 Drops in Productivity Growth
Constant	0.094898 (6.31)	0.095001 (5.39)	0.092963 (5.40)
s.e.e.	0.00329	0.00329	0.00332
$\bar{R}^2$	0.8175	0.8178	0.8142
$D-H$	1.54	1.82	1.64
2SLS 1954–82			
(1.6) $1n\ N_{ne}$			
$1n\ N_{ne-1}$	1.0	1.0	1.0
$1n\ (N_{ne}^*/N_{ne-1})$	0.23819 (17.82)	0.22643 (13.24)	0.23752 (14.82)
s.e.e.	0.00847	0.01101	0.0099755
$\bar{R}^2$	0.7322	0.5477	0.6290
$D-W$	1.30	0.81	1.0034
F-test on constraint on intercept	0.185	0.409	0.047
2SLS 1955–82			
(3.1) $\dot{W}_{ne}$			
$\dot{W}_{ne-1}$	0.38699 (5.55)	0.35715 (5.34)	0.29536 (4.20)
$\dot{p}_a$	0.61301 (8.79)	0.64285 (9.62)	0.70464 (10.01)
$\dot{\Pi}$	0.61301 (8.79)	0.64285 (9.62)	0.70464 (10.01)
$1n\ r_{nu}\ /<r_{nu}>$	− 0.026331 (4.25)	− 0.024642 (4.18)	− 0.022365 (3.85)
$1n\ (W_{um}/W_{ne})/$ $<W_{um}/W_{ne}>$	0.020300 (2.54)	0.021816 (2.74)	0.018241 (2.43)
D_{77}	− 0.038742 (4.89)	− 0.036674 (4.74)	− 0.034215 (4.49)
D_{78}	− 0.023472 (3.25)	− 0.021498 (3.02)	− 0.02055 (3.03)
Constant	0.0041546 (3.23)	0.0042578 (3.47)	0.0039486 (3.30)
s.e.e.	0.00988	0.01048	0.01053
$\bar{R}_2$	0.9106	0.8995	0.8985
$D-H$	− 1.65	− 0.75	− 0.54069
System $(\dot{p}_a, \dot{p}_q, \dot{W}_{ne})$			

Notes

This study was completed in October 1984.

We are grateful to John McCallum, John Sargent, Andrew Sharpe and Tom Wilson for helpful comments on an earlier version, and to Alan Chung for valuable research assistance.

1. The term "great ratios of economics" was used by Klein and Kosobud (1961) to refer to certain key ratios (the savings rate, the capital/output ratio, the labour share, the income velocity of money, and the capital/labour ratio) that they took either as constant or as dependent only on time to establish a model of equilibrium growth. By contrast, our seven ratios are nearly all functions of important endogenous variables. Thus the decomposition of economic growth into the seven ratios is a helpful way of dividing up the story, but does not in itself explain the fundamental causes of changes in the pattern of growth.

2. We use the price of final expenditure, rather than the price of GNP, to define real income, because the price of final expenditure (sometimes called the absorption price) reflects the mix of imported and domestic goods and services actually purchased. The absorption price is the implicit deflator defined by the ratio of the current-dollar to the constant-dollar sums of consumption, investment and government spending.

3. The ratio of real per capita income is equal to nominal per capita GNP deflated by the absorption price index. This ratio is equal to the product of the following seven ratios: the ratio of the GNP deflator to the absorption price deflator; the ratio of real GNP to the real output of the energy-using sector; real output of the energy-using sector divided by the output of the sector when employed factors of production are used at normal rates (normal output); normal real output of the energy-using sector divided by the number of people employed in that sector; number of people employed in the energy-using sector divided by the total labour force; the labour force divided by the source population (the number of people aged 15 and over); and the ratio of the source population to the total population. Since the denominator of each ratio is equal to the numerator of the one that follows it, all of the internal terms cancel out when the seven ratios are multiplied together to give real income per capita. In order to make the decomposition exact, the changes are shown as changes in the natural logarithms of the ratios from the beginning to the end of the period, or from one year to the next in the case of the annual change graphs, divided by the number of years in the time span. When multiplied by 100, these figures approximate the average annual percentage changes in the ratios.

4. Long-term trends in international flows of savings can affect this conclusion. If, for example, Canada became a permanent net exporter of savings, there would be a matching decline in net payments of interest and dividends and a corresponding increase in the ratio of national income to domestic output.

5. How do those results compare with those reported in a previous paper (Helliwell, 1984, p. 191), which attributed 30 percent of the decline in 1982 labour productivity, relative to the steady state growth case, to desired substitution of labour for energy, and most of the rest to cyclical factors? The conclusions differ because the earlier paper compared actual history in 1982 to a steady growth base case that embodied further price-induced increases in energy intensity during the 1970s, whereas in this paper we are comparing actual history in 1982 to the actual history of 1973, and exploring the changes that took place between the two years. This involves a bigger change in cyclical position and a smaller change in the relative price of energy than did the earlier paper's comparison of 1982 with a steady growth benchmark case. Thus the results in the new paper show a higher relative importance of cyclical factors. This is true even though the national accounts data were revised in 1984 to raise 1982 real GNP by more than 1.5 percent above the earlier estimates for the same year, thus reducing the depth of the recession and thereby the importance of cyclical factors in explaining the low output per employee in 1982. The earlier paper (Helliwell, 1984) used the lower value of 1982 GNP, while this paper, and the equation estimates reported in the appendix, are based on the official mid-1984 national accounts data for the entire historical period. In the current paper we have chosen to use the year-to-year or period-to-period basis for our analysis, so as to make it easier to link the 1973–82 results with those from the previous 20 years and with our projections to 1990.

6. The 1982 overestimation reported in the earlier paper (Helliwell, 1984, p. 198) was removed by subsequent revisions to the national accounts data for 1982.

7. Some of the models, especially those that permit unconstrained breaks in productivity growth, also reject the constraint that output should, other things being equal, rise proportionately with normal output. In some cases the intermediate equations for the logarithm of the productivity index have lower standard errors than the corresponding equation for the main model. This happens because of a correlation between the supposed determinants of the long-run slowdown and the cyclical variables excluded from the intermediate equation. These lower standard errors would have significance for the choice of model only if they carried forward to produce lower standard errors for the output equation. As can be seen from the results in the right-hand columns, they do not lead to better fits for the output equation.

8. We have been doing some preliminary testing of another model of technical progress in which the level of labour efficiency is related to the rate of growth of the capital stock, on the presumption that at least some forms of technical progress need to be embodied in new capital goods to attain their maximum effectiveness. Preliminary evidence suggests that this model fits almost as well as the main model, indicating that there is indeed some reason for uncertainty about how the credit and returns for technical progress should be divided.

9. The figures were 1.2 percent, 1.0 percent and 1.5 percent for the United States, the United Kingdom and Canada, respectively. There are two reasons why the number for Canada is lower than the 1.7 percent in MACE. The OECD sample period starts later, thus omitting the high-growth 1950s, and the OECD capital stocks include capital used in the energy sector, which grew faster than the more appropriate series (used in MACE) for the capital stock of the energy-using sector. This second reason also causes the OECD results to understate factor substitution toward labour during the 1970s, since energy capital stocks grew faster than non-energy capital stocks for several countries, and especially for Canada, the United States and the United Kingdom. Efforts are underway to obtain comparable energy investment series for all of the countries to permit the capital stock series to be more appropriately defined.

10. The rates were 3.4 percent, 3.0 percent, 4.2 percent and 3.4 percent, respectively. These rates can be reconciled with Japan's having the highest overall rate of growth of output per employee (Helliwell, Sturm and Salou, 1984, Table 1) by the fact that the growth rates for capital and for energy use (especially before 1973) were much higher in Japan than elsewhere.

Bibliography

Canada. Department of Finance. 1984. *The Canadian Economy in Recovery*. Ottawa: Minister of Supply and Services Canada.

Helliwell, John F. 1984. "Stagflation and Productivity Decline in Canada, 1974–1982." *Canadian Journal of Economics* 17: 191–216.

Helliwell, John F., M.E. MacGregor, and T. Padmore. 1984. "Economic Growth and Productivity in Canada 1955–1990." Discussion Paper 84–30. Vancouver: University of British Columbia, Department of Economics.

Helliwell, John F., Peter G. Sturm, and Gerard Salou. 1985. "International Comparison of the Sources of Productivity Slowdown, 1973–1982." *European Economic Review* 28: 157–91.

Hood, W.C., and Anthony Scott. 1957. *Output, Labour and Capital in the Canadian Economy*. Study prepared for the Royal Commission on Canada's Economic Prospects. Ottawa: Queen's Printer.

Klein, L.R., and R.F. Kosobud. 1961. "Some Econometrics of Growth: Great Ratios of Economics." *Quarterly Journal of Economics* 75: 173–98.

3

Global Futures and Canadian Prospects
A Review of the
Global Modelling Literature

A.R. DOBELL

B.R. KENNEDY

Introduction

> Art and science are both uniquely human actions, outside the range of
> anything that an animal can do. And here we see that they derive from the
> same human faculty: the ability to visualize the future, to foresee what may
> happen and plan to anticipate it, and to represent it to ourselves in images
> that we project and move about inside our head, or in a square of light on the
> dark wall of a cave or a television screen.
>
> (J. Bronowski, *The Ascent of Man*, p. 56)

Toward an Understanding of Global Modelling

Since the Second World War, many scholars working within traditional
disciplines have been confronted by interdisciplinary upstarts who call
themselves "systems theorists" and reject the Cartesian advice to
"tackle the hard task piece by piece." The essence of systems thinking,
they argue, is a search for integrated methodologies, or a reaction
against reductionism in favour of holism. Many of the individual
pioneering efforts in this ambitious endeavour have naturally been prim-
itive or unsuccessful. Nonetheless, systems theories have arisen to
challenge the dominant assumptions and paradigms in many disciplines,
and gradually systems concepts have come to be incorporated into the
mainstream of engineering, management sciences, ecology, computer
sciences and other disciplines.

The need to take an integrated look at natural and social phenomena of
global scale was forcefully promoted by Aurelio Peccei and the Club of
Rome in a series of publications that coincided with growing concern
about the environment and the impact of population growth. Since the

late sixties and early seventies, computer simulation or "global modelling" has been popularly recognized as one of the principal methods of studying such long-range and global phenomena. Several global modelling studies, most notably Meadows's *Limits to Growth* (Meadows et al., 1972) and Barney's *Global 2000* (Barney, 1980) have become widely known and seem to have profoundly influenced the way that the public sees the world.

A casual familiarity with the modelling and forecasting field has led many observers to conclude that global modellers use non-traditional techniques and inevitably project major supply shortages, while sectoral experts using traditional economic techniques repeatedly forecast continuing growth, oversupply and slack markets for the same commodities. Furthermore, the global modellers, as supply pessimists, may appear to be in the same camp as other independent commentators or our future prospects such as the OECD's Interfutures project (1979), the report *Japan in the Year 2000* commissioned by the Japanese government (Okita, 1983), or Tinbergen's RIO report (1976), undertaken for the United Nations. While there is an element of truth in this perception, the reality is not so simple. In fact, the literature on global modelling embraces a vast array of conjecture from which it is not easy to draw concrete guidance as to public policy. Nevertheless, the purpose of this report is to survey that literature, isolate the main themes, and relate them, so far as possible, to the task of policy analysis in the medium term.

It must be emphasized at the outset that this survey can only provide brief reference to selected models, and no original analysis of them. Extensive methodological discussion has been avoided; following a review of model results, we concentrate on an interpretation of their significance for economic policy.

This study begins with a very brief overview of the main modelling activities in the futures forecasting field, and attempts to situate the global modelling literature within that general framework. The bulk of the paper is then devoted to a descriptive outline of particular global modelling efforts to date, followed by an attempt to extract from the results some consensus that might favour certain policies over others. Some general conclusions as to the possible significance of this modelling approach are suggested in the final section.

The Scope of the Study

Since the early seventies, the use of computer simulation techniques to portray various global futures has mushroomed to the point that it has become virtually impossible even to list all of the models worthy of a policy analyst's consideration. A list of only the better known models would include the following:

World2	Forrester
World3	Meadows
WIM	Mesarovic/Pestel
LAWM (Bariloche model)	Herrera
MOIRA	Linnemann
SARUM	Roberts
FUGI	Kaya
UN model	Leontief
Simlink & Simrich	World Bank, Waelbroeck
Global 2000	Barney

It is difficult to know where to draw the line between the above and more obscure models such as:

MRI	Polish Academy of Sciences
ZENCAP	Fritsch/Codoni/Sangy
Bottomley's model	presented at IIASA's Fifth Global Modelling Conference
World IV	Porat and Martin, Stanford
UNIDO World Industry Co-operation model	United Nations Industrial Development Organization
Pirogov's model	All Union Institute of Systems Science, U.S.S.R.
Dayal's Integrated System of World models	Bradford University, United Kingdom

The situation becomes more complex when we realize that many of these models are evolving continuously and may exist in several variations. Furthermore, models or parts of models are frequently cannibalized by other models, and old models can be adapted to new applications, sometimes emerging with a new name. Moreover, any contemplation of global models describing relationships within single sectors, such as MOIRA in the case of agriculture, for example, brings to mind numerous other simulations of relationships within energy, trade, or macroeconomic models. In addition to truly global models there are of course many, like FUGI or CANDIDE, that model regional or national economies. If, under this heading, we admit long-term models of a single sector within a single region or nation, there is almost no limit. For example, there are some 200 known models of the American agricultural sector.

Some of the individual models are so complex that it would take a lifetime for an outsider to check the data and verify the relationships. The largest of these models have tens of thousands of relationships and hundreds of thousands of coefficients. Fortunately some models are relatively simple in structure and many have already been scrutinized by other modellers.

The approach taken in this study has been to select, somewhat arbitrarily, certain models, deemed to be of interest, that are either directly comprehensible or have already been the subject of critical and comparative reviews. For informed comment on the best known models we have relied particularly on *The Global 2000 Report to the President* (Barney, 1980), the proceedings of the Sixth IIASA (International Institute for Applied Systems Analysis) conference on global computer modelling (Meadows, Richardson, Bruckmann, 1982), and one or two recent survey articles (see, for example, Neurath, 1979). In addition, the U.S. Congressional Committee on Technological Assessment has recently conducted a study of five of the nine models reviewed in this report. The committee's report, *Global Models, World Futures, and Public Policy* (U.S. Congress, 1982) was not obtained in time to be used as a source here. However, its treatment of the material is in many ways similar to ours, and several of the main conclusions of the two papers are virtually identical. Their report provides more detailed information on the history and funding of particular models and more detailed illustrations of model structures and outputs.

Readers familiar with the mammoth review reported in *The Global 2000 Report to the President* (Barney, 1980) and *Global 2000: Implications for Canada* (Barney et al., 1981) may wonder how this present small study can contribute anything more. Consider, though, that the recorded history of global modelling goes back only about 15 years. The Global 2000 study began in 1977; as a review of the state of the art it is rapidly becoming dated. Several of the models discussed in this study have appeared since the Global 2000 project. In addition, much of the comparative and critical literature on the models available today was not available to the Global 2000 team. Most notable in this regard are the proceedings of the sixth IIASA conference on global modelling and the critical reviews of the Global 2000 project itself. Many of the earlier computer projections and commentaries, though they are not invalid, have become simply uninteresting in the light of subsequent developments. Thus this study has not attempted to replicate the work of the Global 2000 team and others in digesting the earlier publications; rather it attempts to stand on the shoulders of the more recent commentators and view the field with a Canadian perspective.

Futures Forecasting and Global Modelling

In his opening address to the First Global Conference on the Future, Governor General Edward Schreyer quoted D.W. Brogan's warning: "Never underestimate the stupidity factor as a determinant of history."

This quotation highlights the need for humility in any effort to anticipate or plan for the future. We would do well to remember, for example, that only months before the fall of the Shah of Iran, experts and news magazines seemed to be in virtual agreement that the Iranian regime was secure. Luck has not been all bad, though. Perhaps a corollary to the above axiom is "Never underestimate the importance of sheer luck as a determinant of history." In the energy field, for example, Canada may have avoided a white elephant Arctic gas line, not through foresight, but through unrelated political events. Reliance on luck, however, is hardly to be recommended as public policy. At the same time, the record of futurists is not good either. Can we plan without anticipation? How can we improve our anticipation? How can such anticipation be used fruitfully by a group such as the Royal Commission on the Economic Union and Development Prospects for Canada?

Over the eons a myriad of techniques have been tried for incorporating future considerations into present strategies. The origins of the current crop of techniques can be traced in part to the U.S. Flood Control Act of 1936, which declared that the costs of federal projects should not exceed the benefits, and thus led to the development of methods of analysis designed to measure and to forecast both costs and benefits.

Mathematical formulations of macroeconomic models also led naturally to self-contained systems that lent themselves to numerical simulation, even though the interests of economic theorists generally centred on more basic qualitative properties. Monte Carlo methods, numerical integration and other computational approaches to the study of analytically intractable descriptions of dynamic systems were the obvious forerunners of current simulation programs such as the DYNAMO compiler made famous by Jay Forrester (see Forrester, 1971, and Pugh, 1970). In Europe, the work of Tinbergen in the 1930s emphasized the links between current policies and the eventual consequences for economic goals (see Tinbergen, 1956, for a more recent summary).

During the Second World War a host of futures-oriented systems analysis and operations research techniques emerged in Britain and the United States. After the war they were developed by the RAND corporation, among others, and were eventually adopted by Secretary of Defense McNamara and Assistant Secretary Hitch to emerge with presidential blessing as cost-benefit analysis, PPBS (Planning, Programming, and Budgetting Systems) and other core methods of management science. As our interest in the future increases, our repertoire of techniques continues to expand. We now have delphi techniques, risk analysis, think tanks, computer simulation, gaming, and royal commissions, along with the traditional host of visionaries and mystics. A partial illustration of the techniques current at the end of the sixties for the particular purpose of technological forecasting can be gleaned from

Bright and Schoeman (1972) and the references cited there. A flavour of the more general futures forecasting literature in Canada at the time is offered by Kettle (1970).

Global computer models burst onto the futures forecasting scene in 1970 with the Forrester-Meadows projections sponsored by the Club of Rome. Since that time this class of models may have had more influence than any other technique on how the general public perceives our long-term outlook. Global modelling is primarily a technique, however, not a school of thought. Reviewing the works of futurists who employ global models has more in common with reviewing economic works written in German than, for example, with reviewing socialist economics. That is not to say that such a review is useless. First, it has become imperative for planners to understand the medium and some of the issues that have been expressed through it. Second, and perhaps surprisingly, it is not so easy to distinguish a technique from a school of thought. Consensus with respect to some propositions about the world does seem to be emerging within the global modelling community.

Most global computer modellers deny that they are able to make forecasts. They insist that their interest at this stage lies not so much in the details of the output from their models as in understanding and communicating the mechanisms and relationships. Nonetheless, most observers persist in interpreting the outputs of computer models as forecasts. This situation has led in the past to considerable misunderstanding concerning the global models; the fault no doubt rests with both the modellers and the observers.

In practice, the term "global modelling" has come to refer to computer simulation studies, although in principle much more general activities are embraced by that expression. To understand how such global computer models originate, we must first realize that we all have a limited capacity to understand complexity and that we deal every day with very complex things by modelling them, that is, by constructing a simplified image of the real thing. For example, we carry mental models of our spouse and our employer and our country — not to mention ourselves. In fact, we deal continuously in models and are virtually incapable of thinking without them. Our mental models partially dictate what we will notice and what will be excluded by our perceptual filters. The things we choose to notice will usually serve to reinforce our mental models. Models, therefore, have always been used in the formulation of public policies, both good and bad. A global model is basically a personal "world view" that identifies those aspects of the earth and world society that are important to the modeller and the ways in which they appear to that person to interact. We are all global modellers, though few of us build computer models of the world. The term "the global modelling community," however, usually refers to those who express mental models of the globe through computer simulations. It is the work of this group that is reviewed in the following pages.

Some Methodological Issues

> We could say that rationism is an attitude of readiness to listen to critical arguments and to learn from experience. It is fundamentally an attitude of admitting that "I may be wrong and you may be right, and by an effort we may get nearer to the truth." It is an attitude that does not lightly give up hope that by such means as argument and careful observation, people may reach some kind of agreement on most problems of importance.
>
> (Karl S. Popper in *Philosophy for a Time of Crisis*, edited by Adrienne Koch, New York, Dutton, 1959, p. 263)

Preliminary Concepts in Global Modelling

This section introduces the main concepts that will be used in describing global computer models in the later parts of this paper. To begin, it is useful to note that most global computer models purport to be structural models rather than simply an expression of an empirical regularity observed from existing data. That is, they rest on theories or hypothesized relationships that may or may not be supported by empirical research, but which in any case embody some causal structure. Such models may have a variety of purposes, among them the following:

Forecast   As emphasized in the section entitled Futures Forecasting and Global Modelling, none of the research teams associated with the models studied here claims to be able to make precise quantitative predictions of future developments.

Projection   Several of the models studied here do function as tools of projection, however. These models are provided with a set of assumptions and are then expected to indicate the direction of the main trends that would result. Reference is frequently made in discussion of these models to a set of "baseline assumptions" or a "baseline run." The baseline assumption is generally that present policy and policy trends will continue without change. Baseline runs, however, are not forecasts; indeed, the baseline assumption of "no policy change" is highly unlikely. Change is one thing we know we can expect; particularly as future indicated stresses mount, we can anticipate significant adjustments to the existing policies. In fact, baseline projections are often expected to destroy their own validity as forecasts: the projection results are generally intended to be presented to policy makers with the intention of exposing trends toward future problems that are not yet obvious, thus encouraging governments to change their policies sooner than they otherwise would.

Utopian Models   Some dynamic models, that is, models capable of projecting trends, are not used to describe the world as it is at all, but are expressions of how the world could be. Modellers of this school find it uninteresting to project the consequences of a status quo that they deem unsustainable or intolerable far into the future. Instead they project with models embracing non-existent relationships to show how things could be if the policies they advocate were to be adopted.

Scenarios   Some computer models are not used to develop projections from given initial conditions; in fact, they accept as input the sorts of information that projection models produce as output. These models address the fact that the political process of establishing goals and targets in no way ensures that the targets are mutually consistent, attainable and desirable. Scenario models start with specific target levels of key variables for a future date and check their consistency and implications with respect to such things as the balance of trade and other secondary variables. In effect, they attempt to sketch in some of the missing detail in the projections that would be necessary to realize specific targets.

Communication   In addition to the above functions, the purpose of most models includes a strong communication or demonstration element. For example, Aurelio Peccei, the founder of the Club of Rome, had a strong sense of a "problematique humaine" that he urgently wished to disseminate. The model World3 was an essential medium for achieving this purpose.

Models may also differ in the kind of interaction they permit with the modeller or user and in the degree of aggregation they embody. All models are "interactive" in the sense that there is really no such thing as an objective "baseline run"; all runs require assumptions specified by somebody and usually a preferred set of assumptions is selected after a great deal of experiment with the model. In some models, however, all of the assumptions are supplied initially by the modeller while in others many are left flexible to be supplied iteratively, period by period, by the user or policy analyst as the simulation proceeds.

On the question of aggregation, a difficult decision must be made concerning how much detail should be incorporated into a global model. On the one hand, a model that is highly aggregated is easy to comprehend, though it may fail to make significant distinctions. A highly disaggregated model, on the other hand, may provide more information about individual units or sectors, but may ultimately be as difficult to comprehend as the real world. An example of a highly aggregated model is World3, which contemplates three economic sectors and treats the globe as a single geographic unit. The UN model, by contrast, has 15 geographic regions and 45 sectors for each region. The appropriate level of aggregation and degree will of course vary depending on the purpose of the model. But, as Joan Robinson has observed, to be useful a map must be considerably smaller than the territory it maps. Some models lose more information in the detail than in the aggregation.

Different models used for projection purposes may also have different time perspectives, depending on what phenomena are of interest to the modeller. If modellers are interested in short-term phenomena, such as the normal economic cycles, they will concentrate on different relationships and different time steps from those they will choose if they are interested in some longer-term phenomenon. Modellers with long time horizons, such as the World3 group, will often explicitly omit short oscillations such as economic cycles from their models, while for modellers with a shorter perspective, the same cycles may be of central interest. With these distinctions in mind, we might return briefly to consider global modelling as a technique for building up a consistent world view or mental image of a complex dynamic system, and as a technique for communicating the world view embraced by the individuals who build the model.

In constructing an abstract model or image of salient aspects of "reality," computer simulation offers two advantages: it assures a degree of consistency, and it permits some testing of the consequences implicit in the relationships which make up the model. On the first point, we may safely assume that many of the unexpressed global models that reside within the minds of some 4.5 billion humans abound with paradoxes and inconsistencies. The exercise of expressing models mathematically certainly helps clarify the modeller's ideas. Computer models are, by necessity, the most precisely expressed of all models. Thus, the exercise of creating and manipulating computer models enhances the modeller's understanding of his or her subject. When we have gone through the exercise of expressing our mental model in an appropriate computer language, the computer can, if our model is consistent, help us explore the implications of our model. This of course may help us to redefine our mental model or to make decisions based on our faith in our model and its implications.

There are, however, some difficulties with the process. Michael Mclean has identified what may be an important methodological booby trap inherent in simulation modelling (Mclean, 1978). Mclean contends that in the early, poorly funded stages of a modelling project there is an emphasis on producing a model structure at the expense of adequate conceptual and empirical research. Once a structure is achieved and projections start pouring out, funding often becomes available. By this point the model's structure has taken on an air of permanence and there is a temptation to spend years elaborating it, varying the parameters and experimenting with the unchanging core of the existing model, rather than rethinking its underlying logic.

Perhaps the more important function of global computer models is in the communication, rather than the construction, of a world view. We could choose to express a mental global model through any of a number of media. *Das Kapital* is an example of a global model expressed in literary form, and Keynesian economics might be represented as a global model expressed mathematically.

One reason for choosing computer simulation as a medium of communication is that complex mental models are very difficult to communicate, particularly when the audience is working from a different model and the language of communication is based on existing models. In discussing development issues today, we are dependent on terms like "developing nations," "Third World," "newly industrialized nations" and "east-west relations." All of these terms are tied to certain world views. Dissenting scholars may argue that they do not correspond to their own mental images of what countries should be grouped together. For example, Brian May prefers "spiritually oriented nations" to "developing nations" and "small Neo-Confucian nations" to "newly industrialized nations" (May, 1978). When people come from different cultures employing different languages, different models and different assumptions, it may be difficult to communicate complex ideas. Expressing the model first in an appropriate computer language can help because computers make no assumptions. Every detail must be stated explicitly. If the computer model is simple and well documented, anybody who understands the language can grasp all of the assumptions and relationships being communicated and can study their implications without implicit theory creeping in. Ideally, expressing a mental model in a common computer language in this way puts it into the public domain so that it can be widely studied. Unfortunately, many computer models are so complex and poorly documented that they virtually defy scrutiny.

There is of course another possible advantage (or disadvantage) to communicating by computer simulation — the almost mystical significance that is attributed to anything that comes from a computer. This was perhaps an important reason for the impact of Meadows's *Limits to Growth* in 1972, but it is becoming less and less the case now as increasing computer literacy creates increasing skepticism about computers.

The Problem of Validation

The main methodological problem that must be confronted at the outset is validation. It is generally argued that global computer models have essentially no systematic grounding in empirical evidence; they do not embody a structure inferred from data, or parameter estimates derived by consistent estimation techniques. What can be done with a model, or class of models, whose results "represented an appreciation, not a mathematical proof"? (Peccei, 1981). Schumacher (1964) was outspoken on the matter, with reference to a much earlier long-term perspective or outlook paper: "It is fashionable today to assume that any figures about the future are better than none. To produce figures about the unknown, the current method is to make a guess about something or other — called an assumption — and to derive an estimate from it by subtle calculation. The estimate is then presented as the result of scientific reasoning . . . this is a pernicious practice." In commenting specifically on the World2 model, Norhaus (1973) observes, "Whereas most scientists would require empirical validation of either the assumptions or the predictions of the model before declaring its truth content, Forrester is apparently content with subjective plausibility. This discrepancy in scientific standards of acceptability is probably what lies behind the dispute about the value of *World Dynamics*."

This issue is, of course, part of a deep philosophical controversy concerning the place of counterfactual models as a guide to reasoning. What meaning should be attached to "refutation" of a statistical simulation model employed in a world of uncertainty where individual agents act on the basis of what they expect will happen in the future and governments design their policies on the basis of the actions of individual agents and what they expect those agents will do in the future?

The reply of those defending the work of the Club of Rome, for example, is usually that the purpose of the global models is educational, not formally scientific. Peccei (1980) suggested that *Limits to Growth* "took issue with the self-complacency of industrial society . . . [and] opened a phase of self analysis that brought us to a higher level of understanding" (p. 22). Similar observations abound in almost any review of analytical aids to policy formation. Sanderson (1980) observes that none of the economic-demographic simulation models he surveys can offer serious guidance to policy makers. But "they are not totally without value . . . they are useful as pedagogical aids in teaching government officials about the kinds of long run consequences their decisions could entail" (p. 103). Or at least they are useful for communicating the particular beliefs and values of the model builder on these issues.

In light of these observations, it may appear that computer simulation of global models is hardly a reliable method of seeing into the future. We must bear in mind, however, the bluntness of the other tools we might use for that purpose. In some respects, the movement toward global modelling can be seen as a reaction against the short time frames and high discount rates of conventional project evaluation or management science, and the resulting tendency to downplay distant consequences and the interests of future generations. Similarly, with all their limitations, global modelling methods appeared to offer a way of dealing with ecological, environmental, and social considerations not readily captured in the usual demand-side econometric macro-models centred on quarterly or annual expenditure streams and financial transactions.

With the above battery of distinctions or categories in mind, and with a reminder that global models are expressions of the world views embraced by the individuals who build them, we turn in the next section to a survey of a variety of recent models stemming from a variety of academic disciplines, intellectual paradigms and modelling techniques. This survey attempts to distinguish between the conclusions derived from the output of each global model and the conclusions built into it at the beginning. Recognizing that modelling efforts must be viewed more as special-purpose advocacy than as all-purpose simulation, the survey attempts nevertheless to identify what significant ideas have been contributed to the debate on the problems facing the Royal Commission on the Economic Union and Development Prospects for Canada.

Reviews of Selected Global Models

Myself when young did eagerly frequent
Doctor and saint and heard great argument
About it and about. But evermore came out
By that same door where in I went.

> (*The Rubaiyat of Omar Khayyam*, Verse 27, translated
> by Edward Fitzgerald, New York: Grosset and Dunlop,
> 1899, p. 84)

World3 and its Prototypes

The Forrester-Meadows models were all released between 1970 and 1973 (see Forrester, 1971, for an extended discussion of the original World2 model and the general modelling approach). The series, which was commissioned by the Club of Rome to express its "problematique humaine," culminated in the model World3, which is undoubtedly the most widely known of the global computer models. World3 is highly aggregated and treats the globe as a single geographic unit or region. It is not highly interactive: parameter values are entered by the modeller at the beginning of a run only, and the model runs its own course from that point onward. The model was designed from the top down, as a single unified structure, and is formally capable of reaching virtually unlimited time horizons. World3 is simple, transparent, well documented and easily reproduced. It was also the focus of a substantial debate about growth prospects and modelling methods, and has therefore been subjected to more scrutiny, testing and criticism than probably any other model. Representative critiques can be found in Cole et al. (1973) and Nordhaus (1973).

The baseline runs most immediately associated with World3 were published in *The Limits to Growth* (Meadows et al., 1972). They are best known for the appearance of a global collapse in the twenty-first century or the avoidance of this disaster through population control and policies designed to achieve low rates of economic growth.

The Achievement of World3

The purpose of World3 was largely ideological and directed toward communications. We do not need a computer to predict the consequences of an exponentially increasing population with an exponentially increasing per capita consumption confined on a planet with finite resources. We must realize, however, that in 1973 the fact that something came out of a computer tended to lend scientific authority to it. World3 enabled people who were already concerned about the consequences of growth to capture the popular imagination and to make the issue worthy of serious debate internationally.

There are strong parallels between the World3 phenomena and Malthus's "Essay on the Principle of Population" (1798). As with *The Limits to Growth* (Meadows et al., 1972), Malthus's eighteenth-century pamphlet was taken as a prophecy of doom and provoked extensive debate. Neither publication was particularly original, and both appeared in the midst of a debate that was already underway. Both exploited the most authoritative medium available at the time. In the case of Malthus, it was the mathematical expression of a "Natural Law"; in the case of Forrester and Meadows it was the computer (Neurath, 1979).

World3 has definitely affected popular perceptions of our future prospects and of computer models. There have been subsequent models that are no less pessimistic than World3, but they have not provoked any comparable reaction. Perhaps the main achievement of World3 is simply that it caused the public and even governments to take an interest in the more distant future and the later consequences of current, possibly irreversible, policies. It put to rest the easy assumption of constant returns to scale and unending "golden-age" growth. Though the lesson was probably not needed by serious students of economic growth, it may have had a salutary effect in making the public more conscious of the seriousness of environmental issues and the potentially fragile nature of our renewable resource base.

While the mainstream of global modelling was moved away from some of the mechanisms depicted in World3, some groups are still promoting World3-type simulations, which continue to be catastrophic. For example, a Washington-based group called Carrying Capacity presented a systems dynamics model of U.S. agriculture to the Club of Rome at its Budapest meeting in October 1983. This model projects that within two decades America will have no exportable food surplus.

Thus, in summary, the discussion of the World3 model showed the importance of considering the future implications of present actions.

This conviction that our economic prospects are not simply a matter of projection, but a matter for public decision, reflecting a choice of institutional structures, is perhaps the greatest legacy of the debate generated by work in the modelling tradition initiated by Forrester for the Club of Rome. (This basic point is not original, of course; it can be found in almost any serious appraisal of the scope for public policy.) Work with the model raised questions concerning the possibility and the desirability of depending on perpetually increasing rates of consumption as the driving force behind the economy. And, finally (for better or for worse), World3 encouraged an interdisciplinary integrated approach to interdependent global problems.

Limitations of the Model for Medium-Term Policy

For our purposes, that of seeking guidance for Canadian policy, World3 is primarily of historical significance, for the following reasons:

- A model that has only one region has to be dramatic because it can show only extreme phenomena such as global prosperity or global collapse. Furthermore, time lags and anticipations are key issues in the type of stability analysis undertaken in this modelling effort, and a single-region model does not permit one region to witness problems as they strike another region and thereby either to assist or to alter its domestic policies accordingly. Neither interdependence nor the transmission of change can be represented. Subsequent models have elaborated on regional aspects.

- What comes out of World3 obviously reflects the world view that went into it. As Christopher Freeman has expressed it, "Malthus in — Malthus Out" (Cole, Freeman et al., 1973). Crucial to the World3 model is the view of finite reserves of resources that are readily exploited and easily depleted. This view is reflected in the assumption of exponentially increasing extraction costs as hypothetical limits are approached. Events since 1973 with oil and gas reserves estimates, however, should, if nothing else, lead to mental models with strongly price-elastic reserve estimates or other more sophisticated representations of the dynamics of resource depletion. If we have come to see resource depletion as a process of striving to offset progressively higher extraction costs with progressive technological improvements, then the earlier notion of fixed reserves embodied in the model does not help us project that understanding. Similarly, the starkly drawn pollution sector in World3 is somewhat a product of its decade. This sector in particular has drawn criticism based on charges of too much emphasis and insufficient data. Even given unlimited supplies of food and resources, the pollution sector alone is capable of eliciting the global collapse response in the model (Neurath, 1979, p.112).

- Since World3 — perhaps accelerated in part as a result of World3 —

there has been increasing study of the dynamics of population growth. The continuous exponential growth mechanism embodied in World3 is no longer within the normal range of debate. Demographers now talk of "S-curves" (logistic curves) and demographic transition, and the debate is no longer about whether population will stabilize by 2100 but what the stable population will be.

- World3 rightly drew attention to some of the problems with economists' paradigms. Certainly we cannot explain everything with flow models of supply and demand or short-run financial models. Most modellers have come to realize, however, that price mechanisms and related adjustment processes are central to our understanding and that to ignore them religiously — as does World3 — is just as narrow-minded as to embrace them unquestioningly.
- Even if we accept the global aggregation and conceptual model of World3, there are problems with sensitivity to parameter changes. A central criticism of the work has been that minor adjustments to certain parameters can result in dramatic qualitative changes in the response of the model. These parametric changes are well within the limits of what can reasonably be inferred from existing data bases. The possibility thus exists that the modellers can to some degree elicit the expected or desired results from the model by "fiddling" with parameters. This is a disturbing issue well worth bearing in mind. It is no doubt most associated with World3 simply because World3 has received the most attention. The same can be said of the closely related problem of validation, which has already been mentioned as the most serious problem in assessing the significance of any of the global simulation models.

The Mesarovic/Pestel Model (WIM)

While the World3 model was still being disseminated in 1973, the Club of Rome had already embarked on a follow-up project, the Mesarovic/Pestel model, which is another expression of the "problematique humaine." This model was intended to address some of the criticisms of World3 by elaborating on regional variation, providing more concrete policy proposals and incorporating more hard data. It was also designed to be less controversial and more acceptable to policy makers. The model has been evolving continuously since 1972 and is now referred to as the World Integrated Model (WIM). It was constructed by Mihajlo Mesarovic at Case Western University and Edward Pestel at Hanover Technical University (Mesarovic and Pestel, 1974).

WIM is an interactive model. Whereas World3, once given initial assumptions, ran by itself, WIM is designed to be used as an interactive tool by a policy maker, and consequently it accepts changes of policy and parameters all the way through the run. The model has been applied to a wide variety of analyses on topics ranging from U.S. energy policy to development problems in Africa.

The Mesarovic/Pestel model is highly complex and virtually impossible to depict graphically as there are some 300,000 relationships embodied in it. It uses different analytical techniques to handle different sectors, attempting to use the state of the art from the corresponding disciplines. It is nonetheless reasonably well integrated, having been designed from conception as a single model. It is also considerably disaggregated, detailing, in the original version, ten geographic regions, each with numerous sectors. Resource reserves are treated as a multi-dimensional concept involving probability of discovery, extraction effort and price. There is no pollution sector as such.

One consequence of the enormous complexity and lack of explicit documentation of the Mesarovic/Pestel model is that it has attracted little independent testing and technical criticism. A policy maker using the system who did not have complete confidence in the modellers should feel vulnerable. The model's flexibility and interactive nature also defuse criticism. To some degree, if we do not like an assumption we can change it, though it is hard to know what all of the assumptions are or how they ought to be varied. As the modellers emphasize interaction, they have avoided discussing the results. Nonetheless, standard runs do exist, and we can develop some appreciation for the type of constraints we might encounter in "test driving" the model.

In general, the model is considered to be optimistic and has been well received, though the reasons are difficult to isolate. A partial explanation may be that what an aggregated global model like World3 depicts as a world-wide decline in the standard of living can be more plausibly elucidated by a disaggregated model as the rich getting richer while the poor get poorer. Furthermore, the published run of the Messarovic/ Pestel model has been limited to 50 years, that is, well before the World3 global collapse. If the Mesarovic/Pestel model with baserun assumptions is allowed to run on, it apparently exhibits a collapse comparable to that foreseen by World3 (Neurath, 1979, p. 116). Furthermore, the standard run of this model shows that a 2 percent population growth rate in Asia cannot be sustained without massive food shortages on that continent within 50 years. Is that scenario really any more optimistic than a global collapse in 100 years?

Several reviews of the Mesarovic/Pestel model dwell on the alleged stratified or hierarchical structure of the model and related theory, though it is not clear that the concept adds to an understanding of the model's structure:

I come from a discipline that delights in classification schemes for the description of human behavior and far be it from me to deny the same pleasure to colleagues from another discipline, particularly since theirs appears quite defensible on logical grounds and makes sense in its own right. But I can't see where this somewhat complex scheme fits into their model. How is it needed or helpful for a better understanding of the whole problematique that it sets out to analyse? I can't find any place where the authors themselves used or needed it. (Neurath, 1979, p. 119)

The Achievement of the Mesarovic/Pestel Model

This Second Report to the Club of Rome and its progeny have not affected public opinion to the same extent as World3. The target group for this product has been policy makers, and the team is proud of the growing list of international politicians and officials who have used the model via satellite hook-ups. (One of the groups said to have used the WIM model for forecasting purposes was the regime of the former Shah of Iran, which should impress upon all of us the ultimate limitations of foresight technologies.) The publications associated with WIM have been more academic and less sensational than World3 and consequently have a less wide distribution but probably greater acceptance.

The group has also avoided making projections, a decision which has fostered acceptance and forestalled criticism because it does not provide much to contest. Unfortunately, it does not leave much to report on either. In one sense, WIM is an educational tool. It helps users enrich their understanding and improve their mental models. In the absence of prediction runs and without access to the models, we are left asking the modellers, "What have you learned?" The reply is normative and does not take us much beyond World3. There follow some selected conclusions paraphrased from *Mankind at the Turning Point* (Mesarovic and Pestel, 1974).

- Delays in addressing critical global issues can be disastrous. (This conclusion also emerged from World3.)
- The solution to these crises can be found only in a global context and in the long-term.
- It is possible to resolve these crises through (international) cooperation.
- The futility of narrow nationalism must be appreciated and taken as an axiom in the decision-making framework. (This conclusion perhaps takes on a subtle irony in a country where any effort in the national interest would already be a sign of cooperation and broad-mindedness.)
- A new ethic in the use of material resources must be adopted.
- We must develop a sense of responsibility for future generations if the human species is to survive.

WIM itself is no longer readily available. One of its heirs is a new model called Forecast, which is being developed by Patricia Strauch as a strategic tool for the American Joint Chiefs of Staff. Dr. Strauch apparently intends to "go commercial" with Forecast by 1986. It will be an interactive professional system consisting of a massive global data base and a model of relationships that is expected to include an index of political stability. Strauch reports that her clients have not expressed concern about hidden assumptions or paradigms.

The Significance of the Mesarovic/Pestel Model for Public Policy

- This model does not contradict World3 so much as it elucidates it. It rounds out our understanding of the predicament of mankind.
- The model anticipates that an increasing importance will be attached to the production and distribution of food. Asia is expected to place a tremendous demand for food on North America. It is of particular note that in the standard run of this model, North America's ability to meet this demand is constrained, not by absolute agricultural capacity but by its grain-handling capacity (Neurath, 1979, p. 118). There is also, of course, a question whether North America would be willing to produce and ship the required surplus if Asia were unable to pay. Its ability to pay, in turn, will probably depend upon the extent to which it has been permitted to industrialize and to export industrial products. A run of this model depicting a "liberal world economic order" foresees the emergence of oil-rich nations, grain-rich nations and manufacturing nations. An "isolationist scenario" suggests that domestic food prices can be kept down in North America only at the expense of exacerbating mass starvation in Asia. The isolationist scenario results in no increase in per capita North American income over the grain-rich nation scenario.

The Bariloche Model (LAWM)

The Bariloche model (or LAWM, the Latin American World Model) is a Third World response to World3. The project was carried out under the direction of Amilcar O. Herrera at the Fundación Bariloche in Argentina and received support from the Club of Rome and the International Development Research Centre in Ottawa.

The Bariloche model is a Utopian model. The modellers are humanist socialists whose objective is to describe a new world order and demonstrate its material feasibility. The model is therefore not a projection but a prescription and demonstration. Third World commentators objected to World3 on the grounds that it advocated restricting economic growth just when the Third World had a lot of catching up to do simply to reach acceptable income levels; and that the view that shortages of food and housing were imminent was a parochial, developed-world view since two-thirds of the world's population already have those problems. The model is a demonstration, or rather an assertion, that the limitations on prosperity are not physical but socio-political, and that by adopting an appropriate world order, universal freedom from basic want could be achieved.

In the economic system portrayed by the model, resources are allocated so as to achieve maximum life expectancy at birth, which is the indicator selected as a general measure of well-being. The optimization procedure embodied in the model for making these allocations is of necessity esoteric. This mathematical obscurity seems to have foiled technical critiques as effectively as sheer complexity has done in some other models.

There are two controversial aspects of the model that have led to suggestions that it is excessively optimistic. First, it has no built-in resource constraints other than that of arable land area. Second, population figures are generated by a section of the model that reduces a region's birthrate as its social well-being increases. The resulting population estimates are considerably more optimistic than those used by the United Nations or other modellers. (It should be remembered, though, that the Bariloche model is not intended as a projection model.)

Achievements of the Bariloche Model

The ideas of the Bariloche model have not enjoyed broad popular dissemination. The model's main influence has been at the United Nations and it has been used by the International Labor Organization in some research. It appears to be the most popular of the global models among Third World policy makers and policy analysts.

The insight that the salient aspects of the predicament of mankind are not physical but socio-political cannot be dismissed lightly. The same message comes from the RIO report to the Club of Rome by Jan Tinbergen and from the OECD's Interfutures project. At the sixth IIASA symposium on global modelling, this assessment was the main point of consensus among the seven global modelling teams that participated (Meadows, Richardson, Bruckmann, 1982).

The specific policies related to aid programs, egalitarian Third World income structures, and "optimal" resource allocation are not plausible. What is of considerable interest in this model is the striking familiarity of what comes out of it compared to the novelty of what went into it. The model is able to paint a scenario of stabilization and freedom from want in Latin America and Africa, but by 2040 there are serious food shortages in Asia that could almost be considered a global collapse when we consider that 60 percent of the world's population, according to this scenario, is Asian. Once again, we see North America called on to make up the shortfall in food production. Another interesting observation is that the declining rates of population growth incorporated into this model resemble the restrained population growth scenarios necessary to achieve stability in World3 and advocated as policy objectives by that group (Neurath, 1973).

The Simon Models

This section refers to two small models published by Julian Simon in *The Ultimate Resource* (Simon, 1981b). These relatively unknown models have been included in this review because they demonstrate that the output from a model is not so much a product of the methods and technologies employed as a consequence of the modeller's world view.

Simon has conceived relationships between demographics and economics that he is anxious to communicate. To assist in this dissemination he has used two very simple, easily understood dynamic simulation models. This use of the technology puts Simon in the Forrester-Meadows camp so far as the building and use of computer models is concerned. Beyond that point he parts company with Meadows and many other global computer modellers. To demonstrate this point, consider Simon on World3: "It is a fascinating example of how scientific work can be outrageously bad and yet very influential"; and on Global 2000: "I find the conclusions of Global 2000 almost wholly without merit and the method shoddy" (Simon, 1981a, pp. 286–88).

Simon's contention is that resources, including food, arable land, fuel, minerals and forecasts, can, for economic purposes, be considered infinite. First, we are not really interested in the quantity of a resource but the quantity of a service we get from the resource, and second, the only realistic measure of a resource's scarcity is its price. Simon emphasizes that we can only base future projections on past experience and that the long-term trend for all of the aforementioned resources is one of decreasing prices, that is, decreasing scarcity. Admittedly, we must exploit progressively lower-grade resource deposits, but so far that disadvantage has been more than offset by better methods of extraction and greater economies of scale.

We cannot simply dismiss Simon as a "short-sighted economist." In many ways his time horizons extend further than those of the ecologically oriented. For example, in his work petroleum consumption itself is viewed as a temporary phenomenon that will ultimately give way to alternative forms of energy, which may quite possibly be cheaper in real terms than petroleum.

The consequences of this world view are fascinating. Simon's two models explore the consequences of population growth for both developed and less developed nations. They concentrate on the economic value to society of the marginal child born. A child is depicted as an economic drain on society throughout its period of dependency but at 20 years of age he or she starts to work and contribute to the wealth of society. Economically, the child represents just another form of capital investment like machinery or land improvement, and his or her present value at birth is determined primarily by the rate at which future benefits are discounted.

Population growth is the exogenous or independent variable. The baseline runs of Simon's models display output per worker for various rates of exponential population growth. As we should expect, given a model that concentrates not on diminishing returns mechanisms but economies of scale mechanisms, output per worker rises exponentially and indefinitely for each scenario. The rate of exponential growth does vary, however, depending on the rate of population growth, and a concept emerges of an optimal rate of population growth that is neither too low nor too high (echoing once again a much older literature).

With Herman Kahn, Simon has recently released a study that rebuts Global 2000. Intended originally to be entitled "Global 2000 Revised," it appeared as *The Resourceful Earth* (Simon and Kahn, 1983). This publication reflects both the modelling perspective just described and Kahn's well-known optimism concerning the "technological fix" (see *The Next Two Hundred Years*, Kahn, 1976, for a brief statement of this view). It can be taken as a definitive statement of the arguments against the Club of Rome's perspective.

Significance of Simon's Models for the Royal Commission
The Simon models are interesting because they present an entirely different world view from that associated with the better known global modelling literature. From the latter perspective, one might be tempted to view Canada as a resource-rich society and even a society that can afford to live indefinitely off the resource rents accruing during a future of ever-increasing resource scarcity. This resource society model of Canada implies that per capita income is largely determined by the available resource rents per person, with the obvious implication that population and immigration must be held down. Simon, in contrast, portrays an industrial model where (1) resource rents are transitory and likely to be eroded by technological changes and (2) a nation's wealth is founded upon the efforts of its population. Simon would presumably see Canada as a desperately underpopulated nation in which an interesting assortment of overtaxed citizens are struggling to support a massive infrastructure that is barely adequate to permit industrialization. He would thus advocate greater immigration (as has Canada's foremost economic historian and geographer, Harold A. Innis).

While the Simon models are optimistic, their optimism is qualified. (Of course in the context of a resource-rich country, it is never clear which are the optimistic and which are the pessimistic scenarios to describe the prospects for available resources at a world level.) The price of resources has fallen continuously in the past and will continue to do so — provided that we continue to advance our technical knowledge. There is, overall, less hunger in the world at present than there has been in the past and every indication that this trend will continue. Serious local famines will persist, of course, primarily in regions afflicted by war and political blundering. Simon also acknowledges the possibility of sustained larger famines in the future but points out that if this occurs it will be in part because North America adopts a policy of restricting its food production (Simon, 1981a, p. 80). The problem, in other words, will be one of distribution, not of feasible aggregate production levels. It is primarily to this issue that the next modelling effort is addressed.

MOIRA

Another model that drew its original inspiration from the Club of Rome is MOIRA (Model of International Relations in Agriculture). It is primarily the product of economists at the Free University of Amsterdam and a group of agronomists at the Agricultural University at Wageningen, the Netherlands, who were coordinated by Hans Linnemann. The principal subject of this study is hunger and whether the world can produce enough food for its growing population.

MOIRA is a global model of the agricultural sector only. It bears many resemblances, in fact, to GOL, the agricultural sector model incorporated in the Global 2000 model: both are world models disaggregated into several geographic regions; both are agricultural sector models; both began from estimates of maximum production potential for the geographic units they encompassed; both lean heavily on traditional economic theories for their formulations, and both see the world as being controlled through market adjustments to changing levels of supplies, demands and prices. Likewise, both consider non-agricultural income growth and population growth as exogenous variables (Barney, 1980). It is the difference in the way that the two models are disaggregated that reveals their different orientations. GOL has disaggregated the different types of crops, but it does not distinguish between the incomes of various agricultural consumers. MOIRA quotes all agricultural output in terms of vegetable protein equivalent but has people disaggregated into 12 income groups in each of its 106 regions. The purpose of MOIRA is not so much to model agricultural output as to explain hunger and find policies to deal with it.

As both population and non-agricultural GDP are exogenous variables in MOIRA, it is clearly not a projection model. Rather, it accepts projected population and GDP inputs and then models how the agricultural sector could react to them. The model takes standard econometric techniques that have been routinely applied to relationships among two or three nations and uses the computer to apply them to relationships among many nations. The MOIRA team has taken pains to base the mechanisms in their model on statistical analysis of existing data so far as possible.

A key assumption in the model is the relationship between income and food consumption. It is assumed that, as income rises in the poorer nations, diets will shift toward meat proteins as has happened in the developed nations.

A major contribution of the MOIRA project is the work it has done on the physical limits of agricultural production. Considering only physical limits imposed by available soil, water and solar energy, the group concluded that the earth is capable of producing 30 times as much food as it does at present. This figure ignores such limitations as economics, fuel, labour, fertilizer and skill, but it also assumes current technology, thereby ignoring such potentials as hydroponics and mariculture. Yet people are starving today. How do we reconcile these facts? The important conclusion is that our physical limitations are not in fact the significant barriers. People are starving today, not because we cannot produce enough food, but because they cannot afford to buy the food that is available. The study of famine then is more an exercise in economics and distribution than in agricultural science.

The fact that our physical limitations are remote does not suggest that the problem can be solved easily. The baseline run for MOIRA in fact shows progressively higher numbers of people suffering from hunger. Paradoxically, the baseline run also shows progressively higher *average* protein consumption per capita. To reconcile these observations we must recognize that starvation is primarily an income distribution problem. The ultimate dilemma posed by MOIRA is that to ensure adequate food production it is necessary to have high food prices. High prices guarantee a high average per capita food consumption, but they also increase the number of people who cannot afford to feed themselves adequately.

The standard run also projects that "the trend in developing nations is towards decreasing, rather than increasing, self sufficiency in food. By the year 2000 North America will have strengthened its position as the dominant exporter of basic foods" (Meadows, Richardson, Bruckmann, 1982, p. 62). (It is possible that recent evidence of increasing success in food production both in India and China following economic reforms might lead to reconsideration of this assertion, but it stands as of 1982.)

Sensitivity test runs of MOIRA suggest that world hunger can be reduced by raising the level of economic growth, lowering the rate of population increase, or reducing income inequalities. Several policy scenarios have also been run on MOIRA. Hunger was eliminated most successfully when each of the rich countries used 0.5 percent of its GNP to purchase food on the market and send it as aid to regions that are incapable of producing the food they need. Less successful was a system of international food market regulation. Perversely effective were a trade liberalization in food and a voluntary reduction in protein consumption in the developed countries. Both of these policies backfire because they lower the price of food in the developed countries. This inhibits food production and consequently does not increase food exports to developing countries.

Significance of MOIRA for the Royal Commission

MOIRA again gives strong support to the notion that the salient limitations on human potential are social-political rather than physical. While drawing attention to the long-run importance of our agricultural resource, the model also raises an issue of Canada's moral responsibility to hungry regions. Can Canada ethically restrain its food production as a price-control policy in the light of evidence that this policy will contribute to the starvation of others?

SARUM

A further attempt to extend conventional economic models to take into account changing stocks of renewable and non-renewable resources as well as longer-term environmental considerations within an international trading structure is contained in SARUM, a model constructed by a team in the United Kingdom. The sole source for independent reviews of the SARU model seems to be IIASA. The summary review contained in *Groping in the Dark* (Meadows, Richardson and Bruckmann, 1982), and reproduced below, seems to express its greatest approval for SARUM. (For comparison with other models reviewed in this section it should be noted that *Groping in the Dark* is generally less critical of most models than other sources have been.)

> The mission of the Systems Analysis Research Unit (SARU), located in the U.K. Department of the Environment and headed by experimental physicist Peter C. Roberts, was to "explore the implications for national and international policies of long-term trends in environment and society." One of the ways they filled this mission was to inform themselves about the global models under construction, their methods, data bases, and major assumptions.
>
> Roberts and his team quickly gained respect as constructive critics in the emerging global modelling field. At IIASA conferences, other professional meetings, and in several publications, the SARU staff has provided informed, solid commentary on the principal models. Speaking from an "in-house" perspective, Roberts places particular emphasis on the needs and special requirements of policy-level officials. "How could such models be made more credible?" he asks. "At what point in their development should we expect models to make a really effective contribution to the decision-making process?"
>
> In probing these questions, the SARU staff "came to the conclusion that the difficulties could best be understood by attempting to build a world model within the unit." The result of their efforts, "a simulation model making use of standard rules of economic behaviour and based, as far as

possible, on published empirical data," called SARUM, was first presented at IIASA in September 1976.

The SARU model and the organization of the team have several particularly interesting features. First, the SARU staff self-consciously had limited aspirations for their model. Roberts' skepticism about the utility of pioneering global models extended to his own work. "At this stage of development," he has emphasized, "it is unwise to lay much emphasis on the character of the 'futures' which are simulated. Of more importance is establishing the validity of the data base and the relationships. Not until there is some confidence in the soundness of the basic work is it appropriate to draw conclusions and make recommendations."

A second feature of the project is its built-in self-criticism mechanism. The Science Policy Research Unit (SPRU) at Sussex University, which has gained international visibility with its criticism of *The Limits to Growth* (Cole et al., 1973), was retained by SARU to play a similar role vis-à-vis their model. The SPRU review was included in the IIASA presentation of SARUM — although not in the subsequent *Research Report* describing the model.

The absence of a popularly oriented publication emphasizing conclusions is a third distinguishing feature of this project. The group did publish excellent documentation, however, and has made versions of the model readily available to anyone wanting to implement and run it.

Finally, SARU learned from and built upon the work of other projects. Although the model reflects a commitment to a structure "based on relationships implicit in the neoclassical synthesis," SARUM has incorporated ideas from system dynamics, econometrics, input-output analysis, and the multilevel approach used by Mesarovic and Pestel. Where the model attempts to break new ground, the authors are very explicit about what they are doing and why.

Although an advanced, fifteen-region version of SARUM was used by the OECD Interfutures project (1979) for many of its projections, the model has not received wide media attention or public recognition. In view of the group's philosophy, this is not surprising. But among global modellers, as well as other modelling professionals who are familiar with the model, both the model and the project team are held in very high regard. This group has adhered to high standards of scientific inquiry and good modelling practice. There is much to be learned from SARUM and from the development process that culminated in its completion and documentation.

The Purpose of the Model

To the query, "What are the purposes?" the SARU staff would respond:
1. to learn more about the difficulties of building global models and how to overcome them;
2. to strive for a deeper understanding of the way the global system works; for a greater knowledge of the effects of interaction than can be obtained from analysis of selected isolated problems;
3. to discover the possible areas and dimensions of stress of the development of the global system.

In a general way the focus of SARUM is similar to that of the other global models. It is concerned with long-term developmental trends in the global system, with the impacts of the policies that may be designed to shape these trends, and with avoiding hazards.

The Structure of the SARU Model

SARUM is a multiregion, multisector model, somewhat similar in geographical disaggregation to that of Mesarovic and Pestel. The earliest version was highly aggregated, incorporating only three regions (or strata) based on income levels; however, the latest version defines 15 regions. Regions are linked by trade and aid; both commodity and monetary flows are defined. Each region has an identical structure, comprising 13 interlinked economic sectors. The documented version of the model devotes nine sectors to a rather disaggregated representation of agricultural activity. Non-agricultural activities are more highly aggregated into four sectors: minerals, primary energy, capital, and non-food goods and services. Interregional differences are taken into account by defining different initial conditions and parameter values for each region. The principal exogenous inputs to the model are population, technological growth in capital and labour productivity, technological growth in fertilizer response, and a representation of income distribution within the population of each region.

The Basic Assumptions

A good place to begin discussing the SARU model is with the list of the basic theoretical assumptions, which are based on neoclassical economics, a tradition that traces its roots to Adam Smith's *Wealth of Nations* (1776), and reflects, in particular, the later theoretical contributions of John Maynard Keynes (see *The General Theory of Employment, Interest, and Money*, Harcourt Brace, New York, 1935). Nine basic propositions are identified by the SARU staff:

1. Consumers will choose the goods and services that maximize their utility, given the prices of the goods and services.
2. Entrepreneurs will select the production technique that maximizes their profit, given the factor prices.
3. Producers cannot affect the prices of the goods they sell by adjusting the output.
4. Consumers cannot affect the prices of the goods they buy by adjusting demand.
5. Labour and investment will be attracted to those industries where the wages and profits are highest.
6. Prices are an inverse function of stocks.
7. A set of prices exists that will clear all markets, apart from desired stocks.
8. Consumers will buy more (less) of a good as its price falls (rises), unless the good is "inferior."
9. Entrepreneurs can enter or leave any industry, depending on whether they make a profit or loss.

The overall goal incorporated in the model is to improve the material well-being of deficient members of the population without making anyone worse off (Pareto optimality).

The modellers recognize that these assumptions are not universally accepted and may be regarded as naïve by some. However, they argue that the usefulness of these assumptions, as applied in the model, is supported by empirical data. The detailed arguments are found in SARUM 76, Chapter 3, and make interesting reading for both supporters and opponents of this perspective.

Application of the Assumptions:
The Structure of a Basic Sector

To grasp the way in which the "neoclassical synthesis" has been incorporated in SARUM, it is useful to look more closely at the model's representation of an economic sector. The dominant feedback loops in the model determine labour supply and wages, production levels (output), capital accumulation, and prices. The price mechanism incorporates time delays (smoothed demand and smoothed cost) to take into account the delayed response of prices to changing costs and patterns of demand. Classical Cobb-Douglas production functions are used to relate labour and capital to output. Non-monetarized and monetarized sectors are linked. Computations establish the values of the different variables, and especially the balance (equilibrium) between supply and demand. Sectors within each region are linked by flows of labour, capital, and commodities.

The Linkages Among Sectors

The between-sector flows are determined by prices and profitability. Wage rates determine the flows of labour from sector to sector.

The Linkages Among Regions

Five assumptions about international trade are made in the SARU model:
1. A country may draw its supplies from more than one source, even though significant price differentials exist among them.
2. A country may import and export the same "product" if the product consists of a heterogeneous collection of commodities formed by aggregation.
3. World trade patterns react sluggishly to changes in relative prices because habitual business relations and the massive physical infrastructure (railways, docks, pipelines, etc.) do not change quickly.
4. Some countries regard trade regulations and tariffs as an extension of strategic and diplomatic policy and use trade to further their interests abroad and protect special interests at home.
5. World trade calls for shipping goods over greater distances than domestic trade, and the cost of transport may be a decisive element in the total cost at the market.

A simple "bias matrix" is used by the modellers to take into account deviations from normal price-determined behaviour. Numbers in the matrix correspond to each region and each sector and measure the degree of deviation. This permits the aggregate effects of factors such as distance and tariff barriers to be incorporated. Nations may run trade deficits for a period of time. Heavy debts lead to reductions in domestic expenditures and adjustments in the trade bias matrix to reflect a lack of international credit.

The final international flow, foreign aid, is represented in this version of the model as a simple flow of money. One region's expenditure is increased and another's decreased by a specified proportion of the donor's gross regional product.

Further Developments

SARUM is the only global model among those reviewed that was funded by a government agency and developed in-house. Paradoxically, it appears to have been the project that was most free from external pressures. During the years prior to 1976, Roberts and his colleagues were permitted to go about their work deliberately, to follow an orderly path of development, to devote major resources to validity testing and sensitivity analysis, and to prepare superb documentation.

Following the publication of SARUM 76, a decision was taken to develop — as noted above — a fifteen-region version of the model and to "go public" with it.

SARUM was used by the OECD Interfutures project for a number of long-term scenarios [OECD, 1979]. A SARU staff member joined the OECD team and worked closely with the group in London throughout this phase. With the completion of the Interfutures project, the Unit's activity in global modelling has diminished and its emphasis is now on assisting other research groups wishing to use SARUM, particularly where such groups plan to attempt novel investigations. As an example, a group is using SARUM to study environmental impacts for the Australian Department of Science and Environment. (pp. 66–74)

The UN Model

Like the Bariloche model, the UN model originates in the Third World's rejection of World3. In the early seventies, UN targets for a "development decade" to promote growth and development in the Third World included elements such as the following:

- increasing the share of the developing market economies in manufacturing to 25 percent;
- achieving a 4 percent growth rate of food and agricultural production in the developing countries;
- creating one billion new jobs in the developing countries by the year 2000.

It became a matter of serious concern at the UN that there was no guarantee that the targets would be physically achievable or mutually consistent. In 1973 the United Nations Center for Development Planning, Projections and Policies received financial support from the Government of the Netherlands for a UN modelling project and named Professor Wassily Leontief as project director. The modelling work was done primarily at Brandeis University by Anne Carter and Peter Petri.

Conceptually, this is a simple model, founded on input-output analysis, which is essentially an accounting system for keeping track of flows of goods and services among national sectors and among nations. What is conceptually simple, however, quickly becomes overwhelmingly complicated in the UN model. The accounting system uses both monetary and physical units. These physical flows are fairly disaggregated, monitoring, for example, flows of nine different minerals. Combining this sort of detail with 15 geographic regions results in an immense set of simultaneous equations for which over 10,000 coefficients had to be estimated from the data available. The net result is that it is very difficult for an outsider to judge the assumptions that may be embodied in the model.

The model employs the concept of finite reserves of natural resources; in the published runs, however, the limits on resources have not imposed any constraints. One of the original interests of the project group was pollution, and the model includes provision to monitor the loading of the environment with pollutants. Team member Carter, however, has described the environmental sector of the model as quite superficial, and, in fact, the environmental sector has been eliminated entirely from at least one of the several versions of the UN model in existence today (Barney, 1980, p. 650; Meadows, Richardson, Bruckmann, 1982).

The simultaneous equations structure of the model allows for a great deal of flexibility. For one thing it resembles the spreadsheet application packages available with personal computers in that the user can choose which variables are exogenous and which are endogenous. Given a set of constraints, the model is capable of making projections, but its normal application is as a generator of scenarios.

The model tackles such questions as the consequences of meeting specified targets for growth rates or development levels for less developed countries. How much of the country's mineral resources would be exhausted? How much pollution would be created? What sort of structural changes would be required in regional economies, and what changes to international trade, aid and balance of payments would be implied?

The conclusions that the modellers have reached after experimenting with a variety of scenarios are summarized in *The Future of the World Economy* (Leontief, Carter and Petri, 1977, p. 10–11) as follows:

1. The target rates of growth of gross product in the developing regions set by the International Development Strategy for the Second United Nations Development Decade are not sufficient to start closing the income gap between the developing and the developed countries.
2. The principal limits to sustained economic growth and accelerated development are political, social, and institutional in character. No insurmountable physical barriers exist within the twentieth century to the accelerated development of the developing regions.

3. The most pressing problem of feeding the rapidly increasing population of the developing regions can be solved by bringing under cultivation large areas of currently unexploited arable land and by doubling and trebling land productivity. Both tasks are technically feasible, but are contingent on drastic measures of public policy favorable to such development and on social and institutional changes in the developing countries.
4. The problem of the supply of mineral resources for accelerated development is not a problem of absolute scarcity in the present century but, at worst, a problem of exploiting less productive and more costly deposits of minerals and of intensive exploration of new deposits. . . .
5. With the current commercially available abatement technology, pollution is not an unmanageable problem. . . .
6. Accelerated development in developing regions is possible only under the condition that from 30 to 35 percent and in some cases up to 40 percent of their gross product is used for capital investment. A steady increase in the investment ratio to these levels may necessitate drastic measures of economic policy in the field of taxation and credit, increasing the role of public investment and the public sector in production and infrastructure. Measures leading to a more equitable income distribution are needed to increase the effectiveness of such policies; significant social and institutional changes will have to accompany these policies. . . .
7. There are two ways out of the balance-of-payments dilemma (posed by potentially large deficits in the developing regions). One is to reduce the rates of development in accordance with the balance-of-payments constraint. Another way is to close the potential payments gap by introducing changes into the economic relations between developing and developed countries, as perceived by the Declaration on the Establishment of a new International Economic Order — namely, by stabilizing commodity markets, stimulating exports of manufacturers from the developing countries, increasing financial transfers, and so on.
8. To accelerate development, two general conditions are necessary: first, far-reaching internal changes of a social, political, and institutional character in the developing countries, and, second, significant changes in the world economic order. Accelerated development leading to a substantial reduction of the income gap between the developing and developed countries can only be achieved through a combination of both these conditions. Clearly, each of them taken separately is insufficient, but, when developed hand in hand, they will be able to produce the desired outcome.

Significance of the UN Model for the Royal Commission
The strength of the UN model lies in its input-output flow modelling capacity. Although its treatment of pollution and resources seems somewhat dated, the model adds support to the notion that those physical limitations are not the really salient issues. At the same time, this model has not been able to generate very promising scenarios for the develop-

ing countries within the bounds of the existing international economic framework. The model raises an interesting issue of how we assure that recommendations on economic strategies generated by a political process are mutually consistent, compatible and achievable.

Global 2000

More pessimistic — and more controversial — are the findings of a more recent major study undertaken in the United States. The conclusions of that study — the Global 2000 Report to the President — have been summarized as follows:

> If present trends continue, the world in 2000 will be more crowded, more polluted, less stable ecologically, and more vulnerable to disruption than the world we live in now. Serious stresses involving population, resources, and environment are clearly visible ahead. Despite greater material output, the world's people will be poorer in many ways than they are today.
>
> For hundreds of millions of the desperately poor, the outlook for food and other necessities of life will be no better. For many it will be worse. Barring revolutionary advances in technology, life for most people on earth will be more precarious in 2000 than it is now — unless the nations of the world act decisively to alter current trends. (Barney, 1982, p. 2)

In 1977 President Carter directed a group of American government agencies to assess the "probable changes in the world's population, natural resources and environment through the end of the century." The Global 2000 project was allocated a staff under the direction of Gerald O. Barney, and a tremendous bureaucratic effort was launched involving 11 American federal agencies.

The Global 2000 staff elected not to construct a new global model from scratch but rather to attempt to integrate the various projection models that were already in use by different agencies. It soon became apparent that various groups and individuals throughout the American civil service were involved in futures forecasting. Many of these people had never met or collaborated and were basing their work on mutually inconsistent assumptions. Barney recognized that although it would not be possible to integrate the existing models fully, it was important to use them in order to make the results of the study more acceptable to the bureaucracy.

The Global 2000 staff started with the premise that the best basis on which to anticipate the future is the extrapolation of past trends. They therefore asked each of the participating agencies to produce a forecast in its area of expertise using its existing techniques and models. For example, the Department of Agriculture projected food data and the Census Bureau with the International Development Agency projected population. The results were, of course, inconsistent. The approach used to integrate these forecasts is referred to by the Global 2000 staff as sequential integration. This means that a projection is first made for population without benefit of interaction with other sectors. The population projections are then used as exogenous variables in the economic model to produce GNP and GNP per capita variables, and all of these projections are used as exogenous variables in the next sectoral model. It should be noted that a normally integrated model simulation proceeds in time steps and at each step all sectors have the opportunity to interact and affect conditions in the next step. In Global 2000, however, sectors at the beginning of the integration sequence are virtually unconstrained by other sectors, and sectors at the end of the sequence are so constrained by the precomputed projections of other sectors that the original principle of extrapolating existing data bases is lost. The following statement, for example, does not sound as if it emanated from an empiricist: "After decades of generally falling prices the real price of food is projected to increase 95% over the 1975–2000 period" (Barney et al., 1981, p. 14). It should be realized that with this technique only the initial sectors are really a projection of the data. The remaining figures are scenario developments based on the initial projections. The population and GNP projections therefore deserve primary consideration, since the validity of the entire model depends on them.

The crucial projections of Third World fertility rates were established as follows:

> For the less developed countries the fertility assumptions were made on a judgemental basis by demographers who have worked with the demographic and related socio-economic data for the individual countries over extended time periods. Specifically no mathematical model of fertility change was used. (Barney, 1980, p. 8)

The demographers consulted by Barney must necessarily have found themselves in a difficult situation. Consider for example the problem they must have faced with China, home of approximately one-fifth of humanity:

> Experts differ in their opinion as to what extent the Chinese central government itself knows these facts, but whatever the case may be, national population data are not published. . . . Estimates of China's population range from 800 to 978 million inhabitants, estimates of her crude birthrate range between 14 and 37 per 1,000 inhabitants, her crude death rate between 6 and 15 per 1,000 and the rate of natural increase between .8 and 2.4 percent per year. (Frejka, 1978, p. 540)

At the same time, it clearly does make sense, if one must integrate sequentially, to start with population trends. Barring major disasters, much of the demographic profile of the year 2000 is determined by today's demographic profile and consequently population is the sector that can be forecast most reliably.

Figure 3-1 World Population Growth Trends, 1900–2100

Population   in billions

Traditional Demographic Transition

Rapid Demographic Transition

Illusory Demographic Transition

1900	1950	1975	2000	2050	2100

Year

15	10	5

Source: Thomas Frejka, "Future Population Growth," in *Handbook of Futures Research,* edited by J. Fowles (London: Greenwood Press), p. 546.

The Global 2000 demographers started with a set of assumptions including no change in government policies and an 11 percent increase in global life expectancy owing to health improvements. The projection made indicates that the global population in 2000 will be approximately 6.35 billion, of which 5 billion will live in the developing countries. (In 1975 the world's population was about 4 billion.) Furthermore, most of these people will be living in cities. Some 44 cities will have passed the one million mark, and Mexico City will lead with 30 million inhabitants, two-thirds of whom will be in uncontrolled shanty towns.

These assumptions and projections may suggest a question to some readers. Is it more likely that the assumptions will hold and that the projected scenario will be reached or that in the face of the projected pressures some of the assumptions will break down? Of further concern is the projection that the population growth rate, currently 1.8 percent a year, will have only dropped to 1.7 percent by the year 2000. This result seems to be based on a mental model of the demographic transition phenomenon as a function of family planning policy and economic development. As Figure 3-1 shows, demographic transition is still not well understood. Demographers such as Frejka point out that demographic transition in the developing countries may not follow the expected pattern:

> In a number of developing countries — with varying social, economic, climactic, historical and religious conditions — for which reasonably good documentation of fertility trends exists, a distinctly more rapid decline in fertility has occurred than was the case in the demographic transition of many of the now developed countries. (Frejka, 1978, p. 545)

Furthermore, economists like Julian Simon would argue that demographic transition is not driven by a rising standard of living but by urbanization. This theory maintains that large families are economically rational for rural families but not for urban families, hence the phenomenon of falling birth rates (Simon, 1981b). Supporters of this view could not accept Global 2000's projection of massive urbanization with virtually no change in the population growth rate.

The second factor in Global 2000's sequential integration is GNP. There are several inputs into the GNP projections, but the principal tool is the World Bank's Simlink model. (The Simlink model itself is described later in this paper.) It should be made clear that, while Simlink calculates GNP growth for the world in general and individual nations in particular, it bases its projections on a given growth rate for the western industrialized nations that is read as an exogenous variable. For this key variable, Global 2000 used the 1960–72 trend for its high-growth-rate scenario and the 1973–75 trend for its low-growth scenario, with the actual growth rates reduced slightly in both cases to make them consistent with the population projection. From the current perspective, the "medium" annual growth rate of an average of 4 percent for western industrialized nations for the rest of the century may seem optimistic. From one perspective, what Global 2000 is saying is "given a 4 percent growth rate this is what will happen." An alternative interpretation could be "in view of the strain anticipated, a 4 percent growth rate is unlikely." One cannot say at present whether the assumption of 4 percent growth was overly optimistic, but certainly any errors in the computation of GNP or of population would be reflected in the projections of all the remaining variables. The rest of the model contains a great deal of sectoral detail, probably more than can be justified considering the range of uncertainty.

The principal findings of the Global 2000 Report to the President were the following:

- Rapid world population growth will continue, mostly in the poorest countries. GNP per capita will remain low in most less-developed countries (LDCs) and the gap between rich and poor nations will widen.
- World food production will increase 90 percent from 1970 to 2000, but the bulk of the increase will go to countries with already high per capita food consumption. Real food prices will double.
- Arable land will increase only 4 percent by 2000, and most of the increased food output will have to be from higher yields, which will mean increasingly heavy dependence on oil.
- World oil production will reach maximum estimated capacity, even with rapidly increasing prices. Many LDCs will have difficulties meeting energy needs. Fuel-wood demands will exceed supplies by 25 percent.
- Mineral resources will meet projected demands, but production costs will increase and the 25 percent of world population in industrial countries will continue to absorb 75 percent of world mineral production.

- Regional water shortages will become more severe. Population growth alone will double water requirements in nearly half the world and deforestation in many LDCs will make water supplies increasingly erratic.
- There will be significant losses of world forests as demand for forest products increases. Growing stocks of commercial-size timber are projected to decline 50 percent per capita. By 2000, 40 percent of the remaining forest cover in LDCs will be gone.
- There will be serious world-wide deterioration of agricultural soils. The spread of desert-like conditions is likely to accelerate.
- Atmospheric concentrations of carbon dioxide and ozone-depleting chemicals will increase at rates that could alter the world's climate and upper atmosphere significantly by 2050. Acid rain will continue to damage lakes, soils and crops.
- Extinction of plant and animal species will increase dramatically and 20 percent of all species on earth may be irretrievably lost as their habitats vanish, especially in tropical forests. (Barney, 1982, pp. 1–3)

The Global 2000 staff were aware of the model's lack of mathematical elegance and attempted to compensate for its lack of integration in an interesting way. Experiments were performed on World3 and WIM to see what the effect would be of severing the integrating relationships in those models. It was discovered, naturally, that freeing sectors from constraints imposed by other sectors made World3 and WIM more optimistic. As it was acknowledged that these mechanisms were absent in Global 2000 (probably resulting in multiple allocation of the same resources), it was concluded that the projections generated by Global 2000 and listed above are 20 percent too optimistic. The compensated implications include a decisive global downturn in incomes and food per capita in about 2010 (Barney et al., 1981, p. 35).

The Global 2000 staff also used concurrence with the results of World3, WIM, the Bariloche model, MOIRA and the UN model to defend their results. Although there is definitely some strength to this defence, it also has some weaknesses. World3 is not currently acceptable as a projection, and MOIRA appears to contradict Global 2000's physically constrained food scenario more than it supports it. Further, WIM, Bariloche, MOIRA, and the UN model (in its normal mode) are not projection or forecasting models. In their baseline runs they generally use a population projection similar to that used in Global 2000. Furthermore, the group that "integrated" the various agencies projections in the Global 2000 project includes a number of familiar names such as Anne Carter from the UN group and Mihajlo Mesarovic from the WIM group, and so it would actually be surprising if some of the same sense of the "problematique humaine" did not emerge from this subsequent modelling effort.

Perhaps it is best to view Global 2000 not as a model but as a first attempt to reconcile some of the paradoxes resulting from independent use of the various incompatible models and forecasts developed by various authorities in the United States. It was an ambitious undertaking, and it has perhaps led to greater awareness of some current problems and some ways of correcting them. In the final analysis, though, the U.S. government's mental model of the world — if one may conceive of such a thing — remains virtually as inconsistent as it was in 1975.

Global 2000 has come under heavy criticism in the 1980s. Among other works, *The Resourceful Earth* (Simon and Kahn, 1984) is dedicated to refuting the conclusions of Global 2000.

Implications of the Global 2000 Project

- The early stages of this exercise present a good insight into the sort of unwritten collective global model that may exist in a large bureaucracy. Just as an individual has a mental model, a bureaucracy has a collective image of the world composed of various assumptions and projections accepted in its agencies. Quite probably this model is fragmented and inconsistent, rather like the mental models of a person who is confused or who simply has not thought much about the problem.

- Global 2000 demonstrates how a large group of talented people can spend three years of hard work to produce a model that may have no more inherent validity than a simple individual effort such as Simon's.

- Notwithstanding the problems with the Global 2000 model, a supplementary volume, *Global 2000: Implications for Canada*, is a rare glimpse of how futures-minded outsiders view Canada. The Canadian implications are not based on a special experiment with the model but rather represent the views and advice of some of the key people involved in the project. As such they represent experience gained during the project as well as some of the intellectual capital that was there before the project started. For those who are not familiar with the report, written by Gerald O. Barney and Associates Inc. for Environment Canada and the Canadian Association of the Club of Rome, the following section highlights and discusses some of the implications for Canada of the general trend toward rising population pressure and resource prices anticipated by Global 2000 and several other models.

Implications of Global 2000 for Canada

While Barney and Associates have painted a rather gloomy picture for the United States and the world as a whole, their prognosis for Canada is rosier. Our low population and great resource wealth will secure us not only material well-being but a stronger bargaining position and influence in the affairs of the world. This strength, combined with our enviable diplomatic position as a non-threatening minor power well respected by many nations, will give us an unprecedented opportunity to provide leadership in the difficult times ahead.

Notwithstanding this general optimism, Barney and Associates point out that our own house is not in order and that there are a number of issues we should resolve if we are to face the future with confidence. The following issues may be of particular interest.

Trade

According to *Global 2000: Implications for Canada*, Canada does not have an isolationist option. Indeed, the two nations whose well-being is most dependent on a "liberal world trade order" are Japan and Canada.

One issue to be faced is the possibility of bilateral trade arrangements with the United States. Multilateral advocates will no doubt have raised the following objections to bilateral arrangements:

- Bilateral arrangements may divert trade rather than create it.
- The United States is not likely to be interested in our preferred agenda for negotiation.
- A government publicly committed to securing a bilateral agreement would be in a poor position to negotiate such an agreement.

To this list the Global 2000 group would add the following:

- Seventy percent of Canada's trade is already with the United States. That puts too many eggs in one basket. It is bad enough to be vulnerable to fluctuations in the global economy, as we are, but it is worse to be vulnerable to fluctuations in a single national economy, particularly when the long-range outlook is not so favourable for that economy as for our own.
- Canadian trade opportunities lie with the developing nations, such as Mexico, Venezuela, Indonesia and Taiwan, and entering a common tariff system with the United States would inhibit our ability to pursue these opportunities.
- Increasing pressures, particularly on resources, will cause many problems likely to strain Canadian–U.S. relations in the future. Any industrial relationship based on Canadian–U.S. ties that are vital to us, but optional to them, is likely to compromise our sovereignty seriously. Furthermore, the United States will likely be vulnerable to both external and internal pressures that may sometimes prevent it from treating its neighbours in as civil a manner as it would like to do.

Food

If Global 2000's population and food productions are correct, Canada and the United States will control the world's exportable food surpluses by the year 2000. This portends good grain markets for Canada, but it also creates problems in that, though North America will be grain rich, it will not produce enough to meet the total world demand. In times of scarcity, therefore, Canada and the United States will decide who eats and who does not. If, as would seem likely under these circumstances, the Cold War degenerates into a food war, Canada will unwittingly find itself a major world power. Then what would we do?

Immigration

Canada is likely to come under heavy pressure to accept more immigrants. Barney and Associates ask whether we have a policy on the population and ethnic mix we might consider appropriate for Canada. Another question raised is whether it is possible for Canada ever to have a significantly higher standard of living than the United States. In strictly physical terms, such as of resource wealth per capita, the Global 2000 model would answer affirmatively. The modellers, however, point to the long international border and large American population and, bearing in mind the American experience with Mexican influx, question whether we could ever control our immigration sufficiently to maintain a significantly higher standard of living than such a large neighbour (especially when that differential reflects simply a larger per capita resource base).

Internal Relations

> Canada's internal relations are perplexing to Americans. Sometimes we look with envy at Canada, thinking that it must be wonderful to have the luxury to argue so long and stridently about some of the things that Canadians argue over. (Barney et al., 1981, p. 48)

Notwithstanding that poignant comment, Barney and Associates point out that, since many of our internal disagreements are related to energy, they will be easier to resolve sooner than later. A phenomenon such as rapidly rising prices for natural gas and potash, which is good for Canada in aggregate terms, is likely to benefit some regional economies and provincial treasuries but to harm others. This tension-increasing aspect of future developments may make them extremely difficult to absorb, and politically even more difficult to impose or negotiate. Our current conception of federalism and control of resources is probably still too ambiguous to be able to absorb, for example, a sudden trebling — or halving — of oil prices without a divisive controversy.

The Economy

When resource prices rise, the rents from those resources also rise. Who is to benefit from those rents? Resource extraction is generally capital-intensive, produces relatively few jobs, and rewards primarily those who risk their capital. But most of that capital is from outside Canada. Can

Canada extract more benefit from its resources by requiring more labour-intensive upgrading before the resources are exported? Can very high resource rents be successfully distributed through the traditional industrial economy mechanism of employment? Barney makes it clear that he thinks our economy is different from those of other developed nations and has in many respects more in common with the economies of the resource-exporting developing countries. Rising resource prices will, if anything, tend to accentuate that tendency.

A separate issue discussed under energy in *Global 2000: Implications for Canada* is whether we can rely on our existing market-oriented economic system to guide us to sensible decisions. Having conducted a cost-benefit analysis for a tar-sand plant, given that prices for different forms of energy are set arbitrarily, can we be sure that the plant will actually produce more energy than it consumes? Are we likely to make wise decisions about conservation and substitution when prices are managed or regulated? What proportion of prices in Canada are controlled through some institutional mechanism other than the market?

Technology
Barney et al. raise several interesting issues here as well. Can Canada realistically expect to compete with the United States, Japan and Europe in the "high tech" industries? Which of the high technologies are most important to our resource economy, and how can we plan to excel at those technologies? Though the questions are raised, the answers are not obvious from either the model or the modellers' commentary.

The World Bank Models

In the early 1970s the World Bank was deeply involved in traditional econometric modelling of the economies of the developing nations. The tumultuous events of 1973–74 compelled these traditional modellers to broaden their perspectives and incorporate linkages with the developed and OPEC nations, resource constraints, and longer time perspectives into their models. In so doing, the World Bank modellers propelled themselves from the field of econometric modelling into the global modelling field, or at least into the inevitable grey area that exists between the two. The major remaining distinction between the World Bank and other global modellers is that their time perspectives are still relatively short (five to ten years). This subsection briefly outlines the many models used by the World Bank, with particular references to the developments of the mid-seventies. It draws very heavily on *Global Modelling at the World Bank, 1973–76* (Tims and Waelbroeck, 1982) and *Global 2000* (Barney, 1982).

The business of the World Bank involves it in allocating loans among the developing countries and selecting priority sectors and projects. In addition, the World Bank publishes information pertaining to the credit-worthiness of developing nations for use by other investors. Before 1970, the World Bank had some 75 national economic models of developing nations. These models have been developed independently of one another and reflected the different needs and data base qualities in the different nations. In the early 1970s efforts were made to standardize these models. Rather than making each model identical, the models were simply required to meet a minimum standard of accounting and to use consistent definitions of key statistics. This approach recognized that for the major nations more detail was warranted but for many countries large models would be too expensive and difficult to maintain. The result of the exercise was 45 Revised Minimum Standard Models (RMSM). These RMSMs form the base of an ongoing information system that is updated regularly and automatically produces routine nation reports.

The World Bank was also using a variety of global commodity models. Commodity price forecasting is important to the bank's operations because many developing economies are dependent upon exports of a very few commodities. The commodity models have not been standard-ized. They are used by commodity forecasting experts and weighed with other considerations to produce commodity forecasts.

With the rising influence of OPEC, the World Bank became more aware of the need to model the linkages between developing economies and those of the developed and OPEC nations. There was a need for a more comprehensive modelling to ensure that forecasts were based on an accepted view of the economic mechanisms involved and that the detailed forecasts used in project evaluation were based on a consistent set of assumptions or forecasts. It is important to note that the global models at the World Bank were intended to complement, not replace, the existing models and forecasting methods employed by the bank.

In 1973 when the World Bank assessed the approaches to global model building, it decided that neither the "top down" nor the "bottom up" approach to integration was suited to its needs. It was thought that the top down approach would isolate a small group of model builders, with the result that the vast experience of the staff would not be well used. At the same time, the alternative approach of linking existing models was considered to lack elegance and to show a bias against representing interdependencies. Furthermore, the RMSMs were not suitable for link-ing into a global model because they treated several key issues exogenously and contained too much detail in areas not relevant to the global analysis.

The approach the World Bank eventually adopted is called "parallel simulation of overlapping models." This means that a number of dif-ferent models, exploring different issues, are created by different groups. These models have certain key overlapping variables in com-mon. The common variables are deliberately not used, as we might expect, to link the models. Instead, each model is run independently and the discrepancies in the overlapping variables are examined and used to suggest alterations for subsequent runs. The World Bank believes that this exercise helps its staff understand the workings of the system.

Simlink

The best known of the models in the World Bank global modelling system is Simlink, whose first version was built in 1974. At that time the developing countries were faced with a severe balance-of-payments crisis as oil prices climbed and a recession in the developed countries led to slackening demand for Third World exports. Simlink was to assess the effect of the balance-of-payment problem on growth in the developing nations and to investigate aid policies for offsetting the problem.

Simlink combined elements of existing international trade models, developing country models and commodity models. This is not to say that the existing models were incorporated into Simlink. For example, Simlink's commodity components do not reflect the full commodity forecasting capacity of the other World Bank commodity models. The purpose of Simlink is to integrate national LDC growth projections so that they form a consistent global scenario with respect to available foreign trade earnings and foreign investment capital. Simlink was not intended to be a breakthrough in econometric modelling. It is actually a very simple model employing established techniques and running only about 1500 lines of FORTRAN code including extensive comments. It has been developed on a part-time basis by economists and econometricians at the World Bank. Simlink has been continuously adapted to meet changing needs at the World Bank: Simlink IV pertains to the 1973–76 period under review here and Simlink V was used in Global 2000.

Simlink operates as follows:

- Oil prices and growth and prices in the developed world are provided exogenously.
- Commodity models are used to calculate world prices and demand for primary exports for the developing nations. Some commodity projections are provided exogenously where no model has been developed.
- Exports and prices of manufactures and services from developing countries are calculated on the basis of projected elasticities and inflation.
- Trade volumes and prices are translated into export volumes, export prices and import prices for developing countries, disaggregated into seven groups.
- Regional growth models are then used to relate GDP growth to balance of payments and to determine aid requirements for the target growth rates.

Simrich

Simrich was the systems model that assessed the impact of oil prices on the potential for growth in the developed countries. The purpose of this model is described by Tims and Waelbroeck (1982) as follows:

> The energy price impact is too large to be studied in isolation: the repercussions extend to the whole economy and must be examined in a general equilibrium context. In addition to direct impacts on the energy sector; and on energy-consuming industries in developed countries, it is necessary to take into account the impacts on saving and capital investment, on wages and on the rate of return of capital and the length of life of capital goods. The adjustment process triggered by the increase in energy prices would be lengthy. As a result of the price change, energy users would find themselves impelled to replace energy-intensive capital goods by goods which used less energy per unit of output; energy producers would find it profitable to develop resources of energy which are not profitable before the price increase. A dynamic growth model was required to study this long, drawn-out adjustment process. (pp. 128–29)

Simrich is a neoclassical equilibrium growth model being used to assess the effects of a shock which creates a disequilibrium. Its geographic framework is similar to Simlink except that it emphasizes OPEC–OECD interactions. OPEC oil price was treated as an exogenous variable. Among the principal phenomona it studied were the following:

- The effect of energy price policies in the developed countries on oil imports and GNP.
- The high rents generated by the sudden price increase which prevented a normal supply response through orderly development of alternative energy sources.
- The creation of large foreign exchange balances in OPEC, the investment of these funds in OECD countries, and the after-tax, after-inflation return on these funds in relation to the marginal productivity of capital in the OECD countries.

The global modelling system at the World Bank during the mid-seventies also included some simple developed-country growth models intended to assess the long-term effects of the recession. Of particular interest were the long-term impact of changes in the rate of growth of the labour force and the capital stock. The short-term effects of the recession were analyzed with a system of dynamic multipliers called Multilink. The Multilink system was derived from the Link model of the world economy and the Desmos model of the EEC countries. The multipliers described the impact on GNP of exogenous changes in income and expenditures, which were interpreted as tax and spending multipliers. This added a Keynesian short-run analysis of aggregate demand to the system.

Results of the World Bank Models

It must be emphasized that modelling is a continuous and evolving undertaking at the World Bank. The modelling period described above is now of strictly historic interest since the projection horizon for that project was to 1980. Nonetheless, it is interesting in retrospect to examine some of the assumptions and results.

Simlink, as it turns out, suffered from some bad assumptions. The two most important exogenous variables were growth of the OECD economies and world oil prices. On growth, the optimistic scenario was for 6.1 percent annual average growth between 1975 and 1980. The pessimistic scenario was for 4.6 percent growth, with full employment not being reached until shortly after 1980. The pessimistic oil price assumption was that Saudi light crude would remain at US$9.40 through 1980 while the optimistic assumption was that it would fall to US$7.50.

The overly optimistic assessment of growth prospects for developed economies was generated by the Simrich analysis. The appraisal of the Simrich analysis was that in spite of all the pessimism there was no reason that the developed economies could not resume growth at a rate near pre-1973 levels. Several unexpected developments contributed to the poor performance that actually occurred. The balance-of-payments surpluses accruing to the oil exporters were not recycled through investment in OECD countries as fully as expected. This must be partially related to the observation that much anticipated investment in oil, coal and nuclear power did not materialize owing both to objections from environmentalists and to suppressed domestic oil prices. Another feature was that the developing nations did not curb their imports to manage their balance-of-payments problems in the wake of the rise in oil prices but instead resorted to heavy borrowing. As long as this action was sustainable, it helped to maintain employment in the developed nations but ultimately it had to depress growth in the world economy. Reflecting on Simrich in 1982, Tims and Waelbroeck suggested that the model did not account adequately for the short-run problems caused by struggles concerning income distribution and the management of demand, prices and balance of payments. They also implied that oil consumption is sensitive to domestic oil prices, while OPEC solidarity is in turn sensitive to oil consumption, and thus, had the OECD countries been resolute in passing world prices on to the consumer or reducing consumption in other ways, the later OPEC price rises would not have occurred and the rosy economic projections of the mid-seventies might have come closer to realization.

Implications of the World Bank Models for the Royal Commission

• The World Bank provides an exemplary case of how a policy-making institution can sensibly incorporate a number of models into its analytic operations to improve its staff's understanding of complex relationships without resorting to a single official model to generate forecasts.

- The retroactive assessment of Simrich and the explanation why post-1973 economic performance has not met expectations can only be construed as critical of North American — particularly Canadian — oil-pricing policies at the time.
- A retrospective look at the World Bank models of 1973–76, Global 2000's Simlink run, or even Canada's National Energy Program should impress upon us all how susceptible we are to current impressions of a natural order of things, and how quickly a conventional view as to plausible trends can become entrenched.
- Simlink provides a good example of how a world view comes to be reflected in a model's assumptions and may impose unsuspected limitations on subsequent users. In Simlink, for example, it appears that the growth of Third World nations is largely a function of the growth of the western industrialized countries and that the developing countries can only grow in concert with the West. The model denies other growth options such as those pursued by the People's Republic of China, for example.

Summary

This review, long as it has become, only scratches the surface of the models mentioned and these models themselves are only a sampling from a much vaster literature, not only on global modelling as such, but in related modelling efforts as well. There is, for example, an extensive literature on demographic simulation models and systems models of population; on simulation models of economic-demographic interaction, and economic growth models with an endogenous population component (see Sanderson, 1980, for a review of some of these simulation models and their potential usefulness for policy purposes); and on Monte Carlo methods for simulation of environmental problems (see Fedra, 1983, for an example).

Moreover, as the scope and time horizons of large-scale macroeconometric models are extended, and particularly as their representation of production conditions and the availability of resources (their supply side) is enriched, it becomes difficult to separate the work of modellers working in the tradition of economic analysis from that of modellers working in the tradition of industrial dynamics simply by reference to their computing technology. The MACE model of Helliwell, for example (see Helliwell, 1976) and the CANDIDE model of the Economics Council of Canada are distinguished from the Systems Dynamics National Model of Jay Forrester and his co-workers (see Forrester, 1979), not so much by the sophistication of the computer programs employed in each as by the richness and consistency of the economic theory used in the former.

Furthermore, it has to be said that systems dynamics was preceded by both the qualitative analysis of theoretical models of economic growth and the appeal to simulation (digital and analog) for exploring the dynamic properties of these models where qualitative analysis proved impossible or difficult (see Burmeister and Dobell, 1970, for one example), just as it was preceded by a concern with population growth and environmental problems. Indeed, much of the early criticism by economists of *Limits to Growth* or other work for the Club of Rome was based on the demonstration that theoretical models of economic growth, long familiar to specialists in the field, provided some representation of important adjustment mechanisms and interactions overlooked in the early global modelling literature.

In the present review, the Simon model is discussed as one representative economic growth model, and the World Bank models as one representative of the large class of macroeconometric models, simply because these models have figured more explicitly in the debate concerning the results from global modelling than have some of the other dynamic models emerging from specific disciplines.

Finally, it should perhaps be noted again, as it has been above, that the dynamic modelling efforts reviewed in this study, and indeed the appeal to numerical models itself, represent only one facet of a vast literature on futures studies, futures forecasting, and systems approaches to social problems. Obviously the limitations of space preclude any attempt to develop a synthesis of that literature here.

Modelling as a School of Thought

All moral conceptions revolve around the good of the whole. Morality begins with association and interdependence and organizations; life in society requires the concession of some part of the individual sovereignty to the common order; and ultimately the norm of conduct becomes the welfare of the group. Nature will have it so, and her judgement is always final; a group survives, in competition or conflict with another group according to its unity and power, according to the ability of its members to cooperate for common ends.

> (Plato, paraphrased by Will Durant, *The Story of Philosophy*, New York: Garden City Publishing Company, 1938, p. 49)

A Synthesis of the Global Models

It will be obvious to the reader that there are many points of disagreement among global modellers. After all, global modelling offers merely a technique, one which can be applied by practitioners of all ideological stripes. But is that all that global modelling activities represent? The thesis of this section is that to some degree the global modelling community is becoming a school of thought, has achieved consensus on some important issues, and expresses a common outlook. Unfortunately, it often proves difficult to bring this common outlook to bear fruitfully on concrete problems of public policy, even when they are cast in terms as general as the terms of reference of the Royal Commission on the Economic Union and Development Prospects for Canada.

To view global modelling as a field or school of thought, we must realize that the models presented in the preceding section each represent a snapshot at a certain time of a particular group. Many of the earlier modellers are still active in the modelling community and their opinions have evolved with the field itself. Some of the differences evident in the models have been resolved. Perhaps the most comprehensive recent statement of the points of agreement within the global modelling field is provided in the proceedings from IIASA's Sixth Conference on Global Modelling (Meadows, Richardson, Bruckmann, 1982, pp. xviii–xix):

1. There is no known physical or technical reason why basic needs cannot be supplied for all the world's people into the foreseeable future. These needs are not being met now because of social and political structures, values, norms, and world views, not because of absolute physical scarcities.
2. Population and physical (material) capital cannot grow forever on a finite planet.
3. There is no reliable, complete information about the degree to which the earth's physical environment can absorb and meet the needs of further growth in population and capital. There is a great deal of partial information, which optimists read optimistically and pessimists read pessimistically.
4. Continuing "business-as-usual" policies through the next few decades will not lead to a desirable future — or even to meeting basic human needs; it will result in an increasing gap between the rich and the poor, problems with resource availability and environmental destruction, and worsening economic conditions for most people.
5. Because of these difficulties, continuing current trends is not a likely future course. Over the next three decades the world socioeconomic system will be in a period of transition to some state that will be, not only quantitatively but also qualitatively, different from the present.
6. The exact nature of this future state, and whether it will be better or worse than the present, is not predetermined, but is a function of decisions and changes being made now.
7. Owing to the momentum inherent in the world's physical and social process, policy changes made soon are likely to have more impact with less effort than the same set of changes made later. By the time a problem is obvious to everyone, it is often too far advanced to be solved.

8. Although technical changes are expected and needed, no set of purely technical changes tested in any of the models was sufficient in itself to bring about a desirable future. Restructuring social, economic, and political systems was much more effective.

9. The interdependencies among peoples and nations over time and space are greater than commonly imagined. Actions taken at one time and on one part of the globe have far-reaching consequences that are impossible to predict intuitively, and probably also impossible to predict (totally, precisely, maybe at all) with computer models.

10. Because of these interdependencies, single, simple measures intended to reach narrowly defined goals are likely to be counterproductive. Decisions should be made within the broadest possible context, across space, time, and areas of knowledge.

11. Cooperative approaches to achieving individual or national goals often turn out to be more beneficial in the long run to all parties than competitive approaches.

12. Many plans, programmes, and agreements, particularly complex international ones, are based upon assumptions about the world that are either mutually inconsistent or inconsistent with physical reality. Much time and effort is spent designing and debating policies that are, in fact, simply impossible.

Possibly the most valuable achievement of 15 years of global modelling is expressed in the first point of this consensus. A decade ago global modellers believed that the human race was imperilled by the imminent exhaustion of the most essential resources. Since then a great deal of serious study has led to an emerging model in which, as we consume resources, we are forced to exploit less and less desirable reserves of those resources. This trend would dictate continually rising costs were it not for the possibility of technological and institutional improvements in the extraction and use of resources (see point 8 above). The actual scarcity of resources is not predetermined but is the result of our success or failure in overcoming increasingly difficult challenges in the discovery, extraction and utilization of available resources. This is not a new problem but rather it is the way things have always been.

The environmental consensus as outlined in point 4 is one of uncertainty. On several key issues, such as climatology and desertification, the jury is still out and we must, for the time being, be content to monitor the situation and study it. This point was also a central concern in the report of the OECD's Interfutures project and, indeed, is reflected in the organization of further large research projects such as UNESCO's study of Man and the Biosphere or IIASA's Sustainable Biosphere project (see Holling, 1984, for an outline of the latter).

Points 4, 5, 6, and 7 express another basic element of the global modelling consensus, namely, that real changes are necessary to overcome our current problems. It will not suffice simply to twiddle monetary knobs or tinker with the international financial system.

**FIGURE 3-2 OECD Growth Projections in Successive Years
(Indexes of Real GDP, 1970 = 100)**

4.85 percent p/a					
1974 Projection					
1975 Projection					
1976 Projection					
1977 Projection					
1960–70 Trend extrapolation					
162	152	139	123	100	
1970	1971	1972	1973	1974	
1975	1976	1977	1978	1979	1980
Year	World Bank-24574				

Source: Walter Tims and Jean Waelbroeck, *Global Modelling in the World-Bank 1973–76*,
World Bank Staff Paper 544 (Washington, D.C.: The Bank), p.119.

Most of the remaining points of consensus deal with the fact of interdependencies and the ethic of cooperation and with our responsibility for the consequences of our acts. No doubt the early 1970s offered certain grounds for optimism concerning cooperation. From the global modeller's perspective, some apparent tendencies of the present decade, such as the turning inward of nations, a disregard for national externalities, and a purported interest but lack of action in multilateral channels must be very distressing.

The global modeller's consensus leaves us with human responsibility for our material well-being (or predicament), which is ultimately the fruit of our technological and institutional ingenuity; with a projection that we cannot sustain ourselves by fossilizing the status quo; and with an acute awareness of extra-territorial consequences of actions taken within single nations. These very general insights are not irrelevant to government policy; in fact, they might suggest some direct comment on some contemporary debates such as the introduction of major new technologies, for example. More significantly, the orientation evolving among global modellers relates to one of the major debates of our time in the area of economics and forecasting.

The dominant economic orientation is well indicated by the series of projections depicted in Figure 3-2. From this perspective the rate of postwar economic growth was "normal" and we can expect to get back on track momentarily by sticking to "business as usual."

An alternative interpretation of our predicament is that the early seventies were a watershed between a sustainable growth economy and some other conserver economy or static economy. This indeed was the perspective of the early global modellers. The current global modelling perspective is somewhat different. It is that, in the future, when we look back on the early seventies, they may or may not have been a turning point. If indeed that was the beginning of a significant down-turn leading to sustained stagnation, then we will have failed to make the necessary adaptations. If, however, the economy returns to its past strength, then it will not be entirely the same economy but a modified one with some new ways of doing things.

These different outlooks underlie many of the policy debates in Canada today. A position on such issues as whether governments should subsidize a declining industry through what is expected to be a temporary "bad patch" or instead accelerate the exit and promote the mobility of the ex-workers in that industry follows from adopting one or the other of the orientations mentioned above. The global modelling consensus is clearly in favour of the dynamic orientation, described below, which would advocate greasing the wheels of change. Yet this orientation has inherent implementation problems.

The Dynamic Orientation

All of the points of consensus of the global modelling literature boil down to the assessment that even to maintain, let alone improve, the lot of mankind will require perpetual improvements in technological and institutional efficiency. This perspective is far from unique. The following section will sketch briefly the work of some parallel schools of futurists or economists that arrive at similar conclusions.

The Long Wave
Long-wave theorists can trace their intellectual heritage from Marx's conjunctural theory through the early works of Parvus, van Gelderen, de Wolff and Kondratiev and out through Schumpeter and Tinbergen to Mandel, Mensch, Marchetti and even Forrester (the creator of World2). There are a number of long-wave theories, each professing to explain an apparent cycle with a period of approximately 50 years that exists in various price histories. The claim is also made that the cycle applies to deviations in economic growth from an exponential trend, though this proposition is difficult to demonstrate (see Freeman, 1983, p. 171). The orientation of the long-wave theories, particularly the technology-driven mechanism of Mensch and Marchetti, resembles the global modelling orientation in that each successive growth phase of the wave is based on different technologies or institutions of production. Where the long-wave perspective is unique is in its determinism. Policy makers who were adherents of the long-wave theories and who concluded that they were at the end of a recession would face 10 years of unavoidable depression during which they could only attempt to ease the transition to

the new arrangements that would launch the next growth spurt. This appears to be the position currently held by Jay Forrester, for example.

Interfutures
The Interfutures project is the most recent major study of futures scenarios available. It was conducted by the OECD from 1976 to 1978. Its primary purpose was:

> to provide OECD Member Governments with an assessment of alternative patterns of longer-term world economic development in order to clarify their implications for the strategic policy choices open to them in the management of their own economies, in relationships among them, and in their relationships with developing countries. (OECD, 1979, p. iii)

The orientation of the Interfutures report is very much like that of the global modelling consensus. Interfutures specifically investigated the possibility of limits to growth and concluded that growth could continue without encountering "insurmountable long-term physical limits at the global level" (OECD, 1979, p. 406). The critical issues were seen to be energy transition — the move from fossil fuels to alternative energy sources; the search by developed countries for national policies suited to the next context; common efforts for the development of the Third World; and new forms of international cooperation. Interfutures makes a number of specific recommendations concerning "the need to deal with the rigidities which impede the development of national economies; the redeployment of industry; structural change and new values; and the need to achieve greater equity and better distribution of the world's goods" (p. iv). Ultimately it is acknowledged that pursuing the recommendations is contingent on fostering the necessary political will. The final recommendations, those pertaining to fostering the necessary will, involve actions taken by the media, the scientific community and the educational system, all of which entail policies that may be beyond the direct reach of policy makers in modern democracies. Once again the policy maker might feel fatalistic. At the same time, a royal commission may be a good example of the sort of action that will help to make people more aware of relevant issues.

As may be inferred from Figure 3-2, the dynamic orientation of Interfutures was completed at odds with the business-as-usual orientation that was dominant within the OECD. Interfutures has consequently not had, so far as we can tell from the outside, the influence on the OECD work program that was initially expected.

Economic Historians
The decline of major economies has long been of interest to historians. Carlo M. Cipolla has collected literature from this school. He interprets the problem as centring on the proposition that "while there is a mini-

mum of human needs below which human life is impossible, there is practically no upper limit to human desires" (Cipolla, 1970, p. 5). Furthermore, it is held that the resulting infinite growth of public and private consumption will eventually exceed society's capacity to fill the demand:

> At the beginning of the twentieth century some economists advanced the idea that mature economies are bound to stagnate because consumption cannot expand as production does. The crisis of 1929 and subsequent events seemed to support the theories of stagnationists. There is no doubt that on occasion demand can fall short of productive potential and damage the economy for more than five or ten years — the span of a business cycle.
>
> There may also be long-term disequilibria with overtones of excessive production in some specific sector of the economy. But on the whole, in the long view of history, economic difficulties of mature empires apparently do not stem from insufficient consumption. Quite the contrary! Even if their economic analysis is not unremittingly rigorous, historians have always felt instinctively that the main economic trouble of mature empires stemmed from the supply side. (Cipolla, 1970, p. 7)

This supply-side orientation is the same as that of global modellers and most long-term futurists. The picture painted by economic historians is one of inadequate supplies and insurmountable rigidities despite recognition by many individuals of the nature of the problem.

The Rent-Seeking Literature

There is an emerging school of thought in economics that is generally referred to as "the rent-seeking literature"; it includes, among other works, *Toward a Theory of the Rent-Seeking Society* (Buchanan, Tollison and Tullock, 1980) and *The Rise and Decline of Nations* (Olsen, 1982). The mechanism of decline in this school is very similar to that espoused by the historians just cited. Essentially, a long process of identifiable special interest groups winning institutional recognition weaves a web of entitlements that inhibit the normal adaptability of a capitalist society. As this "entitlement society" emerges, efficiency is progressively sacrificed and decision making is progressively transferred from the economic to the political sphere (Courchene, 1983). This perspective is entirely consistent with the global modelling orientation. Certainly institutional arrangements are believed by global modellers to be the key determinant of human well-being and their quality is believed to be capable of both improvement and degradation. The rent-seeking literature, particularly the world of Olsen, also leaves one with a certain sense of despair, for it argues that political reality favours the acquisition and defence of group entitlements against the common good so that the inevitable direction of institutional evolution is toward decreasing efficiency until a sufficiently traumatic economic shock can clear the system of the accumulated influence of interest groups and associated entitlements. Whether the pursuit of individual self-interest through participation in political processes — the mechanisms of collective action — truly does compromise the general welfare more than the pursuit of individual self-interest through participation in economic processes — the mechanisms of market exchange — is a question that cannot be answered here, however.

Econometric Forecasts

Early in 1984 some members of the research staff of the Royal Commission on the Economic Union and Development Prospects for Canada had the opportunity to review three sets of long-term econometric forecasts. These forecasts portray current opinion as to what is plausible and are, on the whole, optimistic. Though forecasts in themselves do not recommend any particular policy, it is probably safe to assume that the existence of optimistic forecasts generally supports business-as-usual policies. The intention here is not to review the econometric forecasts but merely to point out some areas of convergence between econometric models and global models.

Traditional econometric models are short-term and oriented to the demand side. Traditional global models are long-term and oriented to constraints on supply. Developments since 1970 have brought longer perspectives and considerations of supply constraint to econometric modellers while bringing economist's paradigms to global modelling. Indeed, several of the global models reviewed in this paper could be described as econometric, and it no longer possible to differentiate fully between the two fields. Global models still generally ignore demand-side problems, which may be a suitable approach to long-term projections. Ironically, by this omission, the global models should be relatively optimistic, effectively setting a ceiling under which econometric models would operate, but in practice they are generally more pessimistic than the econometric models. Clearly there are other factors at work — primarily the links to the resource base and the carrying capacity of the biosphere — and we are still a long way from being able to make comprehensive forecasts (let alone consensus forecasts).

Japan in the Year 2000

In 1981 Japan's Economic Council commissioned a "Long Term Outlook Committee" to undertake a major futures study. The primary areas of investigation were Japanese demographics, the Japanese economic outlook, and the outlook for the global economic environment.

The statements in *Japan in the Year 2000* on the global outlook resemble some of the global modelling literature and may be taken by some as independent support of the dynamic orientation. This impression is somewhat misleading, however, because the global scenario was really only a starting point for the study. Little independent research was done in this area, and the main sources relied upon were Global 2000 and Interfutures. *Japan in the Year 2000* does not arrive at a dynamic orientation so much as it starts with one.

What might seem amazing to outsiders is that *Japan in the Year 2000*, a study which professes to have involved 128 experts in the process of research and writing, produced definitive and unanimous statements about Japan's outlook and the "grand design" required to deal with it. The primary plank of the grand design is that Japan as a trading nation is vulnerable to disruptions of the global economic order and that it should therefore be more aggressive in promoting a liberal and open world trade and economic order.

The Hudson Institute

It may appear to some that we have on the one hand the global modellers and other doomsayers, and on the other hand the staff of the Hudson Institute who foretell a rosy future for all. It should be apparent to the reader that this simplification is far from adequate. A more useful simplification may be that the Hudson Institute shares with global modellers and most of the other research groups mentioned above the perspective that progress depends upon real and sometimes painful changes and displacements in the economy. In presentations at the conference Worldview 84 held in Washington, D.C., during June of 1984, the Hudson Institute's director of research, Irvin Leveson, emphasized that the United States was pulling out of the current recession much better than Europe and other nations because its economy is more open and adaptable. Hudson Institute Third World expert, James Wheeler, emphasized that economic growth and instability are inseparable.

What distinguishes the Hudson Institute from many other groups involved in futures forecasting is neither an unqualified optimism nor a faith in the status quo, but a profound faith in the resilience and adaptability of capitalism. Other groups, upon recognizing that economies of the future will have to be very different from those of today, would suggest a need for sweeping changes in government policies. The Hudson Institute, recognizing the same thing, would argue that the natural economic systems will make the necessary changes if permitted to do so. This perspective they seem to share completely with Julian Simon, whose approach to global models has been described briefly above, and whose book with Herman Kahn, *The Resourceful Earth* (Simon and Kahn, 1984), may be taken as the current definitive statement of this position.

The Problem of Sacred Cows

The global modelling literature has painted a picture of mankind poised on a treadmill that requires us to keep running simply to hold our ground.

This we do through technological and particularly institutional innovation. Furthermore, our ability to innovate successfully depends critically on some degree of national and international cooperation. The global modelling literature is not alone in this diagnosis, but rather parallels the perspectives of several other bodies of thought. Unfortunately, many of these groups are pessimistic about the possibility of fostering the political will necessary to take the required steps. This very general perspective provides an orientation that could be applied to many current or future policy issues but is frequently difficult to build upon in practice.

When modellers assert that real changes have to be made and that it is virtually impossible to maintain the status quo, the question arises: "What constitutes real change?" The difference between a business-as-usual orientation and a dynamic orientation is a matter of how receptive a society should be to change — and, indeed, how much collective agreement and active cooperation is necessary. The global modeller's perspective is that we are not flexible enough and our current rate of fiddling with the margins will not produce satisfactory results. There is no doubt a gap between the remedies envisaged by global modellers and the necessary political will. We must realize that institutional reform as the term is used in the broad perspective of global modellers, would require us to take a hard look at many relationships that currently are not exposed to policy debate or may not even be recognized as institutions. To debate policy from the perspective of global modellers, we must be prepared to contemplate to some degree the unquestionable institutions of our time. Where is the five-day week carved in stone? Is employment the only acceptable way to distribute wealth? Do we need an auto industry? Has organized labour outlived its function? Should the sovereignty over resources be vested in the provinces? Are some of the provinces too big or too small? Do we need provinces at all? Are private rights to land or natural resources tolerable at all in a global village? Is the market approach to resource management the only approach? We should realize that from the modeller's perspective we humans, although we embody the opportunity to overcome our problems, are also the source of those problems.

The global modelling literature has frequently been criticized for being long on generalizations and short on recommendations. This problem stems from an orientation whose message is not only that change is necessary but also that we are not changing fast enough. This places the global modellers almost by definition ahead of the political will and nearly beyond the pale of acceptable opinion. It is open to debate whether this orientation follows inevitably from taking the broad perspective of our situation required by the modelling exercise or whether the modellers chose a non-traditional technique to accord with their prior perspective. Many of the implications of the modelling exercises are almost too radical to state explicitly. For example, the UN group working on the RIO model (see Leontief et al., 1977) reported that development could be accelerated in some regions only by steering 40 percent of gross product into capital investment. It seems virtually inconceivable that anything short of a communist revolution could achieve that objective in many of the countries examined. This implication was not mentioned and no recommendation is spelled out in detail. Comments of this nature are, however, clearly revolutionary.

As a school of thought, global modelling is short on what would be considered palatable recommendations. Consider for example that, from a broad global modelling perspective, employment is only one possible mechanism for distributing wealth. Even with an objective of full employment, however, one could conceive of different mechanisms for income distribution. Yet any extensive consideration of such issues is almost certainly beyond the contemplation of the Royal Commission, which is committed to honour many Canadian institutions such as organized labour and aboriginal rights. "Employment" is a prime objective in the contemporary debate; yet to a global modeller it might be merely one means, one among several possible institutional mechanisms, for generating and distributing wealth. If the global modellers were to make a comment on the current Canadian efforts to improve our economy, it would probably be that we do not step back far enough to obtain the necessary perspective on our institutions and that, consequently, we eliminate valid options from discussion.

Conclusions

"All Knowledge brings us closer to our ignorance."
(T.S. Eliot, "Choruses from the Rock," 1934, verse I)

The most useful way to view a global model (in the sense used here) is as a formal representation of subjective perceptions and values. It is an expression of the world view of some modeller or group of modellers (almost certainly all drawn from the same cultural and philosophical background).

As such, a global model offers an excellent mechanism for organizing masses of data in order to create a more orderly picture. In doing so, it makes possible a useful emphasis on dynamic properties, without the limitation to qualitative methods of analysis that often restricted the study of theoretical models of economic growth, for example. Global models can sometimes be used effectively for interfacing or linking a variety of larger-scale disaggregated models of particular sectors or specific phenomena.

Being built on relationships that may express, to some extent, individual or social values, global models can be used to explore the possible consequences of different values. The "Japanese project" at OECD, for example, which became the Interfutures study, was consciously conceived as a means of exploring the implications of development patterns that may be different from those assumed in the demand-oriented economic projections normally employed by the OECD secretariat in the 1970s. Again, however, it must be noted that the institutional changes contemplated in such studies — or implied by the scenarios studied — entail massive changes in individual values and social norms. From this point of view, for example, the whole purpose of the work program adopted by the Club of Rome, including its global modelling efforts, is to achieve the changes in attitudes, perceptions, and values that are considered essential if an acceptable and sustainable path of world development is to be achieved.

Thus, in attempting any summary appraisal of the main themes emerging from the global modelling literature, the following points are central:

- Most writers emphasize alternatives to the present course of action and indeed possibilities outside the actions normally generated by the existing institutional mechanisms. This emphasis on volition, on the need to act decisively and sweepingly, reflects the message that decisions on a national and even international scale are essential to ensure that the desirable futures they portray as physically realizable are in fact achieved. Moreover, most of the global models portray a situation in which a continuation of the kind of policies we have now will make any sustainable future impossible.

    Thus, analytically, we might describe one consequence of the last decade or so of global modelling as the elimination of a variety of infeasible alternatives, and the addition of new possibilities to the range of choice within the feasible region for the world community.
- At the same time, this search for new alternatives may hinge on some dramatic changes in attitudes and values. The constraints on the Royal Commission in its advocacy of policies are probably very much tighter than those which are recognized or assumed by global models. Because these models are usually silent on the institutional details, the alternatives they explore are likely to be feasible only if a process of education alters both the economic goals and the social structures within the communities they study. Thus it might be argued that one effect of the global modelling literature is to force all of us to look more broadly at what action would be acceptable in light of fuller education as to the consequences of our current social goals and mores.

This conclusion as to the dependence of model results on the modeller's prior views has been recognized in many places, but nonetheless deserves emphasis. The following observations are worth noting as illustrations:

> The computerized models themselves perform a simple heuristic analysis that reproduces various input assumptions with few alterations. Thus the

models serve primarily as an accounting framework for displaying the hypotheses and assumptions of the analyst. (Schumacher, 1964)

Global Modelling is an important and viable activity . . . the models developed so far suffer from many drawbacks and considerable improvement is required before serious use can be recommended . . . all models are explicitly normative and conditioned by the social-psychological milieu. . . . (Balakrishnan, 1979, pp.1–2)

The overall conclusion in this paper is that the energy supply projections are opinion, rather than credible scientific analysis, and they therefore cannot be relied upon by policy makers seeking a genuine understanding of the energy choices for tomorrow. (Keepin, 1983)

Global models, then, generate results that are highly sensitive to the assumptions and opinions on which they are based. They tell little that is not already fairly easily predicted from a review of the subjective inputs and structuring from which they start. But building the model does bring out all those implications and may thus be of considerable value in the process of accommodating and adjusting policies and policy debates.

More particularly, what we learn from the debate over global modelling to date is the possible significance of current decisions in shaping future options, and the importance of measures to maintain flexibility in the face of profound uncertainty. The subtitle of the Interfutures report, "Mastering the probable and managing the unpredictable," was carefully chosen. Its emphasis on policies directed toward maintaining options and creating potential, and on institutions with the capacity to adjust to changing circumstances, captures perhaps the central message emerging from computer simulations of many hypothetical futures. What we have learned from the display of global scenarios far into the future is how little we can know of the circumstances we shall confront, and hence how little we can hope to plan now, monolithically and optimally, for that future. What the debate does seem to reveal clearly is the importance of avoiding action now that forecloses future options and limits the scope for future adjustment. It emphasizes instead policies to stimulate experimentation and to facilitate (not stifle) adaptation.

In many respects, therefore, this result suggests an emphasis, not on a predetermined plan or strategy — what in control theory would be called an open loop control — but on feedback mechanisms and self-regulating features. In a social context this emphasis leads to a particular interest in bargaining and negotiation processes, consensus-building institutions, and self-regulatory adjustment mechanisms.

Finally, then, global models should perhaps be assessed not as scientific contributions but as messages on morality. Many are not so much vehicles for forecasting, foresight, or strategic planning as they are attacks on the conventional assumptions or moral attitudes of our time.

Characterized — probably rightly — as "Malthusian" in their heavy emphasis on the carrying capacity of the Earth's resource base, the global models developed in the 1970s are profoundly anti-Malthusian in their emphasis on the need for volition — decisive collective action focussed on a redistribution of wealth — to counter increasing problems of hunger and deprivation stemming from the strains of a growing population pressing against the limits of a finite biosphere. To the extent these models are pessimistic, it is a pessimism about the prospects for continuing technological and institutional innovation sufficient to stay ahead of the demands of a larger, more aware, and more ambitious world population, and a despair as to the possibilities for mobilizing decisive action on a scale sufficiently great as to offset emerging problems. To that extent, the results of these models are seen as calling for collective action and central institutions.

Counterposed against this view is the intellectual tradition represented in this present survey particularly by Julian Simon and Herman Kahn: a tradition of skepticism of collective action, and anti-Malthusian in the conviction that past favourable experience with technological and institutional innovation will continue indefinitely into the future, assuring greater efficiency in production, continuing secular decline in resource prices, and rising living standards for most of even a growing population. But this anti-Malthusian confidence that the carrying capacity of the globe will continue to expand ahead of demand is accompanied — not unnaturally, perhaps — by the quite Malthusian conviction that the existing institutions of capitalist society are the best suited to promote overall welfare, and that decisive collective action directed toward alternative mechanisms for distribution of income, wealth, or entitlements would be not only wrong-headed but counterproductive.

We might argue, then, that the lasting scientific impact of the work on global modelling over almost two decades has been, in the end, relatively small: greater emphasis on analysis of environmental and ecological systems, the biosphere, and the immense uncertainties surrounding major human interventions in the complex interdependent systems which make up the Earth's mantle; and greater emphasis in economic modelling on the quantitative treatment of stocks as well as flows, including population levels, reserves of resources, and accumulations of pollutants, contaminants, and wastes — that is, on the underlying determinants of potential supply. In both cases the uncertainty surrounding future developments, and the need for self-regulating mechanisms to maintain flexibility, resilience, and adaptability in the face of unforeseeable shocks is a paramount feature.

But there is in all this little that tell us whether the present epoch will be seen as a watershed, a time of structural breaks leading to harsh new realities, or of smooth transition to a prosperous post-industrial society. There is no guidance as to whether the terms of trade for resources will maintain a secular decline or enter upon a period of sustained rise reflecting increasing scarcity. If we cannot resolve such basic dilemmas as to future developments — or even the correct identification of our present position — there is little guidance likely on more concrete measures. There is now no consensus in the global modelling literature on any outlook or any strategy save that of "hanging loose" and avoiding committing the nation or any of its regions to any single grand strategy.

The major result of that literature therefore has been to recast an old debate as to the nature of our responsibility for others. The determined scientific pessimism of Malthus was used by Victorian society, just as the determined technological optimism of Kahn and Simon might be by contemporary society, as a convenient convention to avoid confronting the facts of grinding deprivation in the midst of plenty, and in the face of the physical potential to do much better. Malthus served established Victorian society by offering a scientific demonstration of the impotence and even perversity of public policy aimed at charity. With the benefit of the psychological distance created by geographical separation, racial differences, myths of independence and artifacts of nationalism, a doctrine of technological optimism can go a long way toward assuring established contemporary society that present consumption patterns and wealth distribution mechanisms are not only sustainable but in the interests of all concerned, and can thus offer a scientific demonstration of the futility of public policy aimed at redistribution.

It is fundamentally to challenge this assumption that much of the global modelling literature emerged. Its conclusion might be summed up in the assertion that without a more basic equity and justice in the distribution of rights and resources, there can be no sustainable strategies, and no global future, at least for human societies as we know them.

Two types of problems thus stand out from this work. One is the problem of profound uncertainty with respect to critical features of the biosphere and the risk of large-scale irreversible changes caused by human activity. The second is the nature, scope and extent of the social contract, including the mechanisms linking distribution to participation in production. In a way, both problems reflect human progress: the risk of irreversible environmental damage is a consequence of our growing technological power; the difficulty of achieving a stable and sustainable social order is a reflection of rising levels of education, awareness, and information. The global modelling literature reaffirms for us the importance of these problems and underlines the gravity of the situation if we fail to deal with them. For solutions to the fundamental moral dilemmas it poses, however, we must obviously continue to search outside the computer systems, of whatever generation.

Note

This paper was completed in August 1985.

Bibliography

Alchian, Armen, and William R. Allen. 1977. *Exchange and Production: Competition, Coordination and Control.* 2d ed. Belmont, Cal.: Wadsworth.

Balakrishnan, A.V. 1979. "Summary and Conclusions." In *Global and Large Scale Systems Models*, edited by B. Lazarevic. Lecture Notes in Control and Information Sciences, vol. 19. New York: Springer-Verlag.

Barney, Gerald O. 1980. *The Global 2000 Report to the President.* Vol. 2. Washington, D.C.: U.S. Government Printing Office.

_____. 1982. *The Global 2000 Report to the President.* Vol. 1. New York: Penguin.

Barney, Gerald O., et al. 1981. *Global 2000: Implications for Canada.* Toronto: Pergamon Press.

Botkin, James W. 1982. *Global Stakes: The Future of High Technology in America.* Cambridge, Mass.: Ballinger.

Boughey, Arthur S. 1976. *Strategy for Survival, An Exploration of the Limits to Further Population and Industrial Growth.* Menlo Park, Cal.: W.A. Benjamin.

Bright, James R., and Milton E.F. Schoeman, eds. 1972. *A Guide to Practical Technological Forecasting.* Englewood Cliffs, New Jersey: Prentice-Hall.

Bronowski, J. 1973. *The Ascent of Man.* Boston, Mass.: Little, Brown.

Brown, Lester R. 1978. "The Prospects for Food." *Handbook of Futures Research.* London: Greenwood.

Buchanan, James M., Robert D. Tollison, and Gordon Tullock, eds. 1980. *Toward a Theory of the Rent-Seeking Society.* College Station: Texas A&M Press.

Burmeister, Edwin, and Rodney A. Dobell. 1970. *Mathematical Theories of Economic Growth.* London: Macmillan.

Cairns, Alan C. 1983. "The Canadian Constitutional Experiment: Constitution, Community and Identity." Killam Lecture, Dalhousie University, November 24, 1983.

Canadian Association for the Club of Rome. 1978. *Summary of Proceedings of Canadian Conference on Global Modelling.* Montreal: The Club of Rome.

Celasun, Merih, and Frank Pinto. 1975. *Energy Prospects in OECD Countries.* World Bank Staff Working Paper 221. Washington, D.C.: The Bank.

Cipolla, Carlo M., ed. 1970. *The Economic Decline of Empires.* London: Methuen.

Clarke, Ronald O., and Peter C. List. 1974. *Environmental Spectra, Social and Economic Views on the Quality of Life.* New York: D. Van Nostrand.

Cole, H.S.D., Christopher Freeman, Marie Jahoda, and K.L.R. Pavitt, eds. 1973. *Thinking About the Future.* London: Chatto and Windus.

Cole, H.S.D., et al., eds. 1973. *Models of Doom.* New York: Universe Books.

Copithorne, Lawrence W. 1977. *A Neoclassical Perspective on Natural Resource-led Regional Economic Growth.* Discussion Paper 92. Ottawa: Economic Council of Canada.

_____. 1979. *Natural Resources and Regional Disparities.* Study prepared for the Economic Council of Canada. Ottawa: Minister of Supply and Services Canada.

Courchene, Thomas J. 1970. "Inter-provincial Migration and Economic Adjustment." *The Canadian Journal of Economics* 3 (4): 550–76.

_____. 1983. "The Market System in the Age of Entitlements." Unpublished lecture sponsored by the Max/Bell Funding Program and University of Victoria School of Public Administration, November 25, 1983.

Dayal, Ram. 1981. *An Integrated System of World Models.* Vol. 2. Amsterdam: North-Holland.

Dixit, A.K. 1976. *The Theory of Equilibrium Growth*. London: Oxford University Press.

Dolan, Edwin G. 1983. *Basic Micro Economics*. 3d ed. New York: Dryden Press.

Durant, Will. 1938. *The Story of Philosophy*. New York: Garden City Publishing.

Economic Council of Canada. 1977. *Living Together: A Study of Regional Disparities*. Ottawa: Minister of Supply and Services Canada.

_____. 1978. *For a Common Future: A Study of Canadian Relations with Developing Countries* Ottawa: Minister of Supply and Services Canada.

_____. 1982. *Intervention and Efficiency*. Ottawa: Minister of Supply and Services, Canada.

_____. 1983. Submission to the Royal Commission on the Economic Union and Development Prospects for Canada. Unpublished.

Eglington, Peter, and Mavis Uffelmann. 1983. *Observed Costs of Oil and Gas Reserves in Alberta, 1957–1979*. Discussion Paper 235. Ottawa: Economic Council of Canada.

Ellison, Anthony P. 1979. *The Effects of Rising Energy Costs on Canadian Industries*. Calgary: Canadian Energy Research Institute.

Emanuel, A. 1973. *Issues of Regional Policies*. Paris: Organization for Economic Co-operation and Development.

Fedra, K. 1983. *Environmental Modelling Under Uncertainty: Monte Carlo Simulation*. Research Report RR-83-28. Laxenberg, Austria: International Institute for Applied Systems Analysis.

Forbes, Hughes, and P.K. Warley. 1982. *Economic Intervention and Regulation in Canadian Agriculture*. Study prepared for the Economic Council of Canada and the Institute for Research on Public Policy. Ottawa: Minister of Supply and Services Canada.

Forrester, Jay W. 1971. *World Dynamics*. Cambridge, Mass.: Wright-Allen Press.

_____. 1979. "An Alternative Approach to Economic Policy: Macrobehavior from Microstructure." *Economic Issues of the Eighties*, edited by Nake M. Kamirany and Richard H. Day. Baltimore, Md.: Johns Hopkins University Press.

Forrester, Nathan B. 1973. *The Life Cycle of Economic Development*. Cambridge, Mass.: Wright-Allen Press.

Fowles, Jib, ed. 1978. *Handbook of Futures Research*. London: Greenwood Press.

Freeman, Christopher, ed. 1983. *Long Waves in the World Economy*. London: Butterworth.

Freeman, Christopher, and Marie Jahoda, eds. 1978. *World Futures: The Great Debate*. London: W. Robertson.

Frejka, Thomas. 1978. "Future Population Growth." In *Handbook of Futures Research*, edited by J. Fowles. London: Greenwood Press.

Ghantus, Elas T. 1982. *Arab Industrial Integration: A Strategy for Development*. London: Croom Helm.

Grunfeld, Joseph, ed. 1979. *Growth in a Finite World*. Philadelphia: Franklin Institute Press.

Harmin, Robert D. 1980. *Managing Growth in the 1980s: Toward a New Economics*. New York: Praeger.

Hauser, Philip M., ed. 1979. *World Population and Development, Challenges and Prospects*. Syracuse, N.Y.: Syracuse University Press.

Helliwell, John F. 1976. *An Integrated Model for Energy Policy Analysis*. Resources Paper. Vancouver: University of British Columbia, Department of Economics.

Holland, Edward P. 1970. *Simulating the Dynamics of Economic Development*. World Bank Staff Working Paper 90. Washington, D.C.: The Bank.

Holling, C.S. 1984. Resilience of Ecosystems: Local Surprise and Global Change." Unpublished manuscript.

Hoos, Ida R. 1978. "Methodological Shortcomings in Futures Research." In *Handbook of Futures Research*, edited by J. Fowles. London: Greenwood.

Hughes, Barry B. 1980. *World Modelling, The Mesarovic-Pestel World Model in the Context of its Contemporaries*. Lexington, Mass.: Lexington Books.

Kahn, Herman, William Brown, and Leon Martel. 1976. *The Next 200 Years: A Scenario for America and the World*. New York: Morrow.

Kahn, Herman, and Thomas Pepper. 1980. *Will She be Right: The Future of Australia*. Brisbane: University of Queensland Press.

Keepin, Bill. 1983. "A Critical Appraisal of the IIASA Energy Scenarios." Working Paper WP-83-104l. Laxenberg, Austria: International Institute for Applied Systems Analysis.

Kettle, John. 1970. *Footnotes on the Future*. Toronto: Methuen.

Koch, Adrienne, ed. 1959. *Philosophy for a Time of Crisis*. New York: Dutton.

Kogane, Yoshio, ed. 1982. *Changing Value Patterns and Their Impact on Economic Structure*. Tokyo: University of Tokyo Press.

Krcevinac, S., ed. 1981. *Global Modelling: Proceedings of the IFIP-WG 7/1 Working Conference, Dubrovnik, Yugoslavia, Sept. 1–5, 1980*. Berlin: Springer-Verlag.

Laszlo, Ervin. 1978. "Global Futures." In *Handbook of Futures Research*, edited by J. Fowles. London: Greenwood.

Lederman, W.R. 1976. "The Constitution: A Basis for Bargaining." In *Natural Resource Revenues: A Test of Federalism*, edited by A.Scott. Vancouver: University of British Columbia Press.

Leontief, W., A. Carter, and P. Petri. 1977. *The Future of the World Economy*. New York: Oxford University Press.

McCormack, T.W. 1983. "The Next 25 Years." *Canadian Review* (Fall).

McHale, John, and Magda Cordell McHale. 1977. *The Futures Directory*. Surrey, England: IPC Science and Technology Press.

Mclean, J. Michael. 1978. "Simulation Modelling." In *Handbook of Futures Research*, edited by J. Fowles. London: Greenwood.

MacEachen, The Hon. Allan J. 1981. *Federal Provincial Fiscal Arrangements in the Eighties*. Ottawa: Minister of Supply and Services Canada.

Malthus, Thomas R. 1798. "Essay on the Principle of Population" was originally a pamphlet published anonymously. For the final (1826) edition see Malthus, T.R. 1973. *An Essay on the Principle of Population*. London: J.M. Dent.

Manescu, M. 1980. *Economic Cybernetics*. Tunbridge Wells, U.K.: Abacus.

May, Brian. 1978. *The Indonesian Tragedy*. Singapore: Graham Brash.

Meadows, Dennis L., et al. 1974. *Dynamics of Growth in a Finite World*. Cambridge, Mass.: Wright-Allen Press.

Meadows, Donella H., et al. 1972. *The Limits to Growth: A Report to The Club of Rome's Project on the Predicament of Mankind*. New York: Universe Books.

Meadows, Donella, John Richardson and Gerhart Bruckmann. 1982. *Groping in the Dark, The First Decade of Global Modelling*. New York: John Wiley.

Mesarovic, M.D., and B.B. Hughes. 1978. "Testing the Hudson Institute Scenarios: Is Their Optimism Justified?" *Futurist* 20 (November/December).

Mesarovic, M.D., and E. Pestel. 1974. *Mankind at the Turning Point*. New York: Dutton.

Neurath, Paul. 1979. "Models of the World's Problems and Problems with the World Models." In *Growth in a Finite World*, edited by Joseph Grunfeld. Philadelphia: Franklin Institute Press.

Nisbet, Robert A. 1973. *The Quest for Community*. London: Oxford University Press.

Nordhaus, William D. 1973. "World Dynamics: Measurement Without Data." *Economic Journal* 83B (September/December): 1156–83.

Norrie, K.H., and M.B. Perry. 1983. *Economic Rents, Province-Building and Interregional Adjustment: A Two-Region General Equilibrium Analysis*. Discussion Paper. Ottawa: Economic Council of Canada.

Norrie, Kenneth H., and Michael B. Percy. 1981. *Westward Shift and Interregional Adjustment*. Discussion Paper 201. Ottawa: Economic Council of Canada.

Organization for Economic Cooperation and Development. 1979. *Interfutures, Facing the Future*. Paris: OECD.

Okita, Saburo. 1983. *Japan in the Year 2000*. Tokyo: Japan Times Ltd.

Olsen, Mancur. 1982. *The Rise and Decline of Nations: Economic Growth, Stagflation and Social Rigidities*. New Haven: Yale University Press.

Olsen, Mancur, and Hans H. Lansberg, eds. 1973. *The No Growth Society*. New York: Norton.

Parliamentary Task Force on Federal-Provincial Fiscal Arrangements. 1981. *Fiscal Federalism in Canada*. Ottawa: Minister of Supply and Services.

Peccei, Aurelio. 1969. *The Chasm Head*. London: Macmillan.

————. 1977. *The Human Quality*. New York: Pergamon Press.

————. 1980. "Facing Unprecedented Challenges: Mankind in the '80s." IIASA Distinguished Lectures No. 2, p. 3. Laxenberg, Austria: International Institute for Applied Systems Analysis.

————. 1981. *One Hundred Pages for the Future: Reflections of the President of the Club of Rome*. New York: Pergamon Press.

Porat, Marc U., and Wesley Martin, eds. 1974. "World IV: A Policy Simulation Model of National and Regional Systems." *Stanford Journal of International Studies* (Spring): 71–166.

Pross, A. Paul. 1981. "Pressure Groups: Talking Chameleons." In *Canadian Politics in the 1980's*, edited by Michael S. Whittington and Glen Williams. Toronto: Methuen.

Pugh, Alexander L. 1970. *DYNAMO II User's Manual*. 4th ed. Cambridge, Mass.: MIT Press.

Ramsey, F.P. 1928. "A Mathematical Theory of Savings." *Economic Journal* 38 (152): 543–59.

Raven, Peter H. 1984. "Third World in the Global Future." *Bulletin of the Atomic Scientists* (November): 17–20.

Reutlinger, Shlomo. 1975. *Simulation of World-Wide Buffer Stocks of Wheat*. World Bank Staff Working Paper 219. Washington, D.C.: The Bank.

Samuelson, Lee. 1973. "A New Model of World Trade." *OECD Economic Outlook* (December) Paris: Organization for Economic Co-operation and Development.

Sanderson, Warren C. 1980. *Economic-Demographic Simulation Models: A Review of Their Usefulness for Policy Analysis*. Research Report RR-80-14. Laxenberg, Austria: International Institute for Applied Systems Analysis.

Saunders, Robert S. 1974. "Criticism and the Growth of Knowledge: An Examination of the Controversy over Limits to Growth." *Stanford Journal of International Studies* 9 (Spring): 45–70.

Schumacher, E.F. 1964. "Review." *Economic Journal* (March), p. 194.

Schweitzer, Thomas T. 1982. "Migration and a Small Long-term Econometric Model of Alberta." Discussion Paper 221. Ottawa: Economic Council of Canada.

Shearer, Ronald A., John H. Young, Gordon R. Munro and R.A. Matthews. 1973. *Regional and Adjustment Aspects of Trade Liberalization*. Toronto: University of Toronto Press.

Simon, Julian L. 1981a. "Global Confusion, 1980: A Hard Look at the Global 2000 Report." *The Public Interest* 62 (Winter): 3–20.

————. 1981b. *The Ultimate Resource*. Princeton: Princeton University Press.

————. 1989. "Bright Global Future." *Bulletin of the Atomic Scientists* (November): 14–17.

Simon, Julian, and Herman Kahn. eds. 1984. *The Resourceful Earth*. Oxford: Blackwell.

Smiley, D.V. 1980. *Canada in Question: Federalism in the Eighties*. 3 ed. Toronto: McGraw-Hill Ryerson.

Swan, Neil M., and Paul J.E. Kovacs. 1981. *Empirical Testing on Newfoundland Data of a Theory of Regional Disparities*. Study prepared for the Economic Council of Canada. Ottawa: Minister of Supply and Services Canada.

The World Future Society, eds. 1977. *The Future: A Guide to Information Sources*. Washington, D.C.: The Society.

Tims, Walter, and Jean Waelbroeck. 1982. *Global Modelling in the World Bank 1973–76*. World Bank Staff Paper 544. Washington, D.C.: The Bank.

Tinbergen, Jan. 1956. *Economic Policy: Principles and Design*. Amsterdam: North-Holland.

_____. 1976. *Reshaping the International Order: A Report to the Club of Rome*. New York: Dutton.

Trudeau, The Right Honourable Pierre Elliott. 1978. *A Time for Action: Toward the Renewal of the Canadian Federation*. Ottawa: Minister of Supply and Services Canada.

United States Congress. Office of Technology Assessments. 1982. *Global Models, World Futures and Public Policy: A Critique*. Washington, D.C.: U.S. Government Printing Office.

Waelbroeck, Jean L., ed. 1976. *The Models of Project Link*. Amsterdam: North-Holland.

Waslander, Bert H. 1976. *CANDIDE MODEL 1.2M: Summary and Some Simulations*. Economic Council of Canada Discussion Paper 59. Ottawa: The Council.

Whyte, John D. 1982. *The Constitution and Natural Resource Revenues* Discussion Paper 14. Kingston, Ontario: Queen's University, Institute of Intergovernmental Relations.

Weintraub, Andrew, et al., ed. 1973. *The Economic Growth Controversy*. Armonk, N.Y.: M.E. Sharpe.

Wolfson, Margaret. 1978. *Changing Approaches to Population Problems*. Paris: Organization for Economic Cooperation and Development with the World Bank.

4

Savings in Canada:
Retrospective and Prospective

GREGORY V. JUMP
THOMAS A. WILSON

Savings and Investment in an Open Economy

The objectives of this study are twofold: first, to provide an interpretation of the economic significance of recent swings in Canadian savings and investment rates; and, second, to identify some of the things that are likely to influence future savings and investment behaviour. The study offers few new theories. Instead, we attempt to use received economic theory both to interpret the past and to suggest some possibilities for the future. Most of what follows is a synthesis of thoughts and ideas culled from the literature. In a sense, therefore, the study is a survey of recent research pertaining to savings and investment.

An appropriate starting point is a review of the causal relationships that exist between aggregate savings and investment. Economic theory offers two extreme models with which to study these relationships. One of them applies to an economy that is completely closed with regard to foreign trade and capital flows; the other applies to a small open economy where international capital is perfectly mobile. In the former model, savings and investment are closely related in a causal sense; in the latter, savings and investment are determined independently of each other because the real interest rates that allocate savings to productive investments are determined in the rest of the world.

There is a broad consensus among economists that the model of a small open economy offers greater insight into the Canadian experience than the closed-economy alternative. This is not to say that the real rate of return on every Canadian asset or liability is fully determined in U.S. or overseas capital markets. Obviously there are risks unique to specific Canadian assets and liabilities that help to determine their respective real rates of return. However, it is probably safe to regard such factors as being uncorrelated with changes in world-wide financial conditions over the course of the business cycle. If so, the proposition that changes in Canadian real interest rates will closely mirror the changes in real interest rates in the rest of the world provides a reasonable description of the actual state of affairs, at least over the medium and longer terms — and is in accord with the empirical evidence (see Boothe et al., 1985).

Canada's dependence on world real interest rates and world capital markets means that aggregate investment and savings in Canada are strongly influenced by events outside the country. Businesses undertake investment projects up to the point where the (risk-adjusted) real after-tax rate of return on marginal investments is equal to the return available on the next best alternative in financial markets. In a small open economy, this next best alternative is to be found among real interest rates determined in the rest of the world. For Canada this means that aggregate investment will vary inversely with world real interest rates. It also means that domestic monetary policy can have little effect on equilibrium investment flows in the aggregate because of the inability of monetary policy to exert a sustained influence on domestic real interest rates. Regrettable as this appears, it is not entirely bad. Fiscal policy in Canada is also unable to effect sustained changes in interest rates, and this means that there is little danger that government deficits will cause financial pressures that will "crowd out" private investment spending.[1] Many private investors can turn to foreign capital markets for finance in the event of increased government borrowing in domestic bond markets.

The inability of policy makers to influence real interest rates in a small open economy does not preclude the possibility of government influence on investment. Other means than monetary policy are available — in particular, tax policies. It is the after-tax real rate of return that influences investment decisions, and this rate can be altered by domestic authorities. Policy makers can make Canadian investment projects more (or less) attractive by lowering (or raising) the taxation of the proceeds from investments. This can be done by a host of policies, ranging from direct subsidies to investment tax credits, many of which have been used by the Government of Canada at various times.[2]

Let us turn now to the determinants of aggregate savings flows. In an open economy it is essential to distinguish between national saving, that is, saving by domestic sectors of the economy, and net foreign saving. Aggregate saving is the sum of these two components and is, of course, equal to aggregate investment by virtue of the ways in which savings and investment are defined.

National saving is determined by the incomes and preferences of the country's residents, together with the after-tax real rates of return available to them. It is essentially independent of the level of aggregate investment in an open economy.[3] In light of the world real interest rates and domestically determined tax schedules, residents will decide how much to save. Their savings will be channelled into productive investment projects at home and abroad through capital markets.

Net foreign saving is calculated as the difference between gross investment and national saving. If Canadians save less than is invested in Canada, foreign funds will flow into Canada and net foreign saving will be positive. Conversely, if Canadians save more than is invested in Canada, funds will flow out of the country and net foreign saving will be negative.

The mechanism for those relationships is the integration of world capital markets. Investors throughout the major industrial economies of the OECD countries seek the best available returns. Their arbitrage behaviour directs capital flows to the most profitable investments and at the same time causes domestic and international real interest rates to be equalized, at least over the medium and long terms.

Canadian monetary policy has little effect on the level of savings for the same reason that it has little effect on investment, namely, its inability to exert a sustained influence on domestic real interest rates. But unlike investment, aggregate saving in Canada is not very sensitive to tax policies. Policy makers can influence the level of national saving by varying the rate at which the proceeds from savings are taxed, but their influence on aggregate saving is likely to be offset by movements in net foreign saving.

For example, if the Government of Canada were to replace the personal income tax with a consumption tax yielding the same gross revenue, Canadian residents would be likely to save more. National saving would rise, but since domestic investment opportunities would not have been enhanced, the increase would probably be channelled into foreign assets. Net foreign saving would fall by a like amount, leaving aggregate saving unaltered.[4] Canadians would end up owning more of the world's productive resources or, what is the same thing, the rest of the world would own fewer Canadian resources. But investment activity in Canada would be unaffected by this policy.

This example is a good illustration of a fundamental limitation on government policies in a small open economy: it is difficult if not impossible to think of domestic policies that will alter the level of aggregate saving. The government of a small open economy that wishes to increase investment is well advised to attack this objective head-on by tax policies that directly enhance the after-tax returns to physical capital. Attempts to increase domestic investment by incentives for increased national saving are apt to prove disappointing.

This is not to deny that higher national saving might in itself be a worthwhile objective. The effects of increased national saving are, as we have seen, increased asset holdings by domestic residents and higher future incomes. These may be desirable objectives, especially at a time when there is great concern over the inability of many Canadians to provide themselves with adequate retirement incomes.

Patterns of Sectoral Saving since 1962

This section discusses the pattern of saving of the four main sectors of the Canadian economy: households,[5] corporate and government business enterprises, governments, and non-residents over the period 1962–83.[6] The savings data are gross savings flows as published by Statistics Canada in the Financial Flow Accounts. The savings of the household sector are divided into savings through trusteed pension funds and other savings. The government sector is subdivided into the Canada and Quebec Public Pension Funds; the federal government; and the provincial government, local government and hospital sector. The savings of the government sector differ from the government budget surplus as reported in the National Income Accounts by including fixed capital formation by governments.

Table 4-1 presents aggregate and sectoral savings flows over this period, and Table 4-2 presents sectoral and aggregate savings rates expressed as proportions of GNP. Table 4-3 expresses the sectoral savings as shares of total gross domestic saving.

Although aggregate saving increased substantially over the 21-year period, the aggregate savings rate was remarkably stable until the great recession of 1981–82. Since aggregate saving and aggregate investment are identical, the adverse effect of the recession on investment led to substantial reductions in aggregate savings rates over the years 1982–83. Excluding these two years, the aggregate gross domestic savings rate averaged 23.8 percent of GNP, with a range from 20.7 percent to 26.5 percent. There was no apparent trend in the aggregate savings rate.

In 1982 the aggregate savings rate dropped to 19.3 percent, doubtlessly as a result of the severe recession that began in the middle of 1981. In 1983 the savings rate rose slightly to 19.5 percent. The first year since 1954 when GNP actually declined in real terms from the previous year was 1982. In 1983, a recovery began, but the previous peak level of real GNP had not been reached by the year's end, and the unemployment rate remained in the double-digit zone. With aggregate real income below previous peak values in both years, it is not surprising that the savings rate was unusually low.

The stability of the aggregate savings rate was accompanied by significant shifts in the shares of the major sectors. Figure 4-1 presents the savings rates of the four major sectors. Two trends have become apparent since the beginning of the seventies: first, the savings rate of households has increased substantially since 1971; second, the savings rate of the government sector has dropped sharply since 1974. As the next section on inflation-adjusted savings flows makes clear, part of both of these trends is directly attributable to the impact of inflation on savings flows as they are conventionally measured. However, fiscal policies and the cyclical performance of the economy are also important factors.

Figure 4-2 presents a decomposition of the savings rate of the government sector. As is clear, most of the dramatic decline in the savings rate for the consolidated government sector is accounted for by the decline in the savings rate of the federal government. From 1974 to 1983 the total government savings rate declined by 9.0 percentage points, of which 7.2 percentage points are directly accounted for by the federal government. Over the period there was a slight downward trend in the savings rate of the public pension funds, and a tailing off of provincial and local government savings rates under the influence of the 1981–82 recession. Although inflation distortions affect these patterns, the dominant factors are federal fiscal policy and the cyclical performance of the economy, as is confirmed by the data provided in the next section.

Figure 4-3 separates savings through trusteed pension plans from other components of personal saving. Both components of personal saving have increased substantially since the early seventies. However, the relative importance of savings through trusteed pension plans has remained relatively stable. Roughly one-fifth of gross personal saving is accounted for by savings in these plans at both the beginning and the end of the twelve-year period.[7]

The dramatic rise in personal savings rates in Canada is in marked contrast to the savings behaviour in the United States, as is illustrated in Figure 4-4 which compares *net* personal savings rates in the two countries. The net personal savings rate in Canada rose from 5.9 percent of personal disposable income in 1971 to a peak of 15.2 percent in 1982 before tailing off to 13.3 percent in 1983. In the United States, the personal savings rate trended downward over the same period. In 1983 the U.S. net personal savings rate was 5.1 percent, only about two-fifths of the corresponding Canadian rate. This divergent pattern of the personal savings rates in the two countries could be related to fundamental differences in their tax structures, as is considered in a later section of this paper.

The difference in the behaviour of personal savings rates also bears on the issue of the crowding-out effects of government deficits. If reductions in government savings rates are accompanied by equivalent increases in personal savings rates, there can be little or no crowding out of business investment, whereas if personal savings rates and government savings rates both decline, there is a possibility of significant crowding out. However, in an open economy with integrated international capital markets, reductions in national saving will more likely induce an increase in foreign saving than a reduction in business investment.

TABLE 4-1 Annual Gross Savings, Unadjusted for Inflation, 1962–83

	1962	1963	1964	1965	1966	1967	1968	1969	1970	1971	1972
	($ billions)										
Persons & Unincorporated Businesses	3,311	3,596	3,549	4,087	5,164	5,115	5,010	5,535	5,855	6,660	8,368
Trusteed Pension Funds	499	602	644	721	709	817	907	1,025	1,057	1,401	1,589
Other Savings	2,812	2,994	2,815	3,366	4,455	4,298	4,103	4,510	4,798	5,259	6,779
Corporations & Gov't Business Enterprises	4,518	4,870	5,738	6,152	6,558	6,961	7,685	7,994	8,524	9,089	10,114
Total Government	1,195	1,350	2,068	2,638	3,268	3,131	3,516	4,977	3,967	3,845	4,066
Federal Government	−236	−49	555	896	662	381	490	1,508	732	370	59
Provincial, Local and Hospital	1,431	1,399	1,513	1,742	1,897	1,863	2,023	2,356	2,042	2,197	2,634
CPP and QPP	0	0	0	0	709	887	1,003	1,113	1,193	1,278	1,373
Non-residents	779	487	392	1,135	1,232	615	258	1,079	−916	−184	667
Residual Error of Estimate	−125	−39	51	206	182	33	15	−443	345	891	190
Total Savings	9,678	10,264	11,708	14,218	16,404	15,855	16,484	19,142	17,775	20,301	23,405

	1973	1974	1975	1976	1977	1978	1979	1980	1981	1982	1983
						($ billions)					
Persons & Unincorporated Businesses	11,256	14,622	17,411	18,410	20,147	25,450	29,699	35,795	44,755	51,866	49,312
Trusteed Pension Funds	1,934	2,145	2,886	3,865	4,373	5,383	7,337	8,766	9,754	9,288	10,617
Other Savings	9,322	12,477	14,525	14,545	15,774	20,067	22,362	27,029	35,001	42,578	38,695
Corporations & Gov't Business Enterprises	12,484	14,065	15,436	19,801	19,964	22,236	28,110	33,424	29,766	25,251	40,829
Total Government	5,543	8,284	2,306	3,141	1,832	-92	2,832	256	3,917	-7,169	-13,323
Federal Government	1,110	2,084	-2,679	-2,229	-6,236	-9,416	-8,215	-9,380	-6,366	-17,557	-22,484
Provincial, Local and Hospital	2,964	4,429	2,982	3,187	5,730	6,875	8,354	6,633	7,033	6,602	5,990
CPP and QPP	1,469	1,771	2,003	2,183	2,238	2,449	2,693	3,003	3,250	3,786	3,171
Non-residents	242	1,999	5,252	4,655	4,789	5,281	5,384	1,958	7,160	-1,610	-951
Residual Error of Estimate	-44	-629	-300	507	1,265	-1	-612	-1,148	-749	929	278
Total Savings	29,481	38,341	40,105	46,514	47,997	52,874	65,413	70,285	84,849	69,267	76,145

Source: See Appendix.

TABLE 4-2 Rate of Saving as a Proportion of GNE, 1962–83

	1962	1963	1964	1965	1966	1967	1968	1969	1970	1971	1972
					($ billions)						
Persons & Unincorporated Businesses	0.077	0.078	0.069	0.074	0.084	0.077	0.069	0.069	0.068	0.071	0.080
Trusteed Pension Funds	0.012	0.013	0.013	0.013	0.011	0.012	0.012	0.013	0.012	0.015	0.015
Other Savings	0.066	0.065	0.056	0.061	0.072	0.065	0.057	0.057	0.056	0.056	0.064
Corporations & Gov't Business Enterprises	0.105	0.106	0.114	0.111	0.106	0.105	0.106	0.100	0.099	0.096	0.096
Total Government	0.028	0.029	0.041	0.048	0.053	0.047	0.048	0.062	0.046	0.041	0.039
Federal Government	-0.005	-0.001	0.011	0.016	0.011	0.006	0.007	0.019	0.009	0.004	0.001
Provincial, Local and Hospital	0.033	0.030	0.030	0.031	0.031	0.028	0.028	0.030	0.024	0.023	0.025
CPP and QPP	0.000	0.000	0.000	0.000	0.011	0.013	0.014	0.014	0.014	0.014	0.013
Non-residents	0.018	0.011	0.008	0.021	0.020	0.009	0.004	0.014	-0.011	-0.002	0.006
Residual Error of Estimate	-0.003	-0.001	0.001	0.004	0.003	0.000	0.000	-0.006	0.004	0.009	0.002
Total Savings	0.225	0.223	0.233	0.257	0.265	0.239	0.227	0.240	0.207	0.215	0.222

	1973	1974	1975	1976	1977	1978	1979	1980	1981	1982	1983
						($ billions)					
Persons & Unincorporated Businesses	0.091	0.099	0.105	0.096	0.096	0.110	0.112	0.120	0.132	0.145	0.126
Trusteed Pension Funds	0.016	0.015	0.017	0.020	0.021	0.023	0.028	0.029	0.029	0.026	0.027
Other Savings	0.075	0.085	0.088	0.076	0.075	0.086	0.085	0.091	0.103	0.119	0.099
Corporations & Gov't Business Enterprises	0.101	0.095	0.093	0.103	0.095	0.096	0.106	0.112	0.088	0.070	0.105
Total Government	0.045	0.056	0.014	0.016	0.009	0.000	0.011	0.001	0.012	−0.020	−0.034
Federal Government	0.009	0.014	−0.016	−0.012	−0.029	−0.041	−0.031	−0.032	−0.019	−0.049	−0.058
Provincial, Local and Hospital	0.024	0.030	0.018	0.017	0.027	0.030	0.032	0.022	0.021	0.018	0.015
CPP and QPP	0.012	0.012	0.011	0.011	0.011	0.010	0.010	0.010	0.010	0.011	0.008
Non-residents	0.002	0.014	0.032	0.024	0.023	0.023	0.020	0.007	0.021	−0.004	−0.002
Residual Error of Estimate	0.000	−0.004	−0.002	0.003	0.006	0.000	−0.002	−0.004	−0.002	0.003	0.001
Total Savings	0.239	0.260	0.243	0.242	0.228	0.228	0.248	0.236	0.250	0.193	0.195

Source: See Appendix.

TABLE 4-3 Sectoral Saving as a Proportion of Gross Domestic Saving, 1962–83

	1962	1963	1964	1965	1966	1967	1968	1969	1970	1971	1972
					($ billions)						
Persons & Unincorporated Businesses	0.342	0.350	0.295	0.287	0.315	0.323	0.304	0.289	0.329	0.328	0.358
Trusteed Pension Funds	0.052	0.059	0.055	0.051	0.043	0.052	0.055	0.054	0.059	0.069	0.068
Other Savings	0.291	0.292	0.240	0.237	0.272	0.271	0.249	0.236	0.270	0.259	0.290
Corporations & Gov't Business Enterprises	0.467	0.474	0.490	0.433	0.400	0.439	0.466	0.418	0.480	0.448	0.432
Total Government	0.123	0.132	0.177	0.186	0.199	0.197	0.213	0.260	0.223	0.189	0.174
Federal Government	-0.024	-0.005	0.047	0.063	0.040	0.024	0.030	0.079	0.041	0.018	0.003
Provincial, Local and Hospital	0.148	0.136	0.129	0.123	0.116	0.118	0.123	0.123	0.115	0.108	0.113
CPP and QPP	0.000	0.000	0.000	0.000	0.043	0.056	0.061	0.058	0.067	0.063	0.059
Non-residents	0.080	0.047	0.033	0.080	0.075	0.039	0.016	0.056	-0.052	-0.009	0.028
Residual Error of Estimate	-0.013	-0.004	0.004	0.014	0.011	0.002	0.001	-0.023	0.019	0.044	0.008
Total Savings	1.000	1.000	1.000	1.000	1.000	1.000	1.000	1.000	1.000	1.000	1.000

	1973	1974	1975	1976	1977	1978	1979	1980	1981	1982	1983
						($ billions)					
Persons & Unincorporated Businesses	0.382	0.381	0.434	0.396	0.420	0.481	0.454	0.509	0.527	0.749	0.648
Trusteed Pension Funds	0.066	0.056	0.072	0.083	0.091	0.102	0.112	0.125	0.115	0.134	0.139
Other Savings	0.316	0.325	0.362	0.313	0.329	0.380	0.342	0.385	0.413	0.615	0.508
Corporations & Gov't Business Enterprises	0.423	0.367	0.385	0.426	0.416	0.421	0.430	0.476	0.351	0.365	0.536
Total Government	0.188	0.216	0.057	0.068	0.038	-0.002	0.043	0.004	0.046	-0.103	-0.175
Federal Government	0.038	0.054	-0.067	-0.048	-0.128	-0.178	-0.126	-0.133	-0.075	-0.253	-0.295
Provincial, Local and Hospital	0.101	0.116	0.074	0.069	0.119	0.130	0.128	0.094	0.083	0.095	0.079
CPP and QPP	0.050	0.046	0.050	0.047	0.047	0.046	0.041	0.043	0.038	0.055	0.042
Non-residents	0.008	0.052	0.131	0.100	0.100	0.100	0.082	0.028	0.084	-0.023	-0.012
Residual Error of Estimate	-0.001	-0.016	-0.007	0.011	0.026	0.000	-0.009	-0.016	-0.009	0.013	0.004
Total Savings	1.000	1.000	1.000	1.000	1.000	1.000	1.000	1.000	1.000	1.000	1.000

Source: See Appendix.

FIGURE 4-1 Gross Savings by Sector as a Share
of GNE, 1962–83

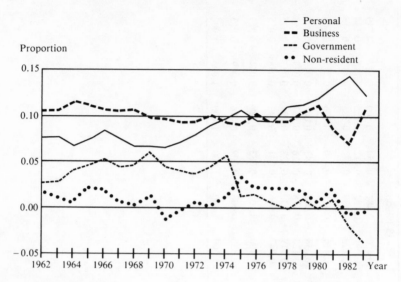

Source: See Appendix.

Domestic saving provided by non-residents has been relatively volatile over the 21-year period. Swings in the savings rate provided by non-residents appear related to swings in the rate of gross private domestic investment, as is illustrated in Figure 4-5. Years of real investment strength, such as 1965–66 and 1974–80, are accompanied by relatively large inflows of foreign capital. The four years of net capital outflow — 1970–71 and 1982–83 — are all years of relatively weak real investment.

These patterns are, of course, consistent with the framework developed in the first section of this paper. In a small open economy with relatively stable national savings rates and relatively volatile investment rates, the rest of the world becomes, in effect, the residual supplier of savings funds.

Nominal gross savings rates of the business sector have been reasonably stable over the past 21 years, except for the recession of 1981–82, when sharp declines in corporate profits led to dramatic reductions in net retained earnings. The rebound in corporate profits with the recovery of 1983 restored business savings rates to more normal levels.

Summary

This brief review of nominal measured savings rates suggests a few tentative conclusions. First, there is no evidence of a trend in aggregate

FIGURE 4-2 **Government Savings as a Share of GNE, 1962–83**

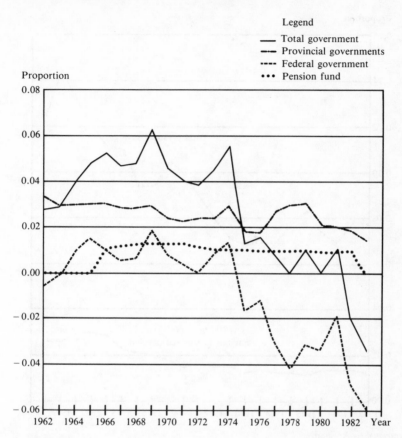

Source: See Appendix.

savings rates; rather, the weakness of savings in 1982 and 1983 is largely attributable to the severity of the 1981–82 recession. Second, there has been a marked shift in the shares of savings, with a reduction in government savings rates virtually offset by an equivalent rise in personal savings rates. Third, there is slight evidence of a reduction in Canada's dependence on foreign sources of savings. In recent years Canada has become a net exporter of capital. However, the rest of the world, being the residual supplier of funds to Canadian investors, may become once again a provider of funds when investment in Canada strengthens substantially. However, this conclusion would be modified if changes in government policies generate additional domestic sources of savings at the appropriate time.

All of these conclusions must be viewed as highly tentative. One

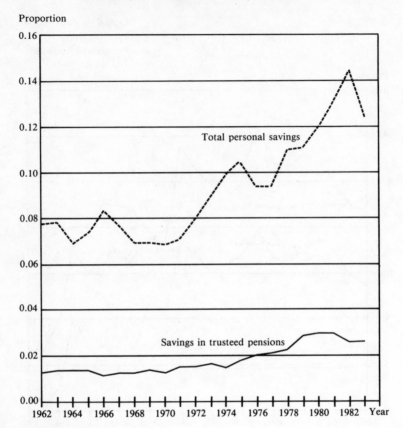

FIGURE 4-3 **Gross Savings (Trusteed Pension and Total Personal) as a Share of GNE, 1962–83**

Proportion

Total personal savings

Savings in trusteed pensions

Source: See Appendix.

important source of distortion in measured savings rates is price inflation. In the next section we present estimated savings flows and rates that are corrected for this distortion.

Inflation-Adjusted Savings Flows

The conventional measures of savings flows provided in the National Income Accounts and Financial Flow Accounts in general do not accurately measure savings if price inflation occurs. This is because the conventional measures do not take into account the inflation-induced reduction in the real value of those assets and liabilities that are denominated in nominal terms. These include all assets and liabilities denominated in domestic or foreign currency, such as deposits, bonds, mortgages and loans.[8]

FIGURE 4-4   Net Rates of Personal Saving, Canada and
United States, 1956–86

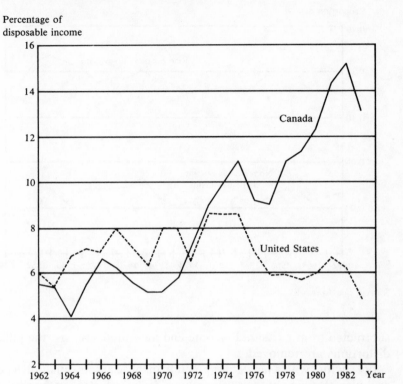

Percentage of
disposable income

Source: (a) Canada: Statistics Canada, *National Income and Expenditure Accounts*.
(b) United States: U.S. Department of Commerce, *National Income and Product
Accounts*.

If a sector is in a net creditor position in such assets, its income
includes interest payments that merely compensate the sector for the
erosion of capital from inflation. This leads to an overstatement of
income and, since savings are calculated by deducting expenditures
from income, to an equivalent overstatement of savings. A sector in a net
debtor position understates its true income by deducting interest payments that really represent the inflation-induced decline in the real value
of its debt; savings are understated by the same amount.

Only for sectors whose net position in such assets is zero, that is,
whose nominal assets are exactly offset by nominal liabilities, is there no
distortion of measured savings flows from inflation. For sectors with a
net creditor position in these assets, inflation leads to an overstatement
of their true savings. If the reduction in the real value of the assets is

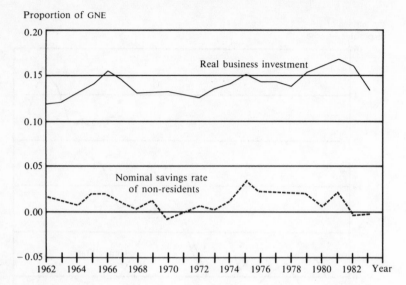

Source: See Appendix.

subtracted from measured income and measured savings, the inflation distortions are removed.

For sectors with a net debtor position in these assets, inflation leads to an understatement of their true savings. If the reduction in the real value of the net debt is added to income and savings for these sectors the inflation distortion is removed.

The details of the inflation correction procedures are given in the Appendix. Two aspects of these corrections are worth noting here:

- The inflation adjustment is based on ex post measures of actual inflation rates. Hence no distinction is made between anticipated and unanticipated inflation, although this distinction may be important in explaining behaviour.[9]
- The inflation adjustment is made for two classes of assets: those denominated in Canadian dollars, and those denominated in foreign currencies. We assume that the latter are all denominated in U.S. dollars. The inflation adjustment used for foreign currency assets is the ex post inflation rate in Canada adjusted for ex post changes in the exchange rate. Once again no distinction is made between anticipated and unanticipated inflation or exchange rate movements.

Since, by definition, all sectors together must have a zero net asset position in each of these classes of asset, the inflation correction for gross domestic savings flows in the aggregate is zero. However, aggregate GNP is affected by inflation adjustment. Since Canada is in a net debtor position on these assets, inflation-adjusted GNP is somewhat higher than nominal GNP. Aggregate inflation-adjusted savings rates are therefore reduced slightly.

Although the aggregate rates of savings are not much affected by inflation adjustment, the savings rates of the main sectors are. The household and non-resident sectors are in a substantial positive net asset position, so that their savings rates are decreased by adjusting for inflation. The government and business sectors, in contrast, are in substantial net debtor positions; therefore their savings rates are increased by the inflation adjustment.[10] These adjustments affect both the levels and the time patterns of sectoral savings rates, since the rate of inflation, albeit always positive, has varied a great deal since 1962.

A few figures will illustrate the importance of these adjustments. In 1983, the savings of the household sector were overstated by $8.3 billion in the conventional measures. As a result of adjusting for inflation, the gross personal savings rate as a percentage of GNP is reduced from 12.6 percent to 10.4 percent. In 1981, when inflation was at its peak, personal savings were overstated by $15.7 billion and inflation adjustment reduced the gross personal savings rate from 13.2 percent to 8.4 percent of GNP.

In 1983 the savings of non-residents were overstated by $4.1 billion. Inflation adjustment reduces the savings rate of non-residents from -0.2 percent to -1.3 percent of GNP. For the years 1979–83, the unadjusted data would have suggested that Canada experienced a capital inflow averaging 0.8 percent of GNP. The adjusted data indicate that the correct picture was a net capital outflow averaging 0.7 percent of GNP.

According to conventional measures, in 1983 the government sector dissaved $13.3 billion, with the federal government dissaving $22.5 billion. After inflation adjustment, the estimates are $7.9 billion and $18.6 billion, respectively.

Business gross saving in 1982 was understated by $11.0 billion and in 1982 by $6.9 billion. As a result of inflation adjustment, business gross savings rates in 1982 and 1983 were 10.0 percent and 12.1 percent respectively (compared to 7.0 percent and 10.5 percent in the unadjusted data).

Adjusted savings flows, adjusted gross savings rates, and adjusted shares of total savings are presented in Table 4-4 to Table 4-6. Figure 4-6 to Figure 4-13 provide a comparison of adjusted and unadjusted savings rates by sector.

For the household sector, the inflation adjustment moderates and delays the recent uptrend in the savings rate but does not eliminate it. In 1982 and 1983 the inflation-adjusted savings rate was at or above 10 percent of GNP, continuing an upward trend that began in 1975, and well above previous levels. Clearly, the real savings behaviour of the house-

TABLE 4-4 Annual Gross Savings by Sector, Adjusted for Inflation, 1962-83

	1962	1963	1964	1965	1966	1967	1968	1969	1970	1971	1972
					($ billions)						
Persons & Unincorporated Businesses	2,885	2,989	2,597	2,856	3,746	3,802	3,673	3,533	3,952	4,746	5,337
Trusteed Pension Funds	439	518	518	528	469	597	679	663	705	1,040	1,102
Other Savings	2,447	2,471	2,079	2,328	3,277	3,206	2,994	2,870	3,247	3,706	4,325
Corporations & Gov't Business Enterprises	4,649	5,095	6,075	6,643	7,132	7,531	8,251	8,793	9,448	9,935	11,496
Total Government	1,507	1,768	2,660	3,486	4,252	4,007	4,435	6,378	5,262	5,085	5,991
Federal Government	59	237	936	1,441	1,293	916	1,018	1,364	1,190	1,050	1,172
Provincial, Local and Hospital	1,448	1,531	1,724	2,045	2,250	2,221	2,453	2,993	2,983	2,902	3,715
CPP and QPP	0	0	0	0	709	870	965	1,021	1,089	1,133	1,103
Non-residents	762	450	325	1,028	1,092	482	110	882	-1,232	-356	391
Residual Error of Estimate	-125	-39	51	206	182	33	15	-443	345	891	190
Total Savings	9,678	10,264	11,708	14,218	16,404	15,855	16,484	19,142	17,775	20,301	23,405

	1973	1974	1975	1976	1977	1978	1979	1980	1981	1982	1983
						($ billions)					
Persons & Unincorporated Businesses	4,607	6,350	10,485	11,878	15,413	19,422	16,699	22,455	29,089	37,458	41,007
Trusteed Pension Funds	633	507	1,526	2,516	3,181	3,745	3,870	5,059	5,343	5,423	8,461
Other Savings	3,973	5,842	8,959	9,361	12,232	15,676	12,828	17,396	23,747	32,035	32,547
Corporations & Gov't Business Enterprises	15,513	18,187	19,314	23,530	22,268	25,458	37,357	43,222	41,497	36,298	47,776
Total Government	9,828	13,133	5,986	6,926	4,133	3,293	11,847	8,542	13,541	828	-7,876
Federal Government	3,696	5,046	-329	74	-3,476	-6,230	-2,075	-2,705	1,600	-10,656	-18,570
Provincial, Local and Hospital	5,345	7,219	5,094	5,441	6,088	7,977	12,929	9,959	10,621	9,343	8,393
CPP and QPP	786	868	1,221	1,411	1,522	1,546	992	1,288	1,320	2,141	2,301
Non-residents	-422	1,300	4,621	3,673	4,918	4,703	123	-2,786	1,472	-6,246	-5,040
Residual Error of Estimate	-44	-629	-300	507	1,265	-1	-612	-1,148	-749	929	278
Total Savings	29,481	38,341	40,105	46,514	47,997	52,874	65,413	70,285	84,849	69,267	76,145

Source: See Appendix.

TABLE 4-5 Rate of Saving as a Proportion of Adjusted GNE, Adjusted for Inflation, 1962–83

	1962	1963	1964	1965	1966	1967	1968	1969	1970	1971	1972
					($ billions)						
Persons & Unincorporated Businesses	0.067	0.065	0.052	0.052	0.061	0.057	0.051	0.044	0.046	0.050	0.051
Trusteed Pension Funds	0.010	0.011	0.010	0.010	0.008	0.009	0.009	0.008	0.008	0.011	0.010
Other Savings	0.057	0.054	0.041	0.042	0.053	0.048	0.041	0.036	0.038	0.039	0.041
Corporations & Gov't Business Enterprises	0.108	0.111	0.121	0.120	0.115	0.113	0.114	0.110	0.110	0.105	0.109
Total Government	0.035	0.038	0.053	0.063	0.069	0.060	0.061	0.080	0.061	0.054	0.057
Federal Government	0.001	0.005	0.019	0.026	0.021	0.014	0.014	0.030	0.014	0.011	0.011
Provincial, Local and Hospital	0.034	0.033	0.034	0.037	0.036	0.033	0.034	0.037	0.035	0.031	0.035
CPP and QPP	0.000	0.000	0.000	0.000	0.011	0.013	0.013	0.013	0.013	0.012	0.010
Non-residents	0.018	0.010	0.006	0.019	0.018	0.007	0.002	0.011	-0.014	-0.004	0.004
Residual Error of Estimate	-0.003	-0.001	0.001	0.004	0.003	0.000	0.000	-0.006	0.004	0.009	0.002
Total Savings	0.225	0.223	0.233	0.257	0.265	0.238	0.227	0.239	0.207	0.215	0.222

	1973	1974	1975	1976	1977	1978	1979	1980	1981	1982	1983
					($ billions)						
Persons & Unincorporated Businesses	0.037	0.043	0.063	0.062	0.073	0.084	0.062	0.074	0.084	0.104	0.104
Trusteed Pension Funds	0.005	0.003	0.009	0.013	0.015	0.016	0.014	0.017	0.016	0.015	0.021
Other Savings	0.032	0.039	0.054	0.049	0.058	0.067	0.048	0.058	0.069	0.089	0.083
Corporations & Gov't Business Enterprises	0.125	0.123	0.117	0.122	0.106	0.110	0.139	0.143	0.120	0.100	0.121
Total Government	0.079	0.089	0.036	0.036	0.020	0.014	0.044	0.028	0.039	0.002	-0.020
Federal Government	0.030	0.034	-0.002	0.000	-0.017	-0.027	-0.008	-0.009	0.005	-0.029	-0.047
Provincial, Local and Hospital	0.043	0.049	0.031	0.028	0.029	0.034	0.048	0.033	0.031	0.026	0.021
CPP and QPP	0.006	0.006	0.007	0.007	0.007	0.007	0.004	0.004	0.004	0.006	0.006
Non-residents	-0.003	0.009	0.028	0.019	0.023	0.020	0.000	-0.009	0.004	-0.017	-0.013
Residual Error of Estimate	0.000	-0.004	-0.002	0.003	0.006	0.000	-0.002	-0.004	-0.002	0.003	0.001
Total Savings	0.238	0.259	0.242	0.242	0.229	0.227	0.243	0.233	0.246	0.191	0.193

Source: See Appendix.

TABLE 4-6 Components of Total Gross Savings as Proportions of Total, Adjusted for Inflation, 1962–83

	1962	1963	1964	1965	1966	1967	1968	1969	1970	1971	1972
					($ billions)						
Persons & Unincorporated Businesses	0.298	0.291	0.222	0.201	0.228	0.240	0.223	0.185	0.222	0.234	0.228
Trusteed Pension Funds	0.045	0.050	0.044	0.037	0.029	0.038	0.041	0.035	0.040	0.051	0.043
Other Savings	0.253	0.241	0.178	0.164	0.200	0.202	0.182	0.150	0.183	0.183	0.185
Corporations & Gov't Business Enterprises	0.480	0.496	0.519	0.467	0.435	0.475	0.501	0.459	0.532	0.489	0.491
Total Government	0.156	0.172	0.227	0.245	0.259	0.253	0.269	0.333	0.296	0.250	0.256
Federal Government	0.006	0.023	0.080	0.101	0.079	0.058	0.062	0.124	0.067	0.052	0.050
Provincial, Local and Hospital	0.150	0.149	0.147	0.144	0.137	0.140	0.149	0.156	0.168	0.143	0.159
CPP and QPP	0.000	0.000	0.000	0.000	0.043	0.055	0.059	0.053	0.061	0.056	0.047
Non-residents	0.079	0.044	0.028	0.072	0.067	0.030	0.007	0.046	-0.069	-0.018	0.017
Residual Error of Estimate	-0.013	-0.041	0.004	0.014	0.011	0.002	0.001	-0.023	0.109	0.044	0.008
Total Savings	1.000	1.000	1.000	1.000	1.000	1.000	1.000	1.000	1.000	1.000	1.000

	1973	1974	1975	1976	1977	1978	1979	1980	1981	1982	1983
						($ billions)					
Persons & Unincorporated Businesses	0.156	0.166	0.261	0.255	0.321	0.367	0.255	0.319	0.343	0.541	0.539
Trusteed Pension Funds	0.021	0.013	0.038	0.054	0.066	0.071	0.059	0.072	0.063	0.078	0.111
Other Savings	0.135	0.152	0.223	0.201	0.255	0.296	0.196	0.248	0.280	0.462	0.427
Corporations & Gov't Business Enterprises	0.526	0.474	0.482	0.506	0.464	0.481	0.571	0.615	0.489	0.524	0.627
Total Government	0.333	0.343	0.149	0.149	0.086	0.062	0.181	0.122	0.160	0.012	-0.103
Federal Government	0.125	0.132	-0.008	0.002	-0.072	-0.118	-0.032	-0.038	0.019	-0.154	-0.244
Provincial, Local and Hospital	0.181	0.188	0.127	0.117	0.127	0.151	0.198	0.142	0.125	0.135	0.110
CPP and QPP	0.027	0.023	0.030	0.030	0.032	0.029	0.015	0.018	0.016	0.031	0.030
Non-residents	-0.014	0.034	0.115	0.070	0.102	0.089	0.002	-0.040	0.017	-0.090	-0.066
Residual Error of Estimate	-0.001	-0.016	-0.007	0.011	0.026	0.000	-0.009	-0.016	-0.009	0.013	0.004
Total Savings	1.000	1.000	1.000	1.000	1.000	1.000	1.000	1.000	1.000	1.000	1.000

Source: See Appendix.

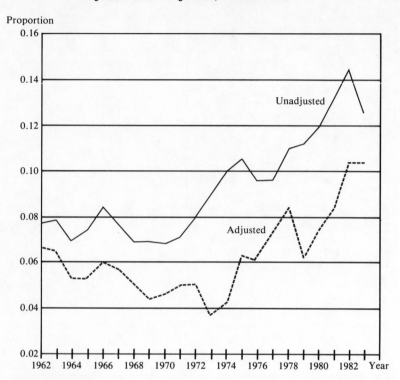

FIGURE 4-6 Gross Personal Savings as a Share of GNE, Unadjusted and Adjusted, 1962–83

Source: See Appendix.

hold sector from 1976 to 1983 increasingly deviated from the pattern established previously. Whether this change can be accounted for by tax incentives introduced over the years is considered in the next section.[11]

Savings rates of the federal government and of the provincial, local and hospital sectors are increased under savings adjustment, and the savings rate of the public pension funds is reduced. For the government sector as a whole, inflation adjustment increases the savings rate in every year of the analysis, with more substantial adjustments in recent years of high inflation. In 1983 the total dissavings rate of the government sector is reduced by two-fifths by inflation adjustment, changing from 3.4 percent to 2.0 percent of GNP. Federal dissaving after adjustment is 4.7 percent in that year, whereas the unadjusted rate is 5.8 percent.

As the figures illustrate, however, the time pattern, as opposed to the level, of government saving is not much altered by the inflation adjustment. Both series reveal a significant decline in savings rates starting in 1975. Since the behaviour of the aggregate government sector is dominated by the behaviour of the federal government, it is not surprising that

FIGURE 4-7   Savings in Trusteed Pension Funds as a Share of
GNE Unadjusted and Adjusted, 1982–83

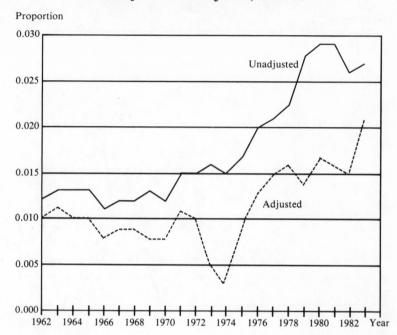

Proportion

Source: See Appendix.

a similar pattern obtains for federal savings rates. When we examine federal fiscal policy in the light of the adjusted data, it is clear that a shift in fiscal policy occurred in the mid-seventies: before 1975 the federal government provided significant net savings (about 2 percent of GNP) whereas from 1975 to 1981 it became a small dissaver (0.8 percent of GNP). In 1982–83, mainly as a result of the impact of the severe recession on federal revenues and transfer payments, federal dissaving increased substantially to 3.4 percent and 4.8 percent of GNP, respectively.[12]

The public pension funds, being net creditors in terms of nominal assets, show the opposite effect: inflation adjustment reduces their savings rates. Although the savings provided by these funds are small in relation to total savings, it is notable that inflation adjustment cuts their recent savings rate in half. The inflation-adjusted data indicate that the savings rates of these plans have been trending downward in real terms since 1968 as the plans have matured. To restore current savings in these plans to approximately the level reached in 1968 would require about a 50 percent increase in contribution rates.

As noted earlier, the inflation-adjusted data provide somewhat more evidence of a downward trend in Canada's dependence on foreign sources of saving. As illustrated in Figure 4-13, non-resident savings as a

FIGURE 4-8   Gross Business Saving as a Share of GNE,
Unadjusted and Adjusted, 1962–83

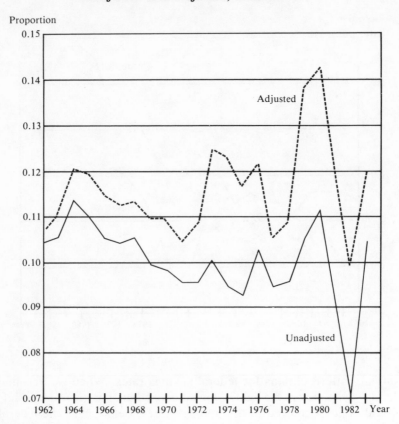

Source: See Appendix.

percentage of Canada's GNP have declined substantially since the 1975 peak. For three of the four years 1980–83 Canada has been a net supplier of real resources to the rest of the world. Whether this is merely a cyclical rather than a secular trend can only be determined after domestic investment spending has recovered more completely.

Business saving is increased in every year as a result of inflation adjustment. As Figure 4-8 illustrates, the inflation-adjusted savings rate of the business sector appears to be secularly stable, but with major cyclical swings reflecting the cyclical volatitility of corporate profits. According to the inflation-adjusted data, business gross saving is financing the lion's share of non-residential investment spending. From 1979 to 1983 the adjusted gross savings of this sector totalled $206 billion, financing over 80 percent of gross fixed-capital formation by business.

Total Government Saving as a Share of GNE,
Unadjusted and Adjusted, 1962–83

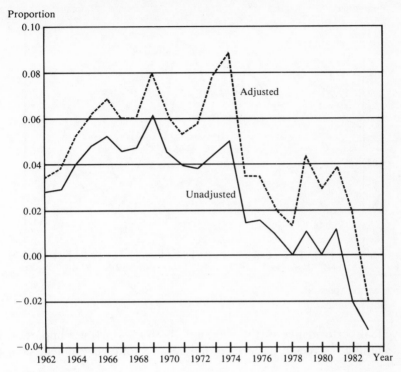

Source: See Appendix.

Summary

Inflation adjustment of the savings data has resulted in some moderation of the upward trend in personal savings rates noted in the previous section. Even after adjusting for inflation, however, personal savings rates moved in an upward trend in 1975, and the years 1982 and 1983 witnessed savings rates higher than in any of the previous 19 years. The balance between savings through trusteed pension plans and other forms of personal savings is not much affected by inflation adjustment.

Although the average level of government saving is raised by inflation adjustment, its recent time pattern is not altered. The federal government moved into a dissaving position in 1975, and except for 1981, has been a net dissaver to the time of writing (1984). During 1982 and 1983 federal dissaving increased substantially, moving the consolidated government sector into a net dissaving position as a result. With the inflation distortions removed, what remains is federal fiscal policy and the

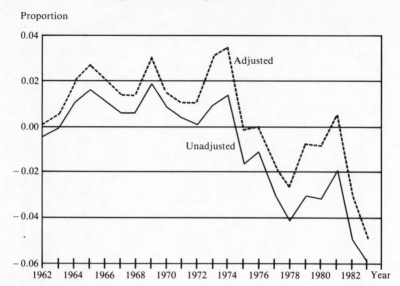

Source: See Appendix.

cyclical performance of the economy, both of which are important in explaining the recent patterns of federal and total government savings rates.

One possible recent trend that is reinforced in the adjusted data is the decline in Canada's dependence on foreign saving. However, the current depressed state of domestic investment activity is doubtless an important contributing cause. We must await a cyclical recovery of business fixed investment in order to determine whether and to what extent a secular trend exists.

Tax Incentives and Personal Saving

Between 1974 and 1976 the Government of Canada instituted a number of personal income tax measures that appear to provide incentives for increased personal saving.[13] They include the $1,000 Investment Income Deduction (IID), Registered Home Ownership Savings Plans (RHOSPs), and higher annual contribution limits on Registered Retirement Saving Plans (RRSPs). A common feature of all the measures is that they permit taxpayers to defer or entirely avoid income taxes on monies used for certain qualifying investments. Another common feature is that each measure is limited to a specified annual maximum contribution.

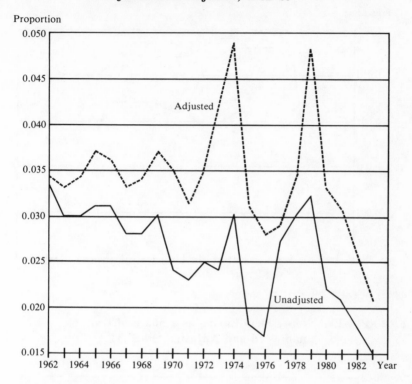

FIGURE 4-11 Provincial Government Saving as a Share of GNE, Unadjusted and Adjusted, 1962–83

Source: See Appendix.
Note: Provincial includes local governments and hospitals.

Whether these tax measures have indeed stimulated increased personal saving is open to debate. Even if they have, the possibility exists that they may have done so at the cost of lower saving by governments or some other sectors of the economy. The evidence relating to this issue is scant and in some cases superficial. We shall review what is known about the matter in this section of the study.

Canadian and U.S. Personal Savings Rates

One piece of empirical evidence in support of the claim that the tax incentives have promoted higher personal saving in Canada is obtained by comparing Canadian rates of personal saving with those in the United States. Both the rates of personal saving and the year-to-year fluctuations were quite similar in the two countries throughout the entire

FIGURE 4-12 CPP and QPP Saving as a Share of GNE, Unadjusted and Adjusted, 1962–83

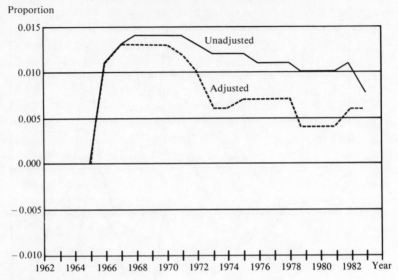

Source: See Appendix.

FIGURE 4-13 Non-resident Saving as a Share of GNE, Unadjusted and Adjusted, 1962–83

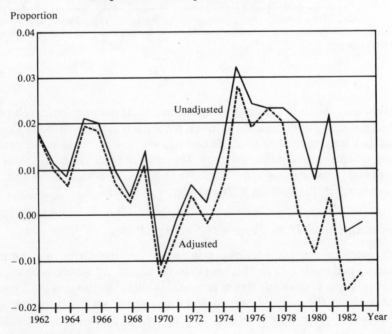

Source: See Appendix.

postwar period until 1975. From 1975 to 1983 the Canadian personal savings rate persistently exceeded the corresponding rate in the United States. The average annual difference between the two rates was 5.5 percentage points (unadjusted for inflation). Before 1975 the average difference was effectively zero. The gap cannot have been due solely to inflation because the two countries experienced similar rates of price inflation. Canadian and U.S. rates of personal saving that are adjusted for inflation show the same divergence starting in 1975.

It seems clear that the gap between the Canadian and U.S. personal savings rates was the result of different behaviour on the part of individual savers. After decades of nearly identical behaviour, something happened in the mid-seventies that caused Canadians and Americans to save different fractions of their disposable incomes. The coincidence in timing with the introduction of the Canadian tax measures cited above seems to suggest these tax incentives as one factor that may be responsible for the phenomenon.

That hypothesis is as good an explanation as any for the savings rate gap. Perhaps this is what prompted the U.S. Congress in 1979 to enact a personal tax incentive of its own, the IRA Accounts, similar to Canada's RRSPs. Even so, the growing spread between Canadian and U.S. personal savings rates is rather superficial empirical support for the notion that tax measures caused Canadians to save more. There has been very little hard economic analysis of this issue, and no detailed empirical studies exist to support the hypothesis.

Moreover, there is ample evidence that something other than — or perhaps in addition to — Canadian tax incentives was involved. If tax incentives were the sole modifier of savings behaviour after 1975, we would expect that the Canada–U.S. savings rate gap would have been the result of a rise in the Canadian rate with the U.S. rate remaining near its earlier postwar average. But that is not what has occurred. It is true that the Canadian personal savings rate was somewhat higher from 1975 to 1983 than its postwar average, adjusted for inflation. The dramatic widening that occurred between the Canadian and U.S. rates, however, is due largely to a sharp drop in the U.S. savings rate. It was the American, rather than the Canadian savers whose behaviour changed most significantly in the mid-seventies. The data strongly suggest that some additional behavioural factor has been at work, at least in the United States. As long as this factor remains unidentified, the case that tax incentives are solely responsible for higher Canadian savings rates will remain circumstantial.

There does exist an extended hypotheses that may explain the data. It is worth relating here, even though it has not been tested formally. This hypothesis maintains that the high and variable rates of price inflation that emerged in the mid-seventies had an unfavourable effect on the risk-return combinations available to individual investor-savers in North

America. After-tax real rates of return available to investors declined from their preinflation values, and the perceived risk on investments rose. The hypothesis contends that the returns to marginal saving have been reduced and people have decided to save smaller fractions of their incomes. In Canada this effect has been offset by personal tax incentives; hence Canadians have maintained their historical saving patterns, while Americans have saved less.

The hypothesis appears to fit the facts but is based upon a number of questionable assumptions. First, it is not clear that high inflation has reduced the ex ante expected rate of return to investor-savers. Nor is it clear that the perceived risks associated with investments have risen. Second, even if risks have increased, economic theory does not unambiguously predict that people will therefore save less. Under certain circumstances, higher risks will lead to more, not less, saving. Finally, the hypothesis considers Canadian tax measures to be a positive stimulus to saving. Yet, it is not at all clear that the measures cited here really are effective stimuli. In fact, there is some evidence to suggest that they may be little more than lump-sum tax subsidies to Canadian taxpayers and provide little or no motivation for higher saving. The latter is the view adopted by Jump (1982) on the basis of an earlier study. The key points of that study are reviewed below with some new thoughts on the issue.

Tax Incentives and the Individual Saver

A measure that reduces the taxation of income generated by saving can cause people to postpone current consumption in favour of additional, new saving if and only if the measure offers them a higher after-tax return than they could otherwise earn on marginal, or incremental, saving. Taxpayers will not postpone current consumption in response to a tax measure that does not produce a more attractive (in terms of yield) investment than already is available to them. Nor will they postpone consumption if the tax measure limits their tax reduction to a level of saving that is less than they are already undertaking. In other words, a tax rebate on saving up to some level will provide no savings incentive for a taxpayer who is already saving more is binding and it represents a lump-sum tax reduction rather than an inducement to save at the margin.

Each of the measures introduced by the Government of Canada in the mid-seventies and referred to at the beginning of this section offers a zero rate of tax on a limited amount of specific annual saving. The first question to be asked is whether these measures have provided Canadian savers with higher rates of return than they could otherwise earn. The second question is whether the annual limits have been binding for those taxpayers who account for the bulk of Canadian personal saving. We shall look at each question in turn.

Many Canadian taxpayers appear to have the ability to earn a tax-free rate of return on marginal savings even without using the $1,000 IID, RHOSPs or RRSPs. All employed taxpayers who participate in contributory pension plans sponsored by their employers potentially have this ability, provided they are able to increase their own contributions to this pension plan. Pension savings earn an after-tax rate of return equal to the before-tax rate of interest — a return equivalent to that available through the $1,000 IID and RRSPs. For people who can make discretionary pension contributions, these tax measures provide few new investment opportunities and are unlikely to prompt them to save more. It is impossible to determine how many Canadians are in such a position, but surely there must be many.[14]

Probably an even greater number of Canadians are able to earn a tax-free rate of return through a mechanism associated with home ownership. Imputed rents on owner-occupied housing are not subject to tax, and mortgage interest payments made by owner-occupants are not tax-deductible in Canada. Anyone who owns a home with an outstanding mortgage can earn a tax-free rate of return on marginal saving by simply using this saving to pay off part of his or her mortgage principal. This possibility constitutes an attractive life-cycle savings strategy. People who borrow to purchase a home early in their working lives can earn a tax-free return on their investment in the form of imputed rents. At the same time they can use future savings to pay off their mortgage over the remainder of their working years — thereby earning a tax-free rate of return on future savings.

The fact that something in the neighbourhood of 60 percent of Canadian households are owner-occupants and that the majority of them have outstanding mortgages suggest that this strategy is an important part of life-cycle saving. For such people, tax measures under consideration may provide very little incentive for increased saving.

Other tax shelters are available in the form of trusts, income averaging annuities and so on.[15] The point is that these shelters, along with employer-based pension plans and mortgages, must certainly limit the number of people for whom the $1,000 IID, RHOSPs and RRSPs offer unique opportunities to earn a tax-free rate of return. The mere fact that great numbers of taxpayers have established RRSPs and RHOSPs or claim the $1,000 IID does not mean that these measures are the only means for sheltering incomes from taxation. A taxpayer may find it simpler to contribute to an RRSP, for example, than to make a marginal contribution to an employer-based pension plan. Or he or she may find it more convenient to use the $1,000 IID than to prepay part of his or her mortgage principal. The fact that the tax measures have been used does not validate the contention that they cause increased saving by Canadians.

We must also consider that taxpayers who do not have tax-free alternatives may find the annual limits imposed upon the $1,000 IID, RHOSPs and RRSPs to be binding. Incentives for increased saving will not exist where the limits are binding. Let us examine this possibility for each of the tax measures.

Introduced in 1974, the $1,000 IID excludes from taxation the first $1,000 of investment income for qualifying Canadian savers during any tax year. The annual limit may be less than $1,000 for a taxpayer with carrying charges, since the exclusion applies to investment income net of deductible expenses. In any event, the limit is small in relation to the incomes of Canadian taxpayers. Revenue Canada (1981) reports, for example, that taxpayers with gross incomes of $20,000 or more in 1979 had investment incomes that averaged $3,624 — well above the $1,000 limit. Even taxpayers with incomes of less than $20,000 in 1979 had an average of $689 in investment income — not far below the limit.

These figures do not prove that the $1,000 annual limit is probably not binding on many Canadians. But how many of these people have no other options for earning tax-free returns? And of those who do not, what fraction of aggregate personal saving can be attributed to them? We do not know the answers to those questions, but it is at least worth considering that the volume of incremental saving attributable to the $1,000 IID may be small.

Jump (1982) argues that the $1,000 IID is largely a lump-sum tax reduction to those who claim it. He has estimated the 1978 tax revenue losses resulting from the $1,000 IID at $90 billion ($64 billion federal plus $26 billion provincial). In other words, had the investment incomes reported by Canadians for 1978 been fully subject to the taxes prevailing then, an additional $90 billion in tax revenues would have been generated. Actually this figure probably overstates the size of any lump-sum tax reduction resulting from the $1,000 IID by a substantial amount. If the IID did not exist, many Canadian taxpayers would have undoubtedly turned to alternative tax-sheltered investments, a possibility that is consistent with the claim made earlier that taxpayers with other tax-free options may still use the $1,000 IID because of its simplicity or convenience.

Taxpayers are eligible to establish RHOSPs only if they do not currently own a "principal residence" and have never had an RHOSP. For someone in this position who also wants to purchase a home within 20 years, an RHOSP is a very attractive proposition. Consider an eligible individual whose marginal tax rate is t. By putting x dollars into an RHOSP, that person is entitled to a tax rebate of tx. Probably the best strategy is to make the maximum annual contribution of $1,000, which requires a net contribution of $(1-t)\$1,000$ from his own funds. If the individual does this for the maximum 10 years and subsequently purchases a home, he or she will earn a rate of return in excess of the tax-free rate of interest (that is, the individual gets both the annual tax rebate of tx, or $t(\$1,000)$ at the optimum, and the investment earnings of the RHOSP are not taxed while accumulating or upon withdrawal). This rate of return is almost certainly higher than any risk-equivalent alternatives the prospective home-buyer could obtain. Under the RHOSP regulations, annual contributions to the plan are limited to $1,000 and a total not to exceed $10,000 over 20 years.

To the taxpayer who is eligible for a RHOSP but does not plan to purchase a home, a RHOSP is not nearly as attractive. After 20 years all of the monies accumulated in a RHOSP become taxable income for the prevailing tax year if a home is not purchased. The taxpayer who is in this position will have earned a rate of return that is probably lower than the tax-free rate of interest but higher than the after-tax rate of interest. The uncertainty here depends upon how the taxpayer's marginal tax rate in the year the RHOSP is dissolved compares with his or her marginal tax rates during contributory years. The computations are somewhat complicated. Suffice it to say that RHOSPs are not likely to be particularly appealing to very many taxpayers who have neither owned a home nor wish to own one in the future.

For the taxpayer who is eligible and who does want to buy a home in the future, there will be an incentive to establish a RHOSP and to make the maximum annual contribution of $1,000. This is consistent with the report by Revenue Canada (Canada, 1981) that the average RHOSP contribution claimed in the 1979 tax year was $989. From our perspective the pertinent question is whether the availability of a RHOSP will induce this taxpayer to postpone consumption and save more.

Note that the annual amount of individual saving necessary to make optimal use of a RHOSP is only $1,000(1-t)$. This is likely to be in the range of $500 to $750 for the typical marginal tax rate. People who have never owned a home but would like to are probably already saving more than that every year. If so, they will benefit from redirecting their savings toward an RHOSP and receiving a lump-sum tax reduction, but they have no incentive to save any more. The only incentive to increase savings generated by RHOSPs applies to would-be home-owners whose annual savings would otherwise be lower than the optimal RHOSP amount. No doubt there are some Canadians who fit this description. But any incremental saving they might do because of this stimulus can hardly amount to enough to alter the aggregate rate of personal saving.

Rules governing RRSP contributions before the 1982 tax year seemed designed to make the 1974 hike in contribution limits an ineffective stimulus to new saving. Until the 1982 tax year, interest paid on monies borrowed to finance a RRSP contribution were tax-deductible against other income. This created a nearly perfect arbitrage situation for taxpayers with investment incomes of more than $1,000 who could make use of the interest deductibility without losing some portion of the IID. A taxpayer in this position could borrow at the after-tax interest rate the funds necessary to finance a RRSP contribution that earned the before-tax rate of interest. This provided a great incentive to make the maximum possible RRSP contribution and thereby earn the greatest gains.

Since the maximum annual RRSP contribution depends upon participation in employer-based pension plans, it is not possible to determine from aggregate taxation statistics for the pre-1982 period how may people took advantage of this arbitrage opportunity. However, judging from the rapid growth in RRSPs and from the high proportion of taxpayers with investment income of more than $1,000 who stood to gain the most, the numbers must have been large.[16] In fact, the numbers are likely to be comparable to the number of Canadians who had investment incomes higher than the $1,000 exclusion limit.

The taxpayers who did take advantage of the arbitrage opportunity between 1974 and 1982 would have found the annual RRSP contribution limits to be binding constraints. For them, RRSPs would have served as lump-sum tax reductions that provided little or no incentive to postpone current consumption and save more. It is conceivable that the bulk of RRSP growth over this interval was generated from this group of taxpayers.

The rules governing borrowing for RRSP contributions were altered in the budget of November 1981. Effective with the 1982 tax year, interest on monies borrowed to finance contributions is no longer tax-deductible. The figures are not yet available, but it is likely that this change will reduce the attractiveness of RRSPs to many investors. The incentive to make the maximum annual contribution may have been removed for some.[17] Whether this means that RRSPs have become an inducement to save more remains unclear.

Under the current rules, the availability of RRSPs should encourage additional saving by that group of taxpayers who have no other means of earning a tax-free return and who would otherwise save less annually than the contribution limit. Since the annual contribution limits here are more generous than those for the IID and RHOSPs, RRSPs may be a stronger saving stimulus. Still it should be noted that these limits were last adjusted in 1976 and have eroded substantially in real terms with the ensuing rise in prices. Whatever impetus to personal saving might have been provided since the borrowing rules were changed in November 1981 is surely much weaker than in earlier years.[18]

Lump-Sum Tax Reductions and Aggregate Saving

In short, it is difficult to disprove the proposition that the Canadian tax incentives introduced in the mid-seventies have been largely lump-sum tax reductions to selected groups of taxpayers and have had little influence on people's decisions to spend or save — at least over the 1974–81 period. And since that possibility cannot be ignored, it is worth conducting an examination of the possible consequences of this type of tax reduction on aggregate saving.

The recipients of lump-sum tax reductions have a right to feel wealthier because of them: they are indeed wealthier. But at the same time, someone else is poorer by a like amount since other taxpayers must foot the bill for these measures by paying higher taxes — either now or in the future. However, the way in which lump-sum tax reductions are financed does have some implications for aggregate saving. Unfortunately, the complexities of government finance do not permit us to determine just what offsetting moves were made by the Government of Canada to finance the tax incentives considered above. We will have to explore two possibilities: (1) that the government has simply allowed the $1,000 IID, RHOSPs and higher RRSP limits to add to its deficit and (2) that general income tax rates have been set at higher values than they would otherwise have been.

If deficit financing has been employed, then the IID, RHOSPs and the increased RRSP limits may actually have contributed to a rise in personal saving in Canada. This might have occurred, not because people have been persuaded to spend less and save more, but because of an entirely passive mechanism. When governments give lump-sum tax reductions and incur deficits, people tend to "save" their tax reductions in anticipation of the higher future taxes required to eliminate the deficit. This action, known as the Ricardian Equivalence Theorem, was proposed by David Ricardo more than 150 years ago. It states simply that deficit-financed lump-sum tax reductions will raise personal saving and simultaneously lower government saving by the amount of the tax reduction.[19] Clearly this kind of action has no real effects other than a possible redistribution of income. We are looking here at a simple transfer of saving between the government and personal sectors.

Jump (1982) has estimated how much personal saving in Canada might have increased in 1979 if all of the revenue losses due to the $1,000 IID and RRSP claims during that year are regarded as lump-sum tax reductions financed by government deficits. RHOSPs were not included in his computation, but they are small enough not to affect the estimates very much. Jump estimated that $2.32 billion worth of personal saving in 1979 might be due to this kind of lump-sum transfer from government saving to the personal sector. This amounts to about 1.3 percentage points in terms of the gross rate of personal saving, which totalled 16 percent of disposable income plus Capital Cost Allowances (CCA) in 1979 on an unadjusted (for inflation) basis. It is a significant portion of personal saving for that year but falls well short of explaining the 5 percentage point gap that existed between the Canadian and U.S. saving rates. Those seeking to explain this gap via Canadian tax incentives will apparently have to look elsewhere.

Perhaps the Government of Canada has financed the $1,000 IID,

RHOSPs and higher RRSP limits by raising income-tax rates above the levels that would have prevailed in the absence of these measures. If so, what can be said of the effect on saving? Very little, except that national saving is likely to have been *lower* than it would otherwise have been. The financing of lump-sum tax reductions with increased marginal tax rates would be a disincentive to save at the margin. The after-tax returns to marginal savings would be lowered, leading to a contraction in both savings and claims on future incomes.

At this time we do not know whether either of these situations actually happened in Canada between 1974 and 1981. Both are based on the proposition that the Canadian tax measures in question act largely as lump-sum tax reductions. The proposition is plausible but remains unproved. An interpretation of the tax measures as providing positive incentives for increased national saving cannot be ruled out entirely but should certainly be received with a great deal of skepticism.

Public Pensions and Private Saving

Since their beginnings in 1966, the Canada and Quebec Pension Plans, combined, have contributed small, positive increments to annual gross savings (see Table 4-1 and Table 4-2). These direct savings flows have resulted from the fact that the annual contributions collected by both the CPP and the QPP have generally been higher than the annual benefits paid by the plans. Between 1967 and 1983 the share of gross national saving generated by these pension plans has ranged from 1 percent to 6 percent.

Such small figures belie the importance that public pension plans will have for future Canadian savings patterns. Perhaps no single factor will exert more influence upon savings behaviour in coming decades than the revisions that will soon be made to the CPP (and also to the QPP.) Unfortunately, a great deal of uncertainty surrounds both the nature of these revisions and their possible effect on future savings.

Let us concentrate on the CPP with the understanding that nearly all of what can be said about this pension plan applies equally to the QPP. Public debate over expanding and/or possibly redefining the eligibility requirements under the CPP has been proceeding for some time. Some changes to the benefit schedules are likely to be made in the near future. It is not yet clear what the changes will be, but it seems unlikely that the benefit structure will be radically altered. The same cannot be said of the structure of contributions. This will change significantly, though not in a manner that can be fully predicted.

The current CPP contribution rate (an employee and employer combination totalling 3.6 percent of annual earnings, subject to a maximum) will be insufficient to finance the obligations of the CPP beyond the next 3 to 9 years (1987–93), even if current benefit schedules remain in place. The 3.6 percent figure was adopted in 1966 as an interim arrangement and

has generated adequate contributions up until now. Eligibility for benefits is based upon a formula involving the number of years of contributions. In the early years of the CPP, few beneficiaries qualified for other
than minimal annual benefits. Total benefit obligations have been so low
that the CPP has accumulated a substantial surplus in the form of a
reserve fund (at the end of March 1982, this fund amounted to $21.5
billion fully invested in provincial and federal government securities).

All that will soon change. As the CPP continues to approach "maturity" in the next few years, benefit payments will outstrip both contributions and the earnings of the reserve fund. Unless contribution rates are
raised, the reserve fund itself will be depleted by 1993 at the latest.[20] This
prospect is not the result of poor planning. It was recognized from the
start that contribution rates would one day have to be increased. That
day is not far off, though the precise time is not certain. It is also
uncertain just how contribution rates will be restructured, and this is the
critical decision with regard to future savings incentives.

In raising contribution rates, policy makers will have to decide
whether the CPP is to be run as a "pay-as-you-go" (or "pay-go") plan or
as a "funded" plan. Under a pay-go plan, contribution rates would be set
to generate exactly the revenues necessary to finance annual benefit
payments with no surplus or deficit. Under a funded plan, contribution
rates would be set (at least initially) at higher values and the CPP would
run a surplus. The surplus would be invested in a fund of assets, the
earnings on which would serve to ensure that future benefit obligations
would be met. As long as either the population or its average annual
earnings continued to grow, the size of the fund would also grow.

The CPP could be put on a fully funded basis, in which case the
actuarial value of the lifetime contributions made by the average contributor would be set equal to the actuarial value of the lifetime benefits
received by the average beneficiary. In this case the required fund would
be quite large — perhaps several hundred billion dollars in size within 20
to 30 years. The CPP could also be put on a blended basis — partially
pay-go and partially funded. In effect, the CPP has been a blended plan
up until now. The larger the pay-go element, the smaller the investment
fund, though any fund is likely to grow over time at approximately the
rate of nominal GNP growth.

Will it make any difference to the Canadian economy which of these
schemes is chosen? This question cannot be answered with certainty,
but the financing choice has a large implication for future savings
behaviour.

Pay-Go and Private Savings Incentives

It has been alleged by a number of economists (most notably, Martin
Feldstein) that a pay-go public pension plan will have a detrimental

effect on private saving. In truth, the evidence pertaining to this claim is quite ambiguous. Let us see why.

Consider the imposition of a mandatory pay-go plan in an economy that previously did not have a public pension plan. People who are currently old (i.e., retired) will be the beneficiaries of the new windfall pensions. The currently young (i.e., workers) will have to bear the costs of these pensions in the form of contributions. How will these two generations react to this new situation? If people are self-centred and do not care about the welfare of later generations, then adverse savings effects can occur: the currently old will simply increase their spending by the amount of their windfall pension receipts. The currently young will attempt to maintain previous consumption patterns and reduce their private saving. The young will save less for retirement, anticipating that they too will receive public pensions after their working days are ended.

In the aggregate, consumption spending will rise and personal saving will decline. The savings decline is potentially equal to pension benefits on an annual basis. Of course this is not the end of the story. With less saving, the currently young will accumulate fewer domestic and international assets. Future income flows must decline as a result. The currently young and all future generations will be worse off while the currently old experience a windfall gain. There will be a transfer to the currently old from all future generations. It is this situation that critics of pay-go pensions fear.

Note that these effects depend upon "selfish" behaviour of the sort in which people are not concerned with the welfare of their heirs. But suppose that people do care about their heirs and attempt to facilitate their well-being by leaving bequests to them. In this case a pay-go public pension will have no aggregate savings effects whatsoever. The currently old will save their windfall pensions in order to pass the proceeds along to their heirs. The currently young will reduce their current saving to accommodate their mandatory contributions, but they will receive enlarged bequests from the old generation in the future. The currently young will, in turn, pass on these enlarged bequests to their heirs, and so on. No generation is made better or worse off in this case. There is no transfer between generations. Nor are there any effects on aggregate savings or incomes.[21]

Economic theory tells us that the effect of a pay-go public pension plan on private saving depends therefore upon whether people wish to leave bequests to their heirs. Unfortunately, economic theory cannot tell us whether that is the case or not. No doubt some people want to leave bequests and some do not. The important question is, which group predominates? The answer can only be determined by empirical observation.

A number of studies designed to detect the effects of pay-go pensions on private saving have been conducted over the past decade. Most of these have used data pertaining to the U.S. Social Security System, a pay-go plan in existence since the mid-1930s. We will attempt to summarize their findings. Readers are referred to the Economic Council of Canada (1979) for more detailed information. In brief, empirical studies have produced mixed and, hence, ambiguous findings. Some researchers, such as Feldstein (1974), have claimed to detect substantial negative effects of Social Security on U.S. personal savings rates. Others, such as Leimer and Lesnoy (1982), have claimed to find little or no effect. The issue remains unresolved.

Perhaps the most that can be said regarding the empirical evidence is that the later studies — which use the more sophisticated techniques — have tended to produce progressively smaller estimates of any adverse effect on private saving that might be attributable to the U.S. Social Security System. This does not mean that progressive future research will lead to the conclusion that pay-go pensions have no effect on private saving. But it does suggest that the rather frightening magnitudes produced in Feldstein's early work probably greatly overstated any decline in saving that the Social Security System might have caused.

It now appears certain that Canadian policy makers will have to decide how to finance the future CPP before any empirical consensus on the effects of pay-go has been reached. This makes that decision a risky one, but at least the risks are reasonably well understood. A decision to put the CPP on a pay-go basis will raise the possibility of an intergenerational transfer that will benefit the currently old at the expense of lower savings and incomes for future generations. It is perhaps worth noting that Canadian policy makers of the 1950s ran exactly this same risk when they established the Old Age Security scheme, which is financed on a pay-go basis through the income tax.

A Funded CPP and Private Saving

What can be said of the funded alternative to a pay-go system? In principle, funding a mandatory pension plan would have no effect on aggregate savings. People could be expected to reduce their private saving by the amounts contributed to the public pension fund,[22] since a public fund guarantees future benefits with actuarial value equal to the present value of the fund. For every dollar that is funded, private individuals need one dollar less private wealth to provide for their retirement. A funded pension plan would simply divert private saving into the public saving of the pension plan.

In actual fact, these results could be expected to hold if and only if the public pension fund invests in the same types of assets that private savers would purchase. The public fund must earn the same rate of return as is available to private investors; otherwise, a dollar invested in the fund would not be a perfect substitute for a dollar's worth of private saving.

The biggest challenge to funding the CPP (or any mandatory public pension plan) is to devise a scheme for ensuring that the criteria used for investing the public funds are identical to the risk-return criteria used by the private sector. It will not be easy to ensure this outcome. Any alternative investment criteria must earn returns viewed as a suboptimal by the participants in the pension plan. And suboptimal returns will have adverse economic consequences. If the public pension fund deviates from the private sector's risk-return criteria, it will allocate a portion of national saving to investments that are less productive than might otherwise have been chosen. This would constitute a misallocation of productive resources with a consequent lowering of national income and welfare. Both the current generation and future generations would be made worse off.

Just how serious a misallocation of resources might result from an inappropriate investment criterion would depend upon several factors, in particular the size of the public pension fund. A fully funded CPP could control a sizable fraction of the nation's savings. A blended plan that was largely pay-go would have a much smaller investment fund. Yet even a small misallocation of resources is to be avoided.

Many financial analysts and private-sector investors are extremely skeptical of the ability of policy makers to device an acceptable management scheme for a public pension fund. The chief fear appears to be that governments will be tempted to allow political considerations to influence their investment decisions. It is easy to imagine how a government might be persuaded to direct pension fund investments toward domestic industries suffering from cyclical or even long-term difficulties without due regard for risk-return considerations. Skeptics point out that the managers of the QPP's reserve fund (and other Quebec public pension funds) have recently favoured heavy equity investment in Quebec industries.[23]

Is it possible to devise a management scheme that would appease the critics of a funded CPP? Little consideration has been given to this issue, but one study (Jump, 1983) contends that the only management system that could avoid suspicion would be one in which CPP funds were managed directly by the private sector. Jump suggests that it might be feasible to "parcel out" CPP funds to private pension funds. Each private fund would be free to invest the public monies in any way it saw fit but would be liable to the CPP for both the principal amount and the average, or market, rate of return. In essence, the private funds would be forced borrowers from the CPP. This would increase their riskiness, but they could receive compensation in the form of a management fee from the CPP.

The advantage of this proposal is that it allows decisions regarding the investment of public pension funds to be retained by the private sector. Each private pension investing the funds would have an incentive to earn the best possible risk-return combination. Its main disadvantage is that even private pension funds must operate under legislative restrictions that do not apply to individuals. For example, private pension funds cannot invest in the equity of a corporation that has failed to make dividend payments in the past three consecutive years. A corporation that fails this test may nonetheless be an attractive investment. By restricting the choices available to private pension funds, legislators may already be contributing to some misallocation of resources — a situation that would be aggravated under Jump's scheme.

This disadvantage could be removed if policy makers were to rescind the legal restrictions that now apply to pension fund investments, though it seems unlikely that this will occur. The current mood of governments appears to favour more, not fewer, restrictions on pension funds assets.

Even if Jump's scheme or some other means of allowing the private sector to control CPP investments could be found, there would still be observable consequences to moving to a funded public pension plan. Earnings from pension investments, be they private or public, are not subject to income tax. Investments attractive to pension funds differ from those attractive to taxable private investors using the same risk-return criteria. Other things being equal, private investors have a preference for equity — as opposed to debt — instruments because of their more favourable tax treatment. Tax-exempt pension funds, however, have the opposite preferences.

A funded CPP would divert savings from the private sector to the public pension fund, and this would probably lead to a decline in the demand for equity investments and a rise in the demand for debt instruments by Canadians. Capital markets could probably accommodate such a shift without altering the relative rates of return on equities and debts owing to the close integration between domestic and international capital markets. Canadians would simply buy more debt, and foreigners would buy more Canadian equities. Canada would reduce its international indebtedness, but at the same time the rest of the world would acquire more Canadian equity assets.

Economically, an international portfolio shift of this sort would be neither good nor bad. However, from a political perspective the result might be viewed as undesirable because it would increase the foreign ownership of Canadian industry. We will refrain from commenting here on the pros and cons of this outcome. Suffice it to say that a funded CPP with privately managed investments might have such a result.

A Funded CPP and Government Debt

No discussion of possible CPP financial arrangement would be complete without some consideration of a funded plan that invests exclusively in public debt. Under the interim financing plan now in effect, any reserve fund generated by the CPP can be co-opted into provincial securities.

Each participating province has the right to borrow from the fund an annual amount equal to the contributions originating in that province. Any monies not absorbed in this manner can be invested in federal government securities. To date, there have been few occasions when the participating provinces have not made full use of this option. The participating provinces negotiated this arrangement at the start of the CPP and have found it to their liking. Past surpluses generated by the pension plan have provided a ready source of finance for provincial deficits. It is likely to prove difficult to persuade all of the participants that a similar arrangement should not be continued in the future. There is a real possibility that the future CPP may continue as a funded system with investments channelled almost exclusively into provincial debt.

The effect of this kind of funded pension plan on saving has been investigated in detail by Jump (1983). This most important finding is that a funded pension plan in which the funds are invested exclusively in government debt is nearly identical to a pay-go plan. It offers the same possibilities for transfers between generations and has the same ambiguous effects on saving as a fully pay-go system with one additional drawback — the possibility of misallocation of resources.

A funded plan committed to purchasing government debt requires governments to run deficits large enough to meet the investment requirements of the pension fund. To generate these deficits, governments must either lower taxes or spend more. If taxes are lowered, the aggregate sum of tax collections and pension contributions will be exactly the same as they are under a pay-go pension plan with identical benefits. In effect the funded plan becomes a pay-go plan where contributors are compensated by reduced taxes. It will have the same effects on aggregate saving as a pay-go system.[24]

If governments meet their deficit requirements by increased spending, they will certainly be contributing to a misallocation of resources. An increase in government spending solely to meet the debt needs of a public pension fund cannot be justified on economic grounds. Money would probably be spent on projects that offered below-market returns, and all generations would be made worse off. This combination of events would result in the savings ambiguities associated with pay-go schemes and would lower national welfare at the same time. Clearly it is the least attractive alternative.

A Look Ahead: Medium-Term Projections of Savings Rates

This section considers the prospects for savings and investment over the next decade. We examine the implications of a long-term projection of the Canadian economy developed in 1983 by our colleague Peter Dungan using the FOCUS econometric model of the Institute for Policy Analysis. This projection is described in detail in Dungan (1984). Although the

**TABLE 4-7 Summary of Projections by Period:
Annual Average Rates of Change**

	1981–85	1986–90	1991–95	1984–95
	(percent)			
Key Indicators	1.9	3.2	2.6	3.0
Real GNP Growth				
Price Inflation	7.5	4.8	4.4	4.7
Unemployment Rate	10.3	8.5	7.1	8.2
Composition of Real GNP Growth				
Consumption	2.2	3.1	2.7	3.1
Residential Investment	3.8	2.9	1.3	2.2
Non-residential Investment	-0.8	8.0	5.1	6.1
Government	1.0	1.3	1.3	1.3
Exports	3.8	3.8	3.7	4.1
Imports	3.3	4.7	4.2	5.0

Source: Peter Dungan, "National Projection through 2005; Provincial Projection Through
1995," Policy Study 8-42 (Toronto: University of Toronto, Institute for Policy
Analysis, April 1984).

Note: These projections are compound growth rates over three five-year periods and one
twelve-year period. For each period the base year is the year before the beginning of
the period.

projection extends to the year 2005, we consider only the period to 1995.
A brief summary of the projection over this interval will provide a useful
backdrop to the subsequent discussion of savings and investment. Relevant statistics are provided in Table 4-7.

As is apparent, the projections entail steady, but moderate, real GNP
growth, following the recovery from the 1981–82 recession. The average
growth rate over the 12-year interval from 1983 to 1995 is 3 percent per
year. This projected growth rate is only sufficient to reduce unemployment gradually. The unemployment rate remains above its estimated full
employment or natural level throughout the period. Price inflation is
gradually reduced to the 4.4 percent range in the early 1990s and averages 4.7 percent a year over the 12-year interval. In the projection, price
inflation has an apparent floor near 4 percent, which Dungan states is "to
allow for the inevitable upward price shocks and for relative price
movements."

These projections are based on a U.S. economic projection with
moderate but steady growth and inflation approaching 4 percent. The
basic assumptions about domestic policy include stable monetary
growth with the money supply (M1) increasing by 7 percent a year and a
moderately restrictive federal fiscal policy, with the inflation-adjusted
federal deficit eliminated by 1992 and with moderate surpluses thereafter. The contribution rates to the public pension funds are assumed to
increase gradually beginning in the late 1980s.

TABLE 4-8 Rate of Saving as a Proportion of GNE, Forecast Period 1983–95

	1983	1984	1985	1986	1987	1988
Persons & Unincorporated Businesses	0.122	0.114	0.094	0.086	0.083	0.086
Corporations & Gov't Business Enterprises	0.105	0.103	0.104	0.107	0.111	0.114
Total Government	−0.026	−0.011	0.004	0.007	0.011	0.013
Federal Government	−0.059	−0.048	−0.033	−0.027	−0.022	−0.020
Provincial, Local and Hospital	0.025	0.029	0.029	0.027	0.026	0.026
CPP and QPP	0.009	0.008	0.008	0.008	0.007	0.007
Non-residents	−0.001	0.002	0.004	0.006	0.006	0.005
Residual Error of Estimate	0.000	0.001	0.001	0.001	0.000	0.000
Total Savings	0.199	0.209	0.207	0.206	0.211	0.218

	1989	1990	1991	1992	1993	1994	1995
Persons & Unincorporated Businesses	0.085	0.083	0.083	0.081	0.081	0.080	0.079
Corporations & Gov't Business Enterprises	0.117	0.119	0.123	0.124	0.125	0.127	0.128
Total Government	0.013	0.015	0.015	0.019	0.020	0.022	0.024
Federal Government	−0.018	−0.016	−0.016	−0.012	−0.010	−0.008	−0.005
Provincial, Local and Hospital	0.024	0.024	0.024	0.024	0.024	0.023	0.023
CPP and QPP	0.007	0.007	0.007	0.006	0.007	0.006	0.006
Non-residents	0.005	0.005	0.003	0.002	0.001	0.000	−0.002
Residual Error of Estimate	0.000	0.000	0.000	0.000	0.000	0.000	0.000
Total Savings	0.221	0.223	0.224	0.226	0.227	0.229	0.229

Source: See Appendix.

The projected composition of real GNP growth indicates that fixed-capital formation by business is the leading component of aggregate demand over the projection period and that it will grow at an annual average rate of 6.1 percent. This does *not* represent a sustained investment boom. Investment does not reach its previous (1981) peak until 1987. In two years, 1987 and 1988, investment grows at double-digit rates, as spending on major energy projects accelerates. However, the effect of even this investment surge on aggregate growth is small, and the continued slack in the economy prevents any resurgence of price inflation. Thereafter the growth of investment gradually subsides to the 4–6 percent range.

This shift in the composition of real demand toward investment causes real import growth to run ahead of real GNP growth. However, favourable movements in the terms of trade allow an excess of real import growth over real export growth without significant changes in the current account of the balance payments.

How is the projected expansion of investment financed? The share of GNP accounted for by total investment (including residential construction and fixed capital formation by government) is projected to increase by 3 percentage points between 1983 and 1985 (see Table 4–8). The breakdown of savings rates by sector indicates that this increase in the share of total investment is more than accommodated by the increased savings of the government and business sectors. The government sector is projected to move from a dissaving rate of 2.6 percent of GNP in 1983 to a positive gross savings rate of 2.4 percent of GNP in 1995 — a swing of 5 percentage points. Business saving is expected to rise by 2.3 percentage points over the same interval. Hence the increase in the savings rates of these two sectors is more than double the increase in total investment. The combined savings rate of the other two sectors must of course decline to preserve the savings-investment identity. Savings by households is projected to drop from the historically high 12.2 percent rate observed in 1983 to 7.9 percent in 1995, a decline of 4.3 percentage points. As a result, there is only a slight decline in the share of savings of the non-resident sector (which, as indicated above, is the residual supplier of funds for investment).

None of the above savings rates are adjusted for inflation, which averages 4.7 percent over the projection period. In order to remove inflation distortions from the projected savings rates, we have constructed projections of the inflation-adjustment factors, using data provided in Dungan's projection. The details of the projection procedures are described in the Appendix. Relevant data are presented in Table 4-8 and Table 4-9 and plotted in Figure 4-14 to Figure 4-17. As is apparent, the trends in the savings rates are not altered significantly by inflation adjustment, reflecting the stability of price inflation over the projection interval. The levels of the savings rates, however, are altered significantly. If we compare the inflation-adjusted savings rates over the projection period with savings rates over the historical period, several significant prospective developments become apparent for each sector.

Sectoral Projections

Households

The recent decline in the inflation-adjusted savings rate of households is projected to continue over the period 1984–86. Personal gross savings as a percentage of GNP are then stable within the 5.2–5.7 percent range

TABLE 4-9 Rate of Saving as a Proportion of Adjusted GNE, Forecast Period 1983–95, Adjusted for Inflation

	1983	1984	1985	1986	1987	1988
Persons & Unincorporated Businesses	0.089	0.082	0.064	0.057	0.054	0.057
Corporations & Gov't Business Enterprises	0.128	0.124	0.122	0.125	0.129	0.132
Total Government	−0.009	−0.007	0.021	0.023	0.026	0.027
Federal Government	−0.044	−0.032	−0.017	−0.011	−0.006	−0.004
Provincial, Local and Hospital	0.030	0.034	0.033	0.030	0.028	0.028
CPP and QPP	0.005	0.004	0.004	0.004	0.004	0.003
Non-residents	−0.010	−0.005	−0.002	0.000	0.000	0.000
Residual Error of Estimate	0.000	0.001	0.001	0.001	0.000	0.000
Total Savings	0.198	0.208	0.206	0.205	0.209	0.217

	1989	1990	1991	1992	1993	1994	1995
Persons & Unincorporated Businesses	0.058	0.057	0.057	0.054	0.054	0.052	0.052
Corporations & Gov't Business Enterprises	0.135	0.137	0.141	0.143	0.145	0.147	0.149
Total Government	0.026	0.028	0.026	0.030	0.031	0.032	0.033
Federal Government	−0.003	−0.001	−0.002	0.002	0.004	0.006	0.007
Provincial, Local and Hospital	0.026	0.025	0.025	0.025	0.024	0.024	0.023
CPP and QPP	0.003	0.004	0.003	0.003	0.003	0.003	0.002
Non-residents	0.000	0.000	−0.002	−0.003	−0.003	−0.004	−0.005
Residual Error of Estimate	0.000	0.000	0.000	0.000	0.000	0.000	0.000
Total Savings	0.220	0.222	0.223	0.225	0.226	0.228	0.229

Source: See Appendix.

from 1986 to 1995. This represents a return to savings rates typical of the historical period before 1975 — from 1962 to 1974, adjusted gross personal savings rates averaged 4.9 percent of adjusted GNP, with a range of 3.7–6.7 percent.

Business
Business savings rates are projected to increase gradually, surpassing their previous historical peak by 1991 and reaching 14.9 percent by 1995. The latter figure is 1 percentage point above the previous peak of 13.9 percent reached in both 1979 and 1980.

Government
The recent deterioration in the adjusted government savings rate is

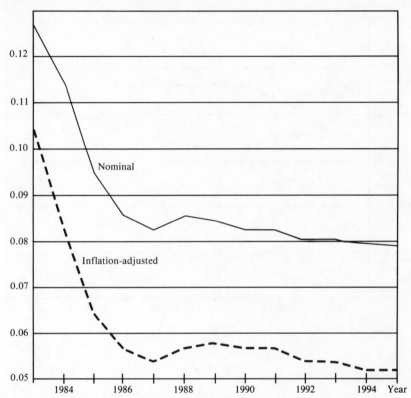

FIGURE 4-14   Gross Personal Saving as Share of GNP,
Nominal and Inflation-Adjusted, 1983–95

Proportion

Nominal

Inflation-adjusted

1984   1986   1988   1990   1992   1994 Year

Source: See Appendix.

reversed over the projection period. However, the projected govern-
ment-sector savings rate of 3.3 percent in 1995 is close to the 3.6 percent
rate achieved for the years 1975 and 1976 but well below the high savings
rates for that sector observed in the 1964–74 period. All of the increase in
government saving is accounted for by the federal government moving
from a large dissaving position in 1983 toward a small positive gross
savings position in 1995.

Non-residents

Recently Canada has become a net exporter of capital on an inflation-
adjusted basis. The projections show net capital exports declining over
the years 1984–86, with a zero net balance achieved from 1986 to 1990.
Thereafter net capital exports gradually increase, reaching 0.5 percent of
GNP by 1995.

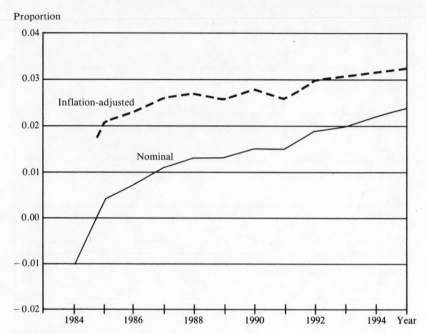

Source: See Appendix.

Summary

Aggregate savings and investments are projected to continue their
recovery toward rates more typical of the period preceding the great
recession of 1981–82. Fiscal policy plays a large part in explaining both
the projected levels and sectoral composition of savings. With a tax
structure favourable to investment, the anticipated cyclical recovery of
investment is reinforced over the medium term. With a fiscal strategy of
reductions in the structural deficit over the medium term, government
savings rates increase sufficiently to provide financial room for the
expansion of investment. Indeed, with business and government savings
both increasing, household savings rates can return to more normal
levels. Perhaps the most interesting contrast with the past is that Canada
is a small net exporter of capital to the rest of the world over the
projection period. Given the capital requirements of the developing
countries and the crowding-out effects of U.S. fiscal deficits on U.S.
capital exports, the other OECD countries must take up some of the
slack. These projections indicate that Canada should make a modest
contribution in this respect.

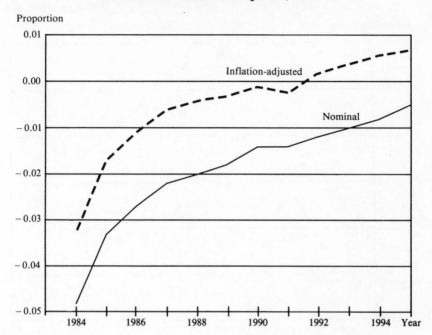

FIGURE 4-16 Federal Government Saving as Share of GNP, Nominal and Inflation-Adjusted, 1983–95

Source: See Appendix.

Conclusion

This study maintains the orthodox view that real interest rates are largely determined externally in a small open economy such as Canada's. Investors, seeking the best possible returns, act to equate the real interest rate in Canada with that in the rest of the world.

When investment prospects in Canada are especially attractive or unattractive vis-à-vis the rest of the world, international capital flows into or out of Canada, thereby augmenting or absorbing national savings flows. Net international capital flows represent net foreign saving and serve to ensure that Canadian gross saving and investment are equivalent.

National saving and investment (i.e., saving and investment by Canadian residents) need not be equal. In fact, national saving and investment are essentially determined independently in a small open economy. This has important implications for government policy.

If, for example, the Government of Canada were to succeed in promoting an increase in national saving through tax incentives, the likely consequences would be an offsetting reduction in net foreign saving but little or no change in gross investment in Canada. Similarly, tax policies that led to increased investment would probably produce a matching

FIGURE 4-17 Non-resident Saving as Share of GNP,
Nominal and Inflation-Adjusted 1983–95

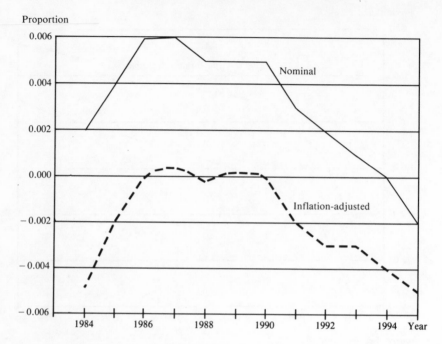

Source: See Appendix.

increase in net foreign saving with few effects on national saving in Canada.

The historical data since 1961 reveal no trends in the aggregate savings rate, once allowance is made for the recession of 1981–82. The sectoral shares of savings have shifted significantly since the early 1970s, however. Large reductions in government saving have been accompanied by large parallel increases in personal savings rates. In recent years, savings from the rest of the world have represented a declining share of total savings.

These divergent trends of the personal and government savings rates are moderated, but not eliminated, in the inflation-adjusted data. These data, which adjust to conventional measures by adding or subtracting real capital gains and real capital losses on assets denominated in nominal units, represent more accurate measures of true savings rates. Even after such inflation adjustment, the personal gross savings rate rose from 6.3 percent in 1975 to 10.4 percent in 1983, while the government gross savings rate declined from 3.6 percent to a dissavings rate of 2.0 percent over the same period. The lion's share of the decline in the government sector savings rate over that period is accounted for by the federal government, which moved from a small dissavings position (0.2 percent) in 1975 to a large dissavings position (4.7 percent) in 1983.

The substantial rise in the personal savings rate in Canada is a marked contrast to the situation in the United States. This divergence occurred during a period of accelerating inflation, which could have altered the relationship between effective real after-tax yields to savings in the two countries. In addition, the Government of Canada introduced a number of tax incentives designed to promote personal saving.

The hypothesis that the divergence of personal savings rates in the two countries is fully explained by these tax incentives is examined and rejected. The tax incentives — the $1,000 Investment Income Exclusion, RHOSPs and higher limits for RRSPs — can be argued to be more akin to lump-sum tax reductions than schemes for effectively increasing after-tax returns to savings at the margin. This argument rests on the fact that each of the tax measures imposes an annual limit on the amount eligible and that these limits appear to be binding on many Canadian taxpayers. Even where the limits are not binding, it is not obvious that these measures offer tax shelters that do not already exist in other forms. Finally, even if the tax measures have provided incentives for higher personal saving, they have probably been blunted or completely offset by the higher government deficits or increases in other taxes necessary to finance them.

A dominant influence on future national saving in Canada will come from the as yet unannounced revisions to the way in which the Canada Pension Plan is financed. Some increases in CPP contribution rates will have to be made in the next decade in order to meet the growing liabilities of the plan. How these increases are made will have an important bearing on the future savings behaviour of the private sector.

The CPP will have to adopt either a pay-go, a fully funded, or a partially funded system. If a pay-go scheme is adopted, there may be adverse effects on private saving through transfer of wealth between generations. Critics of pay-go have long argued that this system of finance undermines private incentives to save for retirement and leads to a reduction in total domestic saving. Actually, there is no definitive evidence to support this claim, but neither is there clear evidence to refute it. The question of whether pay-go does or does not cause reductions in domestic saving in a closed economy remains unanswered. However, in an open economy, changes in personal savings rates would be offset by changes in savings provided by non-residents.

Moving the CPP to a fully funded basis would avoid the uncertain implications for saving that are associated with pay-go finances but only if the investment fund controlled by the plan were to be invested in the same assets the private sector would choose. This would be extremely difficult to achieve. The investment of CPP funds in a manner other than that dictated by the private sector would be a misallocation of resources — a consequence that may be more unattractive than the savings risks of a pay-go system.

Any blended, or partially funded, scheme to finance the future CPP represents a combination of both the pay-go and full funding methods. The continuation of the present partially funded system in which the funds are invested exclusively in provincial government debt would have similar savings effects to a pay-go system, but with some risk of a misallocation of resources if increased government spending occurred as a result.

Savings prospects over the next decade were examined in the context of a recent macroeconomic model projection. In the projected climate of continued moderate economic growth and moderate inflation, aggregate savings and investment rates are projected to return gradually toward historical average levels. With the medium-term federal fiscal strategy of gradual reductions in the ratio of the structural deficit to GNP, government savings rates should rise as the economy grows. At the same time, household savings rates should decline from their recent historically high levels. Business savings rates, stimulated by various tax incentives, should surpass their previous peak ratios some time within the projection period. Finally, Canada's relationship with the rest of the world has shifted qualitatively. Over the projection period, Canada is either a small net exporter of capital in real terms or is in rough balance on its real capital account.

Of course, this projection, like all projections, depends upon certain assumptions regarding domestic policy and the external economic environment. The recent federal proposals to raise the contribution limits for RRSPs and RPPs could delay the downward adjustment of personal savings rates for a considerable time. Continued high real interest rates as a result of a continuation of the present influence of U.S. monetary and fiscal policies could also stimulate personal saving while slowing economic growth in Canada, thereby reducing business and government sector savings rates as a consequence.

Appendix

Inflation Adjustment

Gross sectoral savings in the financial flow accounts are simply gross income less current spending. In this study we analyze gross savings flows only; hence no adjustment is needed for any understatement of capital cost allowances due to inflation.

In a period of general price inflation, sectoral gross income flows will be overstated for sectors that have positive net asset positions denominated in nominal units and understated for sectors that have negative net asset positions denominated in nominal units. The purpose of the inflation adjustment is to remove these measurement errors from the income flows and hence from the savings flows, since the measurement of current spending is not distorted by inflation.

The generally accepted definition of income is the maximum that could be spent on current consumption (or distributed to other sectors) without altering the net asset position of the sector. Conventional accounting measures of income presume that the relevant net asset position being held constant is defined in terms of *nominal* units. It makes more sense, however, to define income as the amount that could be spent on consumption or distributed without altering the *real* net asset position of the sector. Note that, by either definition, the resulting income flows can be measured either in current dollars or in constant dollars by simple deflation.

In a period of general inflation, an individual with a positive net asset position denominated in nominal units of currency must increase that net asset position in proportion to the price level in order to maintain his real net worth unchanged. Similarly, an individual with a net liability position denominated in nominal assets must reduce his net asset position (i.e., increase his net liability position) in proportion to the price level in order to maintain his real net worth unchanged. The increase in net nominal assets that is required to leave the individual's real net worth unchanged is defined as the inflation adjustment factor in this appendix.

Two types of nominal assets and liabilities are distinguished: those denominated in Canadian currency and those denominated in foreign currency. The inflation factors differ by the rate of appreciation or depreciation of the exchange value of the Canadian dollar. When conventional savings flows are adjusted by removing these inflation distortions, we obtain the inflation-adjusted savings flows analyzed in this paper.

Definitions of Gross Saving by Sector (unadjusted for inflation)

SP	Saving by persons and unincorporated businesses including grain transactions.
SPP	Saving by persons and unincorporated business through trust-eed pension funds.
SPO	Other saving by persons and unincorporated business.
SB	Saving by corporations and government business enterprises.
SG	Saving by governments.
SGE	Federal savings.
SGO	Provincial, local and hospital savings.
SGP	Canada and Quebec pension plans savings.
SNR	Saving by non-residents.
REE	Residual error of estimate.
S	Total saving.

Source: Financial Flow Accounts. Statistics Canada, 13-002, Fourth Quarter including Year-End Outstandings : Table 1-3 (annual totals) or Tables 1-1 or 1-2 for quarterly totals, which must be summed across calendar years.

Let the suffix X denote an inflation-adjusted variable. For example:

SPX denotes the inflation-adjusted value of personal savings in Table 4-4 above.

RSPX denotes $\frac{\text{(SPX)}}{\text{(GNEX)}}$, the inflation-adjusted gross personal savings rate and appears in Table 4-5, where GNEX denotes inflation-adjusted GNE and is explained below.

Let the prefix I denote an inflation-adjustment factor such that:

SJX (adjusted saving of sector J) = SJ (unadjusted savings of sector J) − ISJ (adjustment factor for sector J).

The adjustment factors for the individual savings components must be computed in a way that varies from component to component. However, the basic idea is as follows:

$$\text{ISJ}(t) = \text{NDAJ}(t-1){}^{*}\text{P}(t) + \text{NFAJ}(t-1){}^{*} [\text{P}(t) + \text{E}(t)].$$

P(t) denotes the rate of change in the GNE price index over the four quarters centred on the fourth quarter of year t; e.g., if t is 1978, the P(t) is the rate of change in the GNE price index between the end of 1977 and the end of 1978. More explicitly:

$$\text{P}(1978) = \frac{[\text{PGNE}(78{:}4) + \text{PGNE}(79{:}1)] - [\text{PGNE}(77{:}4) + \text{PGNE}(78{:}1)]}{\text{PGNE}(77{:}4) + \text{PGNE}(78{:}1)}$$

Hence P(*t*) is the four-quarter rate of change in prices, expressed as a fraction rather than as a percentage.

E(*t*) is the four quarter rate of change in the foreign exchange rate (U.S. dollars per Canadian dollars) computed over the same interval as P(*t*).

Using the price of a U.S. dollar rather than a weighted average of several foreign currencies assumes that these assets are primarily denominated in U.S. dollars.

NDAJ(*t* − 1) denotes the net stock of fixed-income assets denominated in Canadian dollars held by sector J at the end of period *t* − 1; e.g., the computation of ISJ(1978) is based on the net stock of domestic assets at the end of 1977.

NFAJ(*t* − 1) denotes the net stock of fixed-income assets denominated in foreign currencies held by sector J at the end of period *t* − 1.

With this general format we now specify the calculation of values for NDAJ and NFAJ for each of the sectors. The basic data all come from Financial Flow Accounts, Table 4-3, for Year-End Outstandings by Sector and Subsector.

The Household Sector

This sector is a consolidation of sectors I and II (persons and unincorporated business) with adjustments for the net foreign asset and net equity position of sector VII (insurance companies and pension funds).
The net stock of assets denominated in U.S. dollars (NFAP) is assumed to consist of:

> net foreign currency deposits of sectors I, II and VII
> + net foreign investments of sectors I, II and VII.

All other assets and liabilities (other than equity assets and claims on assorted enterprises) are assumed to be denominated in Canadian dollars. Household life insurance and pension assets are adjusted to exclude the foreign currency, foreign investment and net equity holdings of sector VII.
The subdivision of adjusted personal savings into savings through trustee pension funds (SPPX) and other personal savings (SPDX) requires estimates of the two net asset positions of trusteed pension funds (sector VII.3).
The net stock of assets denominated in U.S. dollars (NFAPP) is the net foreign investments of sector VII.3. All other assets except equities are assumed to be denominated in Canadian dollars.

The Government Sectors

The federal government sector is a consolidation of sectors V and X (i.e., the Bank of Canada is consolidated with the federal government). For this sector as for all other sectors, claims on associated enterprises are treated as equity.

The net stock of assets (NFAGF) denominated in U.S. currency consists of:

> official international reserves + net foreign currency
> deposits
> + net foreign investments.

All other assets and liabilities except equity are assumed to be denominated in Canadian dollars. The assets of the public pension funds sector were divided in the same way, using data for sector XII.

The provincial government, local government and hospital sector's assets (sector XI) were divided in the same way as those of the federal government, except that the amount of provincial and municipal bonds held by the non-resident sector was assumed to be denominated in U.S. dollars.

The Non-resident Sector (Sector XIII)

The stock of assets denominated in Canadian dollars (NDANR) is assumed to consist of:

> Net holdings of bank deposits (exclusive of foreign currency deposits)
> + Government of Canada bonds and treasury bills.

All other assets and liabilities (other than equity assets) of this sector are assumed to be denominated in U.S. dollars.

Inflation adjusted GNE is computed as follows:

$$\text{GNEX}(t) = \text{GNE}(t) + \text{NFANR}(t-1)^*[\text{P}(t) + \text{E}(t)] \\ + \text{NDANR}(t-1)^*[\text{P}(t)].$$

In this way nominal GNE is corrected for inflation-induced changes in the real value of Canada's net foreign debt.

The Business Sector

Since the aggregate inflation adjustment is zero by definition, the inflation adjustment for the remaining sector, the business sector, may be computed residually:

$$\text{ISB} = -(\text{ISP} + \text{ISGF} + \text{ISGP} + \text{ISGO} + \text{ISNR}).$$

Inflation-adjusted gross savings of the business sector are calculated as:

$$\text{SBX} = \text{SB} - \text{ISB}.$$

Projection of Inflation Adjustment Factors

The projection prepared by Dungan (1984) includes data on savings flows and price inflation. As the FOCUS model does not include data on net financial asset position of the four main sectors (household, government,[25] business and non-resident), these series had to be constructed. We combined the foreign and domestic components of the net financial asset position of the household, government and non-resident sectors, denoting the net financial asset position of sector J at end of period t by NCAJ(t), and projected these data for each of these sectors as follows:

Households

$$NCAP(t) = NCAP(t-1) = [SP(t) - SPX(t)]$$
$$+ \ 0.403 \ SPX(t).[26]$$

Governments

$$NCAGF(t) = NCAGF(t-1) + SGF(t) - IGF(t),$$

$$NCAGO(t) = NCAGO(t-1) + SGO(t) - IGO(t),$$

and

$$NCAGP(t) = NCAGP(t-1) + SGP(t).$$

where IGF and IGO represent gross fixed capital formation by the federal sector and the provincial, local and hospital sectors, respectively.

Non-residents

$$NCANR(t) = NCANR(t-1) + SNR(t).$$

The inflation-adjustment factors for the projection period for the above sectors were then calculated using the inflation rates[27] in the projection. The inflation-adjustment factor for the business sector was derived residually.

Notes

This study was completed in November 1984.

Since the paper was written while one of the authors was on leave at the University of California at Berkeley, distance as well as research efficiency dictated a strict division of labour. Thomas Wilson assumed responsibility for the sections that discuss the historical and inflation-adjusted data and the section that presents projections to 1995. Gregory Jump assumed responsibility for the introductory section on savings in an open economy and for the sections on tax incentives and pensions. The authors want to thank Nancy Hanada for research assistance; John Sargent, members of the research advisory group at the Royal Commission, and four anonymous referees for helpful comments; and Julia Wilson for preparation of the manuscript. Any errors are, of course, the responsibility of the authors.

1. This is not to say that government deficits may have no adverse effects on private expenditures in a small open economy. Deficits may indirectly inhibit domestic investment by creating fears that they will lead to higher taxes in the future. In addition, deficits that drive private borrowers out of domestic and into foreign capital markets may lead to a phenomenon known as exchange-rate crowding out, in which higher foreign borrowing forces an appreciation in the foreign exchange rate and adversely affects production and investment by export-based industries. It is worth noting, however, that any exchange-rate crowding out that might occur can be expected to be short-lived. This is because higher foreign borrowing today gives rise to higher flows of interest and debt repayment abroad in the future. The interest and debt repayment flows will serve to restore and perhaps even reduce the future values of the foreign exchange rate.

2. One difficulty sometimes associated with the use of tax-based investment policies in Canada is the presence of wholly owned Canadian subsidiaries of U.S. corporations. U.S. tax laws require the parent company to consolidate its earnings received from foreign subsidiaries into its own taxable (in the United States) income. Some Canadian tax measures appear to be ineffectual when applied to these subsidiaries. For example, a reduction in income tax rates for Canadian corporations could result in a transfer of tax revenues to the U.S. Treasury if Canadian subsidiaries were simply to pass on their tax savings to their U.S. parents. Any subsidiary that behaved in this manner would, however, be at a competitive disadvantage in relation to any Canadian firms in the same industry. This might prompt the subsidiary to retain a larger fraction of its Canadian earnings in order to make competitive expansions in investment. Alternatively, the parent of such a subsidiary might decide to sell out to Canadian interests, since the subsidiary would now be worth more to Canadian owners than to the U.S. parent. In either case, the policy objective of higher investment in Canada is likely to be realized. The existence of subsidiaries is less problematic with policy stimuli such as an investment tax credit on net new investment. In order to gain the benefits of such a credit, a subsidiary firm would have to expand its investments and would presumably finance this expansion (at least in part) by retaining a larger fraction of its Canadian earnings.

3. The independence of national saving and investment is questioned in Feldstein and Horioku (1980). Using pooled cross-section and time-series data for 17 OECD countries, they observe a high correlation between national rates of saving and investment. In their view this constitutes damning evidence against the hypothesis that domestic saving and investment are determined independently. However, their arguments are not entirely convincing, and their conclusions are rejected in this study as premature. Domestic saving and investment do share similar cyclical movements, but this does not necessarily imply a cause-and-effect relationship between them. While Feldstein and Harioku cast some ambiguity on the matter, we maintain the orthodox view in this study that domestic saving and investment are determined independently in a small open economy.

4. The affect on aggregate demand of this hypothetical action would be a decline in consumption spending matched by an offsetting increase in exports as Canadian goods are diverted to foreign markets. This describes the medium- to long-term response and ignores any possible disruptions that might occur in the short run.

5. As in the Financial Flow Accounts, the household sector includes unincorporated enterprises.

6. The Financial Flow Accounts adopt the convention that the retained earnings of foreign-owned enterprises are part of gross business savings.

7. Note that these are gross savings; if capital cost allowances are excluded, savings via trusteed pension plans in 1983 accounted for about 30 percent of net personal savings.

8. The conventional measures also do not take into account real capital gains and losses made on all assets. However, while there may be some connection between such real gains and inflation, the relationship is indirect and certainly not one-to-one. We therefore ignore such real gains and losses in our analysis.

9. When an increase in inflation is fully anticipated, interest rates will fully reflect the increase in inflation rate, and rational investors should not regard this apparent extra income as part of their true income. For an individual in a net creditor position, the ordinary unadjusted savings rate will rise but the inflation-adjusted rate should remain the same. If the increase in inflation is unanticipated, interest rates will not fully reflect the increase. The individual suffers an unanticipated reduction in real income and wealth, and the inflation-adjusted savings rate may change as the individual adjusts his or her behaviour in response to the real change in his or her economic position.

10. Although the gross savings of the business sector are understated because of inflation, the net savings of the business sector are subject to an offsetting inflation distortion. Since capital cost allowances of that sector are on an historical cost basis, these allowances understate true depreciation when inflation occurs. The net effect of inflation on business net savings therefore depends on the relative strengths of the two sources of inflation distortion.

11. The trend in the adjusted personal savings rate could reflect some increase in precautionary savings owing to greater uncertainty regarding inflation, interest rates and real economic growth. Another factor that could have become operative in recent years is the changing age structure of the population, in particular the maturing of the baby boom generation into age brackets with higher savings. For a recent discussion of these demographic influences see Foot and Trefler (1983).

12. Note that federal fiscal policy cannot be read directly from these estimates, since federal fixed capital formation is included in federal gross savings and the data have not been adjusted for the business cycle.

13. A desire to promote higher personal saving does not appear to have been the government's chief reason for introducing these measures. A desire for improved equity in the tax system was probably at least as important a consideration.

14. An employment-based pension plan that is recognized as a tax deferral is called a Registered Pension Plan (RRP) in Canada. The contribution limits for RRSPs are lower for people who participate in an RRP than for those who do not.

15. The availability of income averaging annuities after 1982 was eliminated by the federal budget of November 1981.

16. Recently released data pertaining to the 1981 taxation year reveal that 44 percent of individuals with RRSPs (but without RPPs) contributed to the limit in that year. Thirty-three percent of those with both RRSPs and RPPs contributed to the limit.

17. Although interest on direct borrowing to buy an RRSP is no longer deductible, indirect borrowing (achieved by asset swaps) effectively continues to generate deductible interest expenses.

18. The February 1984 budget proposes a substantial schedule of increases for RRSP/RPP limits starting in 1985.

19. In fairness, the empirical viability of the Ricardian Equivalence Theorem has never been proved. Many economists argue that individual recipients of lump-sum tax reductions will be too short-sighted to recognize the offsetting future tax liabilities implicit in a higher government deficit. The empirical evidence on this issue is ambiguous.

20. See National Council of Welfare (1982) for a discussion of this possibility.

21. Note that bequest-motivated individuals will satisfy the Ricardian Equivalence The-orem on an intergenerational basis; that is, current saving is adjusted to offset higher contributions faced by future generations. Individuals without bequest motives will not comply, though they may satisfy the theorem on an intragenerational basis; for example, an individual with no bequest motive might increase current saving to off-set higher tax liabilities he expects to face later in his own life.

22. The decline in private saving will be equal to pension fund contributions under the assumption that individuals are not restricted in their abilities to borrow against future incomes at market rates of interest.

23. Even the Government of Canada apparently fears the potential manipulation of QPP investments. It recently passed Bill S-31, which prevents the QPP and certain other pension funds from acquiring more than a 10 percent equity position in certain corporations.

24. Jump does not consider the possibility that governments may run deficits, regardless of the type of public pension plan in effect. If governments do this, then a funded plan committed to buying government debt is not identical to a pay-go plan. A funded plan would absorb government debt that would be issued in any event and would not require any change in government taxation or spending. However, this situation still leads to the possibility of an intergenerational transfer under a funded plan. The reason is that government deficits, for whatever reasons they occur, mean that future genera-tions will have to pay higher taxes in order to service the national debt. If people do not wish to leave bequests to their heirs, the current generation will benefit at the expense of future generations. If bequest motives prevail, the current generation will alter its saving so as to protect future generations. The two possibilities offer the same choices as exist under a pay-go pension plan coupled with a balanced budget.

25. Only the net debt of the federal government is available in the FOCUS model.

26. This equation was fitted to data for the period 1962–83. It would suggest that roughly 40 percent of inflation-adjusted household gross saving flows into assets denominated in nominal units, with the remainder being capital cost allowances and net changes in equity assets (including housing and the net equity positions of insurance companies and pension funds). Note that all of the inflation-adjustment component of normal savings flows is added to the stock of assets denominated in nominal units.

27. Since we were unable to separate assets denominated in Canadian and U.S. dollars in the projection, we used the inflation rate for the GNE deflator to calculate the inflation-adjustment factor for each sector. Given that the annual rate of appreciation of the Canadian dollar over the projection interval is only 0.4 percent, this approximation should introduce only minor errors.

Bibliography

Boothe, Paul, Kevin Clinton, Agathe Côté, and David Longworth. 1985. "International Asset Substitutability." In *Post-War Macroeconomic Developments*, volume 20 of the research studies prepared for the Royal Commission on the Economic Union and Development Prospects for Canada. Toronto: University of Toronto Press.

Canada. Revenue Canada. 1981. *Taxation Statistics* (1981 edition). Ottawa: Minister of Supply and Services Canada.

Dungan, Peter. 1984. "National Projection Through 2005; Provincial Projections Through 1995." Policy Study 84-2. Toronto: University of Toronto, Institute for Policy Analysis.

Economic Council of Canada. 1979. *One in Three: Pensions for Canadians to 2030*. Ottawa: Minister of Supply and Services Canada.

Feldstein, Martin S. 1974. "Social Security, Induced Retirement and Aggregate Capital Accumulation." *Journal of Political Economy* 82 (September/October): 905–26.

Foot, David, and Daniel Trefler. 1983. "Life-Cycle Saving and Population Aging." Working Paper 8308. Toronto: University of Toronto, Department of Economics and Institute for Policy Analysis.

Jump, G.V. 1982. "Tax Incentives to Promote Personal Saving: Recent Canadian Experience." In *Saving and Government Policy*, Conference Series 25. Boston: Federal Reserve Bank of Boston.

————. 1983. "Financing Public Pensions: Some Capital Market Implications." Toronto: Ontario Economic Council, mimeo.

Leimer, Dean, and Selig Lesnoy. 1982. "Social Security and Private Saving: A Re-examination of the Time Series Evidence Using Alternative Social Security Wealth Variables." *Journal of Political Economy* 90 (June): 606–29.

National Council of Welfare. 1982. "Financing the Canada Pension Plan." Ottawa: The Council, mimeo.

5

A Note on Demographic Projections for Canada
Review and Implementations

DOUGLAS GREEN
JUDITH GOLD
JOHN SARGENT

The much-discussed "aging" of the Canadian population which is expected to take place over the next 40–50 years has implications for many aspects of Canadian life. This brief study reviews some current projections of the demographic outlook and provides a general discussion of their implications for government expenditures in general and for such components as health, education and income maintenance for the elderly.

Following this introduction, we sketch the demographic history of the 1921–81 period. The next section examines a number of projections for population growth and age distribution prepared by Statistics Canada (1985) and by the federal Department of Insurance for Canada Pension Plan (CPP) purposes (Canada, 1982). This is followed by a review of several studies that have attempted to draw out the implications of anticipated demographic developments for government expenditures and the CPP. We then go on to compare the anticipated demographic pressures in Canada to those in the United States and selected European countries. The study concludes with some cautionary notes on the uncertainties surrounding long-term demographic projections.

As has been widely reported, CPP contribution rates will have to rise substantially in order to cover benefits (partly as a result of the maturing of the plan and partly as a result of the changing demographic profile). The implications of projected demographic developments for total government expenditures are not as clear. Because of aging, the costs of operating social security and health service programs will rise more rapidly than the rate of growth of the population. Other government expenditures, however, may decline relative to the size of the economy, thus offsetting, at least partially, the increases induced by the aging population.

Demographic Developments, 1921–81

This section describes the growth of the Canadian population and changes in its age distribution from 1921 to 1981. Table 5-1 presents average annual population growth rates between decennial census years; average birth rates, death rates, net immigration rates, fertility rates, and life expectancy at birth over the intervals between censuses; and the percentage distribution across age groups for the census years 1921 to 1981.

The table shows the continuous decline of the death rate and the concomitant increase in life expectancy for both men and women over the entire 1921–81 period. Both the birth rate and the fertility rate displayed substantial variation, declining through the 1930s and 1940s, increasing in the 1950s and 1960s, and then declining steeply to 1976. Both have declined further since but at a much slower pace. Net immigration has exhibited no clear trend.

In 1921 those 14 and younger accounted for a slightly higher proportion of the population than did this group in 1961 — toward the end of the baby boom. The percentage share of those 65 and older was lower in 1921 than in any of the later census years. The latter proportion has risen gradually throughout virtually the entire 1921–81 period.

Between 1921 and 1931 the total population grew at an average annual rate of 1.7 percent. By 1931 the population share of those 14 and younger had declined significantly, while the shares for the 15–24 and 65-and-older age categories rose. The total population grew at an average annual rate of approximately 1 percent between 1931 and 1941. By 1941 the population share of those 14 and younger had declined again while the proportion of those aged 15–64 increased.

The slowing of population growth over the period 1921 to 1941 was associated with a decline in the share of those aged 14 and younger. As the large 0-14 cohort of 1921 matured, a "bubble" effect was created, first increasing the proportion of the 15–24 age group and later leading to an increase in the share of the 25–64 age group.

Between 1941 and 1951 the average annual rate of population growth increased to 2 percent, reflecting the beginning of the baby boom and a step-up in immigration in the second half of the 1940s. The share of the 14 and younger group jumped to 30.3 percent in 1951 from 27.8 percent in 1941. Another significant development was the substantial drop in the share of the 15–24 age group.

The population growth rate increased again to 2.7 percent between 1951 and 1961. By 1961 the population share of those aged 14 and younger had burgeoned to 34 percent, while the shares of the other three age categories declined slightly.

In the decade between 1961 and 1971 population growth slowed to an average annual rate of approximately 1.7 percent. The share of the

TABLE 5-1 Historical Demographic Data

	Total									0 to 14		15 to 24		25 to 64		65+	
		Average Annual Growth Rate[a]	Per 1,000 Population			Fertility[d] Rate per Woman	Life Expectancy at Birth[e]		Average Annual Growth Rate[f]	% of Population	Average Annual Growth Rate[f]	% of Population	Average Annual Growth Rate[f]	% of Population	Average Annual Growth Rate[f]	% of Population
			Average Birth Rate[f]	Average Death Rate[f]	Average Immig.[c] Rate[f]		Male	Female								
Year	Population (000s)															
1921	8,788	2.0	N.A.	N.A.	1.9	3.5	N.A.	N.A.	2.4	34.4	0.8	17.3	1.2	43.5	2.3	4.8
1931	10,377	1.7	25.2	11.1	2.8	3.2	60.0	62.1	0.8	31.6	2.6	18.8	1.8	44.0	3.2	5.6
1941	11,507	1.0	21.0	9.9	-0.8	2.8	63.0	66.3	-0.3	27.8	1.0	18.7	1.7	46.8	2.9	6.7
1951	14,009	2.0	26.1	9.5	1.3	3.5	66.3	70.8	2.9	30.3	0.0	15.3	1.9	46.6	3.5	7.8
1961	18,238	2.7	27.7	8.2	7.0	3.8	68.4	74.2	3.8	34.0	2.0	14.3	2.1	44.1	2.5	7.6
1971	21,568	1.7	20.2	7.5	3.6	2.2	69.3	76.4	0.3	29.6	4.4	18.6	1.6	43.8	2.3	8.1
1976	22,997	1.3	15.7	7.4	4.5	1.8	70.2	77.5	-1.6	25.6	2.3	19.5	2.4	46.1	2.8	8.7
1981	24,342	1.2	15.4	7.1	3.1	1.7	71.9	78.9	-1.5	22.5	0.8	19.1	2.2	48.6	3.4	9.7

Sources: Statistics Canada, "Historical Statistical Compendium," prepared for the Royal Commission on the Economic Union and Development Prospects for Canada (Ottawa, 1984), 1.6, 1.7; Statistics Canada, *Historical Statistics of Canada*, 2d ed. (Ottawa, 1983), B1–B22; Department of Finance, *Economic Review April 1984* (Ottawa, 1984), p. 121.

a. Average annual ratio of live births per 1,000 population.
b. Average annual ratio of deaths per 1,000 population.
c. Average annual ratio of immigrants less emigrants per 1,000 population.
d. Average number of live births per woman during child-bearing years if, over the course of her lifetime, each woman has a probability of giving birth in each child-bearing year equal to the proportion of woman at that age in the given year who gave birth.
e. Expected age of death, i.e., probability of dying at each age weighted by that age.
f. For preceding ten years with the exception of 1976 and 1981 which is for the preceding five years.

FIGURE 5-1 Percentage Share of Selected Age Groups, 1921–81

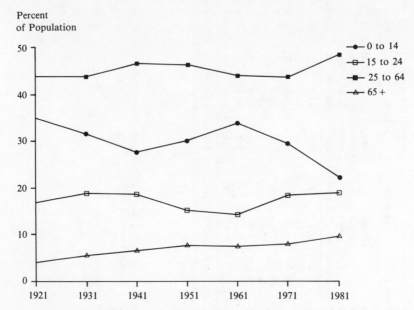

Source: Statistics Canada, "Historical Statistical Compendium," prepared for the Royal Commission on the Economic Union and Development Prospects for Canada (Ottawa, 1984), 1.6, 1.7; Statistics Canada, *Historical Statistics of Canada*, 2d ed. (Ottawa, 1983), B1–B22; Department of Finance, *Economic Review April 1984* (Ottawa, 1984), p. 121.

population represented by those 14 and younger declined significantly to 29.6. The maturation of the baby boom generation, however, led to a considerable expansion of the proportion of those aged 15–24, to a share of 18.6 percent in 1971 compared to 14.3 percent in 1961.

The average annual population growth rate declined to approximately 1.3 percent over the decade 1971–81; this decline was associated with a further sharp contraction of the share of the population 14 and younger to 22.5 percent. The proportion of the population represented by those aged 15–24 rose until the mid-1970s and diminished thereafter to 19.1 percent by 1981. The aging of the baby boom cohort led to a significant increase in the share of the population aged 25–64, while the share of the 65 and older group continued its upward trend. The 1970s are unique in that the proportion of the young was at its lowest level, while the proportion of the elderly was at its highest; some two out of three Canadians were of working age, also a record high.

A glance at Figure 5-1 provides an illustration of the "bubble effect," which occurs when a large age cohort matures. The baby boom, represented, roughly speaking, by those aged 14 and younger in 1961, resulted in a peak in that census year in the share of the total population in this age category. As this cohort matured, there was first an increase in the proportion of those aged 15–24; this share increased until 1976 and then declined. By 1981 the "bubble effect" was having its impact on the next oldest age group, those aged 25–64. Figure 5-1 also shows the gradual increase in the proportion of the population aged 65 and older over the period 1921–81.

Population Projections, 1981–2030

This section presents four of the latest, official demographic projections of Statistics Canada for the period 1981–2030.[1] These projections differ in their assumptions with respect to the fertility rate, the mortality rate, and net immigration. Also presented are the base case[2] demographic projections underlying the Statutory Actuarial Report No.8 of the Canada Pension Plan (Canada, 1982; hereinafter, SAR). The five projections are presented in Tables 5-2 to 5-6.

Analysis of the Projections

The four Statistics Canada demographic projections are based on the following set of assumptions:

1. Low fertility, low immigration case: this projection assumes a fertility rate which declines to 1.4 by 1996 (from the current level of 1.7) and thereafter remains constant; net immigration is assumed to be 50,000 per annum throughout the projection period.
2. Medium fertility, low immigration case: this projection assumes a fertility rate of 1.6 throughout the entire projection period; net immigration is assumed to be as in point 1.
3. Medium fertility, high immigration case: this projection assumes the same fertility rate as point 2, and net immigration is assumed to increase from 45,000 per annum in 1983 to 100,000 per annum in 1994 by increments of 5,000 per annum after which it remains constant.
4. High fertility, high immigration case: this projection assumes a fertility rate of 1.6 until 1985, increasing to 2.2 by 1996 and remaining constant thereafter; net immigration is assumed to be as in point 3.

All four projections use the same mortality rates, which are assumed to decrease in the future at a slower pace than experienced between 1976 and 1981. The male/female difference in life expectancy at birth narrows slightly. By 1996 life expectancy at birth is assumed to rise to 74.9 (from 71.9 in 1981) for males and to 81.5 (from 78.9 in 1981) for females. It is assumed to remain constant thereafter.

The CPP (SAR) projection assumes that the fertility rate will increase to approximately 2.0 by 1999 and remain constant thereafter; net immigration throughout the entire projection period is assumed to equal 0.32

TABLE 5-2 Population Projections by Age Group Level, Rate of Growth and Percentage Share: Low Fertility, Low Immigration

	Total		0 to 14			15 to 24			25 to 64			65+		
Year	Population (000s)	Average Annual Growth Rate[a]	Population (000s)	Average Annual Growth Rate[a]	% of Population	Population (000s)	Average Annual Growth Rate[a]	% of Population	Population (000s)	Average Annual Growth Rate[a]	% of Population	Population (000s)	Average Annual Growth Rate[a]	% of Population
1981	24,342	1.2	5,477	−1.5	22.5	4,649	1.5	19.1	11,830	2.3	48.6	2,361	3.1	9.7
1990	26,428	0.9	5,404	−0.1	20.4	3,842	−2.1	14.5	14,097	2.0	53.3	3,086	3.0	11.7
2000	27,741	0.5	4,730	−1.3	17.1	3,716	−0.8	13.4	15,462	0.9	55.7	3,830	2.2	13.8
2010	28,203	0.2	4,006	−1.6	14.2	3,435	−0.8	12.2	16,315	0.5	57.9	4,449	1.5	15.8
2020	28,004	−0.1	3,755	−0.6	13.4	2,797	−2.0	10.0	15,725	−0.4	56.2	5,733	2.6	20.5
2030	26,948	−0.4	3,285	−1.3	12.2	2,663	−0.5	9.9	13,950	−1.2	51.8	7,064	2.1	26.2

Sources: Statistics Canada, "Historical Statistical Compendium," prepared for the Royal Commission on the Economic Union and Development Prospects for Canada (Ottawa, 1984), 1.7; Statistics Canada, *Population Projections for Canada, Provinces and Territories, 1984–2006*, cat. no. 91–520 (Ottawa, 1985), Projection Series Number 1; and unpublished data from Statistics Canada, Demography Division.

a. For preceding ten years with the exception of 1990 which is for the preceding nine years.

TABLE 5-3 Population Projections by Age Group Level, Rate of Growth and Percentage Share: Medium Fertility, Low Immigration

Year	Total Population (000s)	Total Average Annual Growth Rate[a]	0 to 14 Population (000s)	0 to 14 Average Annual Growth Rate[a]	0 to 14 % of Population	15 to 24 Population (000s)	15 to 24 Average Annual Growth Rate[a]	15 to 24 % of Population	25 to 64 Population (000s)	25 to 64 Average Annual Growth Rate[a]	25 to 64 % of Population	65+ Population (000s)	65+ Average Annual Growth Rate[a]	65+ % of Population
1981	24,342	1.2	5,477	-1.5	22.5	4,649	1.5	19.1	11,830	2.3	48.6	2,361	3.1	9.7
1990	26,558	1.0	5,534	0.1	20.8	3,842	-2.1	14.5	14,097	2.0	53.1	3,086	3.0	11.6
2000	28,397	0.7	5,377	-0.3	18.9	3,727	-0.3	13.1	15,462	0.9	54.5	3,831	2.2	13.5
2010	29,447	0.4	4,884	-1.0	16.6	3,789	0.2	12.9	16,325	0.5	55.4	4,449	1.5	15.1
2020	30,005	0.2	4,817	-0.1	16.1	3,369	-1.2	11.2	16,086	-0.1	53.6	5,733	2.6	19.1
2030	29,839	-0.1	4,587	-0.5	15.4	3,315	-0.2	11.1	14,873	-0.8	49.8	7,064	2.1	23.7

Sources: Statistics Canada, "Historical Statistical Compendium," prepared for the Royal Commission on the Economic Union and Development Prospects for Canada (Ottawa, 1984), 1.7; Statistics Canada, Population Projections for Canada, Provinces and Territories, 1984–2006, cat. no. 91–520 (Ottawa, 1985), Projection Series Number 1; and unpublished data from Statistics Canada, Demography Division.

a. For preceding ten years with the exception of 1990 which is for the preceding nine years.

TABLE 5-4 Population Projections by Age Group Level, Rate of Growth and Percentage Share: Medium Fertility, High Immigration

	Total		0 to 14			15 to 24			25 to 64			65+		
Year	Population (000s)	Average Annual Growth Rate[a]	Population (000s)	Average Annual Growth Rate[a]	% of Population	Population (000s)	Average Annual Growth Rate[a]	% of Population	Population (000s)	Average Annual Growth Rate[a]	% of Population	Population (000s)	Average Annual Growth Rate[a]	% of Population
1981	24,342	1.2	5,477	-1.5	22.5	4,649	1.5	19.1	11,830	2.3	48.6	2,361	3.1	9.7
1990	26,648	1.0	5,561	0.2	20.9	3,859	-2.1	14.5	14,144	2.0	53.1	3,084	3.0	11.6
2000	29,011	0.9	5,565	0.0	19.2	3,814	-0.1	13.1	15,822	1.1	54.5	3,811	2.1	13.1
2010	30,730	0.6	5,229	-0.6	17.0	3,988	0.4	13.0	17,108	0.8	55.7	4,404	1.5	14.3
2020	32,034	0.4	5,290	0.1	16.5	3,682	-0.8	11.5	17,365	0.1	54.2	5,696	2.6	17.8
2030	36,672	0.2	5,193	-0.2	15.9	3,711	0.1	11.4	16,647	-0.4	51.0	7,122	2.3	21.8

Sources: Statistics Canada, "Historical Statistical Compendium," prepared for the Royal Commission on the Economic Union and Development Prospects for Canada (Ottawa, 1984), 1.7; Statistics Canada, *Population Projections for Canada, Provinces and Territories, 1984–2006,* cat. no. 91–520 (Ottawa, 1985). Projection Series Number 4; and unpublished data from Statistics Canada, Demography Division.

a. For preceding ten years with the exception of 1990 which is for the preceding nine years.

TABLE 5-5 Population Projections by Age Group Level, Rate of Growth and Percentage Share: High Fertility, High Immigration

	Total		0 to 14			15 to 24			25 to 64			65+		
Year	Population (000s)	Average Annual Growth Rate[a]	Population (000s)	Average Annual Growth Rate[a]	% of Population	Population (000s)	Average Annual Growth Rate[a]	% of Population	Population (000s)	Average Annual Growth Rate[a]	% of Population	Population (000s)	Average Annual Growth Rate[a]	% of Population
1981	24,342	1.2	5,477	−1.5	22.5	4,649	1.5	19.1	11,830	2.3	48.6	2,361	3.1	9.7
1990	26,749	1.1	5,662	0.4	21.2	3,859	−2.0	14.4	14,144	2.0	52.9	3,084	3.0	11.5
2000	29,967	1.1	6,519	1.4	21.8	3,814	−0.1	12.7	15,822	1.1	52.8	3,811	2.1	12.7
2010	32,690	0.9	6,736	0.3	20.6	4,440	1.5	13.6	17,109	0.8	52.3	4,406	1.5	13.5
2020	35,360	0.8	7,177	0.6	20.3	4,669	0.5	13.2	17,815	0.4	50.4	5,699	2.6	16.1
2030	37,846	0.7	7,818	0.9	20.7	4,830	0.3	12.8	18,071	0.1	47.8	7,127	2.3	18.8

Sources: Statistics Canada, "Historical Statistical Compendium," prepared for the Royal Commission on the Economic Union and Development Prospects for Canada (Ottawa, 1984), 1.7; Statistics Canada, *Population Projections for Canada, Provinces and Territories, 1984–2006*, cat. no. 91–520 (Ottawa, 1985), Projection Series Number 5; and unpublished data from Statistics Canada, Demography Division.

a. For preceding ten years with the exception of 1990 which is for the preceding nine years.

TABLE 5-6 Population Projections by Age Group Level, Rate of Growth and Percentage Share: CPP Base Case Projection

	Total		0 to 14			15 to 24			25 to 64			65 +		
Year	Population (000s)	Average Annual Growth Rate[a]	Population (000s)	Average Annual Growth Rate[a]	% of Population	Population (000s)	Average Annual Growth Rate[a]	% of Population	Population (000s)	Average Annual Growth Rate[a]	% of Population	Population (000s)	Average Annual Growth Rate[a]	% of Population
1981	24,342	1.2	5,477	-1.5	22.5	4,649	1.5	19.1	11,830	2.3	48.6	2,361	3.1	9.7
1990	27,333	1.3	5,935	0.9	21.7	3,966	-1.7	14.5	14,463	2.3	52.9	2,969	2.6	10.9
2000	29,991	0.9	6,319	0.6	21.1	4,059	0.2	13.5	16,042	1.0	53.5	3,571	1.9	11.9
2010	32,352	0.8	6,345	0.0	19.6	4,477	1.0	13.8	17,349	0.8	53.6	4,181	1.6	12.9
2020	34,666	0.7	6,726	0.6	19.4	4,461	0.0	12.9	17,881	0.3	51.6	5,598	3.0	16.2
2030	36,688	0.6	7,043	0.5	19.2	4,694	0.5	12.8	17,762	-0.1	48.4	7,189	2.5	19.6
2040	38,424	0.5	7,277	0.3	18.9	4,977	0.6	13.0	18,615	0.5	48.4	7,555	0.5	19.7
2050	40,134	0.4	7,673	0.5	19.1	5,111	0.3	12.7	19,618	0.5	48.9	7,732	0.2	19.3
2060	41,895	0.4	8,006	0.4	19.1	5,387	0.5	12.9	20,352	0.4	48.6	8,150	0.5	19.5
2070	43,811	0.5	8,346	0.4	19.1	5,641	0.5	12.9	21,337	0.5	48.7	8,487	0.4	19.4
2080	45,827	0.5	8,754	0.5	19.1	5,862	0.4	12.8	22,335	0.5	48.7	8,876	0.4	19.4
2090	47,890	0.4	9,136	0.4	19.1	6,155	0.5	12.9	23,281	0.4	48.6	9,318	0.5	19.5
2100	50,069	0.4	9,548	0.4	19.1	6,429	0.4	12.8	24,381	0.5	48.7	9,711	0.4	19.4

Sources: Statistics Canada, "Historical Statistical Compendium," prepared for the Royal Commission on the Economic Union and Development Prospects for Canada (Ottawa, 1984), 1.7; Department of Insurance, Canada Pension Plan Statutory Actuarial Report No. 8 as at December 1982 (Ottawa, 1982).

a. For preceding ten years with the exception of 1990 which is for the preceding nine years.

percent of the total population, and the mortality rate is assumed to decline moderately.

A cursory examination of these tables reveals a number of similarities among the various projections:

- The proportion of those aged 65 and older rises continuously in all projections over the period 1981–2030, with particularly large increases from 2010 to 2030. This is a continuation of the trend in the 1921–81 period. Increases in the population share of this age group are substantial over the 1980s. The 1990s, however, are characterized by a slower rate of increase in the share of this age group as a result of the relatively large number of births to the baby boom generation and the existence of a relatively small age cohort from the 1930s. After 2010, as the baby boom generation begins to reach retirement age, the 65-and-older share in the total population once again expands significantly.
- All projections indicate that the shares of the population represented by the two younger age categories (0–14 and 15–24) will decline continuously, or virtually continuously, until the year 2030.
- The share of the population aged 25–64 increases until the year 2010 and declines thereafter (with the exception of the high fertility, high net immigration case, where this share decreases throughout the entire projection period).
- An additional point of interest is that in none of the projections is the proportion of the working age population (15–64) less than recorded in 1961; for three of the four projections this proportion falls below the 1971 proportion only in 2030.

A major difference between the various projections is in the extent of the above noted general population share changes and in the rapidity with which they occur. As expected, the higher the fertility rate assumption, the higher the proportion of the population aged under 25 relative to the 25–64 and 65-and-older age categories throughout the entire projection period. For example, in the low fertility, low immigration projection for the year 2030, the share of those aged 14 and under is 12.2 percent, while for the high fertility, high immigration projection the comparable figure is a substantially higher 20.7 percent. Correspondingly, the 65-and-older age group share is much higher under the low fertility, low immigration projection than under the high fertility, high immigration projection — 26.2 percent compared to 18.8 percent by 2030. Figure 5-2 clearly illustrates the implications of the various fertility assumptions in the year 2030 and also provides a comparison with 1981.

The projections above differ substantially in their implications for total population growth. The low fertility, low immigration case shows the total population starting to decline after 2010, and the medium fertility, low immigration case shows a slight decline starting after 2020.

FIGURE 5-2 **Percentage Share of Selected Age Groups in 1981 and Alternative Projections for the Year 2030**

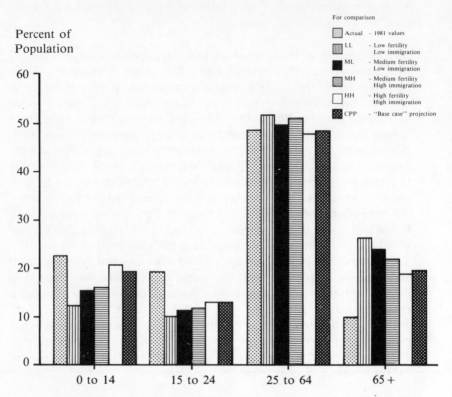

Sources: Statistics Canada, "Historical Statistical Compendium," prepared for the Royal Commission on the Economic Union and Development Prospects for Canada (Ottawa, 1984), 1.7; Statistics Canada, *Population Projections for Canada, Provinces and Territories, 1984–2006*, cat. no. 91–520 (Ottawa, 1985); Department of Insurance, *Canada Pension Plan Statutory Actuarial Report No. 8 as at December 1982* (Ottawa, 1982); and unpublished data from Statistics Canada, Demography Division.

In contrast, the other cases project continuing, though modest, growth of total population.

The immigration assumption also has some effect on the age structure of the population, since the proportion of immigrants under 65 typically has been, and is assumed to continue to be, higher than that for the entire population. Looking at Figure 5-2, a comparison between the medium fertility, high immigration and medium fertility, low immigration projections shows that, with the higher net immigration assumption, the proportions of groups in the 0–64 range is higher than with the low net immigration assumption. The situation is reversed for the remaining age category, aged 65 and older.

Given constant age-specific fertility and mortality rates (and constant age-specific immigration rates), a population can be expected to approach eventually a steady state, characterized by a constant growth rate (+ or -) and constant age-group shares. Most of the projections assume something like constancy in fertility and mortality rates after 2000, and we can see from the very long-term CPP projection (Table 5-6) that a steady state is approached after about 2030 (by which time there would be relatively few survivors of the baby boom cohort of the 1940s–60s).

Whether such steady state projections show continuing growth or decline in total population depends (subject to a qualification for immigration) on whether the fertility rate exceeds or falls short of the replacement value (2.1). (The fertility rate, as noted above, is the number of live births per woman during her child-bearing years. The fact that replacement value is slightly higher than 2 reflects the slightly above 0.5 probability of having a male baby and the mortality for females prior to reaching child-bearing age.) In the CPP projection shown in Table 5-7, the assumed fertility rate (2.0) is marginally below the replacement value, but this is more than offset by the assumption that net immigration will occur at an annual rate somewhat greater than zero (0.32 percent).

Conclusions

On the basis of the various demographic projections we have reviewed, what general conclusions might be drawn respecting Canada's population outlook?

We would note first that the medium fertility assumption (1.6 children per woman, a rate very close to the latest observed rate) seems a reasonable central assumption, but clearly we cannot exclude the possibility of fertility dropping on a sustained basis below the low fertility case (1.4) or rising on a sustained basis back above the high fertility (2.2). Still, the following generalizations seem reasonable:

- A substantial increase in the population share of those 65 and over, over the next 50 years, is a virtual certainty, but the increase in this share by 2030 could range from a doubling to somewhat less than a tripling relative to the current ratio. The most dramatic increase in the share will occur between 2010 and 2030.
- A period of several decades of virtually continuous decline in the absolute number of the 0–14 and 15–24 age groups (and hence a more dramatic decline in their shares) is a very real possibility.
- If fertility and net immigration rates were to stabilize in the near future, the population would approach a steady rate configuration by about 2030, that is, age-group shares would remain approximately constant at their 2030 levels.

- The total population will almost certainly continue to grow but at continuously declining rates, until at least 2010 (by which time it will likely be in the 28 to 32 million range). With low fertility, the total population will then tend to decline slowly. With medium fertility (still below the replacement rate), the total population will eventually start to decline, assuming a low net immigration rate (lower than the range experienced, on average, over the postwar period, where the rate is defined relative to total population). However, with medium fertility, and if the net immigration rate continues in the postwar range, then the total population will stabilize or continue to grow very slowly.

Impact of Demographic Change on Government Expenditures

The previous analysis indicates that the Canadian population has been aging for the past six decades and that this trend will continue over the next fifty years and be particularly marked between the years 2010 and 2030. The aging of the population has many implications for government expenditures; in particular, it will tend to increase the cost, as a share of GNP, of CPP/QPP benefits and of expenditures on Guaranteed Income Supplement (GIS), Old Age Security (OAS) and health care. Partially offsetting this trend may be a relative reduction in expenditures on education as the proportion of people under the age of 25 declines.

This section examines a number of studies which consider the magnitude of anticipated expenditure increases. These studies are by Foot (1982; 1984), Denton and Spencer (1985), Hamilton and Whalley (1984), and the Economic Council of Canada (1979). The Foot studies use the "dependency ratio" concept to analyze the total expenditure burden for all levels of government and the burden for different levels of government resulting from changes in the age composition of the population. The Denton and Spencer study examines projected total expenditures disaggregated into components of expenditures that are age related and other types of expenditures, for various population growth projections and for three different productivity growth assumptions. The Economic Council summarizes a number of other works on the subject, and the Hamilton and Whalley study deals only with expenditures related to the elderly and with associated financing problems. The lack of comparability among the different studies, with respect to their indicators of the burden that demographic pressures place upon government expenditures, precludes a direct quantitative comparison of results. Instead, we compare their results in more qualitative terms.

Impact on Aggregate Expenditures

What impact might structural changes in age distribution have on aggregate government expenditures? If this impact is not significant, then it can be inferred that the alleged financing pressures arising from certain types of expenditures, such as those on GIS, OAS and health care, will be offset by declines in expenditures on education and other expenditure components.

In his 1982 study, *Canada's Population Outlook*, Foot makes use of dependency ratios, the ratio of the population under the age of 15 and over the age of 64 to the population aged 15 to 64 years. Table 5-7 presents an unweighted ratio, and two weighted ratios, for Foot's base case population projection (which is characterized by a fertility rate of 1.75, life expectancy consistent with the 1971–76 trend, and net immigration of 65,000 per annum; these assumptions are similar to the Statistics Canada, 1985, medium fertility and low net immigration case presented in Table 5-3). After a minor increase in 1991, the unweighted ratio declines to 2011 and rises only to previously experienced levels thereafter. These general trends in the unweighted dependency ratio hold for a variety of different demographic assumptions.

However, Foot does not find the unweighted ratio a particularly useful analytical tool, since several studies have shown that, on a per capita basis, total government expenditures are approximately two and one-half times as great for the elderly (persons 65 and older) as for the young (under the age of 18) (Foot, 1982, pp. 138–39). Foot thus constructs weighted expenditure dependency ratios where the weights "bracket" the two and one-half current ratio of the relative cost of servicing the over-65 age group and the young. Table 5-7 presents the historical and projected expenditure dependency ratio for two alternative assumptions concerning the relative cost of government services for the young and the elderly: the assumptions that the relative cost of servicing the elderly is twice ($W = 2$) or three times ($W = 3$) that of servicing the young. Under both assumptions, the ratio rises gradually to 2011, after which it increases substantially. Under $W = 3$, the ratio reaches 1961 levels somewhat before 2021, and under $W = 2$ the 1961 level is reached somewhat after 2021. The year 1961 was a year in which the share of the young in the total population was abnormally high; under all the alternative relative cost assumptions (including the first discussed case where there is no difference in the relative cost, i.e., $W = 1$), the 1961 dependency ratio was the highest for the twentieth century. By 2031 the dependency ratio for both the $W = 2$ and $W = 3$ relative cost assumptions reaches levels not previously experienced. These projections imply that some time after 2021, Canada will face demographic pressures on government expenditures substantially heavier than any previously experienced. Up to that point, however, these pressures are within the historical experience and should not present undue problems despite the higher relative costs of servicing the elderly compared to the cost of servicing the young.

It should be noted that the dependency ratio is only a rough indicator of pressures on the "working population" for support of the dependent population. The general trend of the pressure would be reduced to the

TABLE 5-7 Historical and Projected Expenditures Dependency Ratios for Canada, 1851–2051

Census Year	Expenditure Dependency (Wa = 1)		Expenditure Dependency (Wa = 2)		Expenditure Dependency (Wa = 3)	
	Ratio	Index (1979 = 1.0)	Ratio	Index (1979 = 1.0)	Ratio	Index (1979 = 1.0)
History						
1851	0.909	1.86	0.960	1.53	1.011	1.32
1861	0.834	1.71	0.890	1.42	0.945	1.23
1871	0.829	1.70	0.895	1.43	0.962	1.26
1881	0.749	1.53	0.821	1.31	0.893	1.17
1891	0.692	1.42	0.769	1.23	0.846	1.10
1901	0.651	1.33	0.734	1.17	0.818	1.07
1911	0.603	1.24	0.678	1.08	0.753	0.98
1921	0.644	1.32	0.723	1.15	0.802	1.05
1931	0.592	1.21	0.680	1.08	0.769	1.00
1941	0.526	1.08	0.628	1.00	0.730	0.95
1951	0.615	1.26	0.741	1.18	0.866	1.13
1961	0.712	1.46	0.842	1.34	0.973	1.27
1971	0.604	1.24	0.734	1.17	0.864	1.13
Projection						
1981	0.475	0.97	0.618	0.98	0.760	0.99
1991	0.489	1.00	0.658	1.05	0.828	1.08
2001	0.464	0.95	0.645	1.03	0.826	1.08
2011	0.446	0.91	0.641	1.02	0.836	1.09
2021	0.519	1.06	0.778	1.24	1.037	1.35
2031	0.593	1.21	0.926	1.47	1.258	1.64
2041	0.586	1.20	0.915	1.46	1.245	1.62
2051	0.590	1.20	0.919	1.46	1.247	1.63

Source: D.K. Foot, *Canada's Population Outlook* (Toronto, 1982), pp. 129, 138, 139.
a. W denotes the relative cost of servicing the elderly compared to servicing the young.

TABLE 5-8 Population Growth and the Demographically Induced Growth in Real Government Expenditures by Level of Government, 1941–2021

Period	Population	Federal	Provincial	Municipal	Total
	(% Growth Per Decade)				
History					
1941–51	21.7	27.8	24.6	28.5	26.3
1951–61	30.2	29.2	32.9	38.7	32.0
1961–71	18.3	21.0	15.6	9.6	17.1
1971–81	12.9	21.3	9.3	-1.0	13.2
Projection					
1981–91	10.6	17.6	10.5	8.5	13.4
1991–2001	6.5	10.4	5.8	2.4	7.6
2001–11	4.0	8.5	3.5	0.1	5.6
2011–21	2.4	15.5	4.9	4.3	9.9

Source: D.K. Foot, "The Demographic Future of Fiscal Federalism in Canada" (Toronto, 1984), Table 3, p. 16.
Note: Hypothetical calculation for both historical and projection periods, assuming constant real per capita expenditures in each age group at 1976 relative levels.

extent that labour force participation rates increase (through further increases in the participation of women and/or any trend toward later retirement). It would be increased if average participation rates were to fall (for example, through a continuing trend toward early retirement).

Foot concludes that these findings underline the importance of the government's designing policies which will lead to the eventual transfer of resources from youth-related programs to programs for the elderly. More specifically, this would imply reducing, at least in relative terms, expenditures on education relative to expenditures on health care, housing and income maintenance schemes for the elderly.

In a second study, "The Demographic Future of Fiscal Federalism in Canada" (1984), Foot points out that the projected shifts in population shares will lead to changes in the relative levels of expenditures at different levels of government. This occurs because the share of age-related expenditures in the federal budget is considerably larger than in the budgets of other levels of government. This of course will likely imply a need for some shift in revenue shares.

Foot also calculates hypothetical trends to demographically related government expenditures for 1941 to 2021 under the assumption that recent (1976) per capita will continue to prevail in the future. These estimates, presented in Table 5-8, indicate that, over the next three decades, growth rates of all demographically induced government expenditures will decline from the rates that would have been historically experienced given the constant per capita level of expenditures. (However, growth rates of real output may also be declining given the slowing in growth of the working-age population. As shown, federal government expenditures grow significantly faster than the expenditures of other levels of government. The rate of growth of total government expenditures, and for each level of government, declines to the year 2011, after which it increases. According to Foot in this study, the projected results are robust for alternative population projections and for substantial variations in relative per capita expenditures.

Denton and Spencer (1985) have also analyzed the impact of demographic projections on total government expenditures, using a model which includes a set of age-sex specific weights for all government expenditure categories. The derived weighted index is designed to reflect expenditures required if nothing changes except the size and structure of the population. Denton and Spencer refer to this index as the "constant quality" index. Expenditures over and above those needed to allow for population growth and compositional shifts are referred to as the "quality change" components of expenditures. This component was projected on the basis of an assumed constant propensity of the government sector to claim a share of increases in the real national product for quality improvement.

Denton and Spencer estimate constant quality and total government expenditures for various demographic assumptions and for three potential output growth scenarios. The standard projection assumes that the fertility rate will remain at a level of 1.7 through the projection period; that mortality rates will continue to decline but that the rates of decline will fall off — eventually reaching zero by the year 2026; and that annual net immigration will be 80,000 per annum. The underlying assumptions of this projection correspond most closely to the Statistics Canada medium fertility, high net immigration scenario in Table 5-4. Denton and Spencer's high fertility projection assumes that the fertility rate will rise from 1.7 to 3.0 by 1991, while the low fertility projection has the fertility rate falling to 1.5 by 1991; the net immigration assumption is common to the three cases.

The three potential output growth scenarios are a no growth scenario; a medium growth scenario which assumes an annual rate of growth of 1 percent in real GNE per individual aged 20–64, (in other words, total real output in the economy, or real GNE, would grow, in this case, at an annual rate of 1 percent plus the rate of growth of the population aged 20–64); and a high growth scenario which assumes an annual rate of growth of 2 percent of real GNE per individual aged 20–64.

Denton and Spencer find that, for the standard demographic projection, constant quality government expenditures rise by 7.3 percent between 1980 and 1990, 14.0 percent by the year 2000, and 31.4 percent by the 2030 (Denton and Spencer, 1985, Table 2, p. 73). These increases are exceeded by both the rate of growth of the total population and the rate of real GNE growth to the year 2020. (If we assume any growth at all in productivity, they are significantly below the GNE increases over the entire projection period. See Table 5-9.) Increases in total expenditures, however, are greater than real output growth in all cases. Thus, the authors conclude that demographically induced expenditures will be quite manageable in the future and that the more serious problem may be that of controlling quality-related increases in government expenditures.

These results hold over a wide range of population projections. Table 5-9 presents the estimates of total expenditures and constant quality expenditures for all three productivity growth scenarios and for the standard demographic assumptions. The table also shows these estimates for the low and high demographic assumptions and the medium GNP growth scenarios. As can be seen in the table, total expenditures grow faster than both the constant quality component of expenditures for all three demographic assumptions, and faster than GNP for all three productivity assumptions. However, the constant quality component of expenditure grows more slowly than GNP for all three demographic projections when productivity is assumed to grow at medium rates. In the case of the low productivity, low fertility assumptions, constant quality government expenditure growth exceeds GNP growth (not shown in Table 5-9).

Hence Denton and Spencer conclude that population aging is important at the aggregate level, but it is not the most critical consideration; since the quality change component rises more quickly, it is relatively more important than the constant quality (or demography related) component. Both Foot (1982) and Denton and Spencer (1985) could be taken as suggesting that the implications of population aging for aggregate expenditures will not be too difficult to manage.

The 1979 study by the Economic Council of Canada is somewhat less optimistic. The council's low projection case assumes a fertility rate of 1.5 and net immigration of 20,000 per annum (this projection lies between Statistics Canada's low fertility, low immigration and medium fertility, low immigration projections). In this case, benefits to the elderly are estimated to rise from about 3 percent of GNP in 1976 to as much as 10 percent by 2031. This projection assumes that the present age of eligibility and present target level of income replacement provided by the Canada Pension Plan (CPP) and the Quebec Pension Plan (QPP) are maintained, and that Old Age Security (OAS) payments continue to bear the same relationship to the average industrial wage as in 1978 (providing a combined replacement ratio with CPP/QPP of about 39 percent for an unmarried worker earning the average industrial wage). The average annual productivity growth was assumed to be 1.8 percent, but, given the assumption that OAS is increased in line with real wages, the results would not be expected to be very sensitive to the productivity assumption. Under the same program specification assumptions, the Economic Council's medium demographic projection (the fertility rate is assumed to be 2.1 and net immigration is 80,000 per annum; this projection is most similar to Statistics Canada's high fertility, high immigration case) results in elderly benefits representing over 7 percent of GNP in the year 2031. In contrast, the Denton and Spencer estimation of faster GNP growth than growth of demography-related government expenditures implies that income security costs for the elderly, when combined with other demographic related expenditures, will decline as a share of GNP.

In addition to assuming the maintenance of OAS payments in relative rather than in real terms, the Economic Council also differs from Denton and Spencer in that it does not foresee much opportunity for decrease in expenditures related to youth (or in other government expenditures) which would offset projected increases in absolute and relative levels of income-security costs for the elderly. The Economic Council also notes that aging population in itself will lead to some downward pressure on the potential growth of the economy in terms of real income per person, particularly after the year 2000. Hence, while the Economic Council's overall tone is not alarmist, it does caution that Canadians will face hard choices in setting priorities for pension reform. The Economic Council recommends that any changes should be taken well in advance so that

TABLE 5-9 Denton and Spencer's Indexes of Population, Real GNP and Government Aggregate Expenditure, 1980–2030: Various Projections

			All Expenditures	
Year	Population	GNP	Total	Constant Quality Component
			(Indexes: 1980 = 100)	
Historical				
1950	57.0	25.6	12.9	69.1
1960	74.3	40.4	27.6	79.4
1970	88.6	67.1	57.2	90.3
1980	100.0	100.0	100.0	100.0
Standard Population Projection: No Productivity Growth				
1980	100.0	100.0	100.0	100.0
1990	111.5	112.2	117.5	107.3
2000	120.4	122.5	132.6	114.0
2010	126.8	132.2	146.9	120.2
2020	131.5	131.9	152.2	126.5
2030	133.2	125.3	150.5	131.4
Standard Population Projection: Medium Productivity Growth				
1980	100.0	100.0	100.0	100.0
1990	111.5	120.3	125.2	107.3
2000	120.4	145.1	153.9	114.0
2010	126.8	172.9	185.4	120.2
2020	131.5	190.6	207.6	126.5
2030	133.2	200.1	221.0	131.4

TABLE 5-9 (cont'd)

			All Expenditures	
				Constant Quality
Year	Population	GNP	Total	Component
		(Indexes: 1980 = 100)		

Standard Population Projection: High Productivity Growth

1980	100.0	100.0	100.0	100.0
1990	111.5	128.9	133.3	107.3
2000	120.4	171.6	178.8	114.0
2010	126.8	225.6	235.0	120.2
2020	131.5	274.4	286.6	126.5
2030	133.2	317.9	332.1	131.4

High Fertility: Medium Productivity Growth

1980	100.0	100.0	100.0	100.0
1990	116.0	120.0	125.9	108.7
2000	135.9	144.8	158.0	120.5
2010	154.3	182.8	205.5	135.2
2020	179.5	227.3	260.6	151.5
2030	206.1	271.9	317.7	170.7

Low Fertility: Medium Productivity Growth

1980	100.0	100.0	100.0	100.0
1990	110.7	120.3	125.0	107.0
2000	117.6	145.2	153.2	112.8
2010	122.0	171.1	181.8	117.6
2020	124.0	184.0	198.3	122.4
2030	122.6	187.6	204.9	125.5

Source: F.T. Denton and B.G. Spencer, "Prospective Changes in the Population and their Implications for Government Expenditures," in *Ottawa and the Provinces: The Distribution of Money and Power* (Toronto, 1985), Table 2, pp. 73–74.

individuals can take them into account when planning for their retirement.

Impact on Specific Government Expenditures

Canada Pension Plan (CPP)

Table 5-10 provides estimates of the elderly dependency ratio (population aged 65 and over divided by the population aged 15 to 64) to the year 2100 using two projections from the December 1982 CPP Statutory Actuarial Report (SAR) released by the federal Department of Insurance. As can be seen from this table, this ratio increases more or less continuously until the year 2030, after which it levels off. The elderly dependency ratio estimates are higher under the lower fertility rate assumptions, since this assumption generates an older population than the higher fertility assumption. In 1980 there were approximately seven

TABLE 5-10 Two Alternative Projections of the Elderly Dependency Ratio

Year	CPP Base Case Projection[a]	CPP Alternative Projection[b]
1980	.143	.137
1990	.164	.161
2000	.178	.178
2010	.189	.194
2020	.245	.261
2030	.311	.344
2040	.314	.358
2050	.307	.366
2060	.312	.375
2070	.311	.369
2080	.311	.367
2090	.313	.366
2100	.312	.361

Source: Department of Insurance, *Canada Pension Plan Statutory Actuarial Report No. 8 as at December 1982* (Ottawa, 1982), p. 46, and Department of Insurance printouts.

Note: The elderly dependency ratio is defined as the population over 65 divided by the population between the ages 14 and 65.

a. Assumptions: fertility rate = 2.0 after 1999; net immigration = 0.32 percent of population.

b. Assumptions: fertility rate = 1.7 after 1999;net immigration = 0.32 percent of population.

working-age persons for every person of retirement age; by the year 2030 this ratio will decline substantially to something like three persons of working age for one person of retirement age. This provides a vivid illustration of the potential increase in the burden of financing pensions.

The SAR (Canada, 1982) presents some estimates of the degree to which CPP contribution rates must rise under alternative funding arrangements using the base case demographic projection. The increases in contribution rates are greater than the increase in the "pension ratios" as a result of the compounding of the impacts of the latter increase with the maturing of the plans. To illustrate this general point, Table 5-11 shows the SAR projections of contributions under two alternate funding assumptions.

It is not our purpose here to examine the various issues that arise with respect to choice of approach to funding. Our illustrative funding cases might be considered to be intermediate between full funding and "pay-as-you-go," though closer to the latter than the former. Under funding arrangement B, contribution rates are so set that net cash flow to the provinces does not become negative, that is, new loans to the provinces never fall below the level of interest payments by the provinces. This provision requires contribution rate increases starting in 1985. The size

TABLE 5-11 Projected Contribution Rates Under Various Assumptions

Year	Standard Assumption (Fert. Rate of 2.0 after 1999; Net Immig. 0.32% of Pop.)		Net Immigration 75,000 per Year		Total Fertility Rate of 1.7 after 1999	
	Fund B	Fund C	Fund B	Fund C	Fund B	Fund C
1983	3.60	3.60	3.60	3.60	3.60	3.60
1984	3.60	3.60	3.60	3.60	3.60	3.60
1985	3.65	3.60	3.65	3.60	3.65	3.60
1986	3.85	3.60	3.85	3.60	3.85	3.60
1987	4.11	3.60	4.12	3.60	4.11	3.60
1988	4.39	3.60	4.39	3.60	4.39	3.60
1989	4.60	3.60	4.60	3.60	4.60	3.60
1990	4.81	3.60	4.82	3.60	4.81	3.60
1991	4.98	3.60	4.99	3.60	4.98	3.60
1992	5.15	3.60	5.16	3.60	5.15	3.60
1995	5.58	3.97	5.60	3.98	5.58	3.96
2000	6.08	4.95	6.11	4.98	6.07	4.95
2005	6.43	5.75	6.49	5.80	6.43	5.75
2010	6.99	6.52	7.08	6.60	7.02	6.55
2015	7.95	7.60	8.10	7.73	8.06	7.69
2020	9.03	8.76	9.26	8.97	9.27	8.98
2030	10.92	10.76	11.34	11.17	11.58	11.40
2040	10.76	10.66	11.26	11.16	11.85	11.75
2050	10.47	10.41	11.01	10.95	12.00	11.94
2075	10.70	10.69	11.35	11.33	12.25	12.23
2100	10.82	10.82	11.55	11.54	12.15	12.15

Source: Canada, Department of Insurance, *Canada Pension Plan Statutory Actuarial Report No. 8 as at December 1982* (Ottawa, 1982), Tables 1, 11, 12.

of the fund under this arrangement increases perpetually as the interest on the current fund compounds. Under funding arrangement C, contribution rates are so set that the provinces are not required to repay outstanding loans, but the net cash flow to the provinces is negative starting in 1985 because of the interest charges to the provinces on the outstanding loans. This approach is currently projected to require contribution rate increases starting, at the latest, about 1994. Initially, the size of the fund shows some further increase (as interest earnings exceed the "deficit" on contributions versus benefits). It then levels off at a fixed current dollar amount. Contribution rates rise significantly faster under arrangement B than under arrangement C, but, eventually, they converge.

The Department of Insurance (Canada, 1982) made additional projections which illustrate the sensitivity of these contribution rates to alternate demographic assumptions. These projections are also presented in Table 5-11 for funding arrangements B and C. As can be seen from this table, the assumption that net immigration will be 75,000 per annum leads to higher contribution rates over the projection period relative to the base case assumption that net immigration will be 0.32 percent of the population, since lower net immigration will lead to an older population. For similar reasons, the assumption that the fertility rate remains at a level of 1.7 after 1999 also leads to higher contribution rates relative to both the base case and the alternate net immigration assumption case.

Old-Age Security (OAS) and Guaranteed Income Supplement (GIS)

Problems similar to those that affect the CPP confront OAS and GIS. The important differences between these programs and the CPP are that the OAS and GIS are "mature," whereas part of the reason for increasing CPP expenditures is that not all the population over 65 is as yet eligible for full benefits; that CPP is partially funded, while OAS and GIS are pay-as-you-go schemes; and that OAS and GIS are financed out of general revenues, while the CPP is financed by employees' and employers' contributions and interest on the fund. Currently, OAS and GIS expenditures are somewhat more than twice the size of total CPP/QPP payments to the elderly.

Employing a low population projection (fertility rate 1.5, net immigration 20,000 per annum), which has the percentage of those aged 65 and over representing nearly one-third of the population by the year 2050, Hamilton and Whalley (1984, p. 125) estimate that the succeeding generation of workers could face a surcharge on their combined federal and provincial income tax of approximately 30 to 40 percent to pay for OAS/GIS. This calculation assumes either no productivity growth or increases in the OAS/GIS payments in real terms in line with real earning. In addition, it ignores the fact that, as the CPP matures and women enter the labour force in larger numbers, GIS payments will not likely increase at the same pace as the share of the population of those over 64. To prevent the large surcharge, Hamilton and Whalley (1984, pp. 120–121, 132) recommend the modification of the universality of these income support programs. This could result in a dramatic reduction in expenditures.

Denton and Spencer (1985), using the model described above, also find that the changing age structure will entail substantial increases in constant quality social security expenditures. In particular, for their standard demographic projection, they find that social security expenditures (which, in their work, includes CPP, QPP and OAS but not Family Allowance or GIS) will experience a 30 percent increase between 1980 and 1990 and that, by the year 2030, they will be three times their 1980 levels (Denton and Spencer, 1985, Table 4). As can be seen in Table 5-12, this increase is greater than the increase in both population and real GNP for all cases with the exception of the high productivity growth projection.

Health Care

Expenditures on health care, which are about twice the current combined expenditure on CPP/QPP/OAS/GIS, are also expected to increase as a result of the changing age structure of the population. This assertion is based, to a large extent, on the fact that it is seven times more costly, on a per capita basis, to provide health services to persons over the age of 65 relative to individuals under 18 (Hamilton and Whalley, 1984, p. 125). Using their low population projection, Hamilton and Whalley estimate that, in their most pessimistic demographic case, health care expenditures could rise by 75 percent by the year 2050, which, according to their calculation, would require a further income-tax surcharge of 20 to 25 percent. Again, Hamilton and Whalley acknowledge that their surcharge is likely to be an overestimate, since they have ignored possible relative-cost changes between health care and other costs. This surcharge is also likely to be an overestimate because of failure to account for increases in the per capital tax base.

Foot (1982, p. 221) suggests increases in the real per capita cost of physicians' services of 5.6 percent, and hospital services of 15.9 percent, by the year 2000, with further increases of 7.5 and 30.9 percent, respectively, between 2001 and 2031.

Denton and Spencer (1985) estimate, with the standard demographic projection, that "constant quality" health expenditures will increase by 16.2 percent over the period 1980–90, 30 percent between 1980 and 2000 and by 69.8 percent over the entire projection period (1980–2030). These increases are less than the increase in real GNP in all but the no productivity growth case. From Table 5-12 it can be seen that these results hold for two alternate demographic projections. In all projections, health cost increases are large and are second only to those in the social security category.

In an earlier study, Denton and Spencer found projected total health cost increases to be substantial but not of crisis proportions, and they pointed out that, while the share of total health costs in GNP peaks in the year 2025, it will be equivalent to the percentage allocated by West Germany in the mid-1970s and only slightly above that spent in the United States and Sweden at that time (Denton and Spencer, 1983, p. 161). Their standard projection in this case has the fertility rate rising to 2.1 by 1991 and remaining constant thereafter. Alternative demographic assumptions (such as a lower fertility rate) chiefly affect the timing of the increase in the ratio but do not greatly increase the magnitude. For instance, with the lower fertility rate assumption, the health-care cost ratio does not increase at all until 2001 but is increasing faster by the end

TABLE 5-12 Denton and Spencer's Indexes of Population and "Constant Quality" Government Expenditure, 1980–2030: Various Expenditure Classes

(Indexes: 1980 = 100)

Year	Population	GNP	No[a] Growth	Medium[a] Growth	High[a] Growth	Total "Constant Quality" Expenditures	Social Security	Health	Elementary & Secondary Education	Post-Secondary & Other Education
Historical										
1930	42.5					60.2	25.7	44.2	60.8	57.7
1940	47.3					64.1	34.0	49.8	62.6	61.6
1950	57.0	25.6				70.3	47.6	61.0	64.6	64.1
1960	74.3	40.4				80.3	60.8	75.5	85.1	68.5
1970	88.6	67.1				90.8	74.9	86.1	105.0	86.1
1980	100.0	100.0				100.0	100.0	100.0	100.0	100.0
Standard Demographic Projection										
1980	100.0		100.0	100.0	100.0	100.0	100.0	100.0	100.0	100.0
1990	111.5		112.2	120.3	128.9	107.3	129.2	116.2	91.5	94.6
2000	120.4		122.5	145.1	171.6	114.0	153.3	130.4	95.6	90.9
2010	126.8		132.2	172.9	225.6	120.2	176.7	144.9	90.9	94.4
2020	131.5		131.9	190.6	274.4	126.5	233.0	158.9	88.4	89.7
2030	133.2		125.3	200.1	317.9	131.4	295.7	169.8	88.6	88.6

High Fertility Projection

1980	100.0	100.0	100.0	100.0	100.0	100.0
1990	120.0	108.7	128.9	122.0	93.5	94.5
2000	144.8	120.5	153.0	140.6	124.9	92.7
2010	182.8	135.2	176.4	162.0	141.2	120.9
2020	227.3	151.5	232.5	189.8	151.8	128.3
2030	271.9	170.7	295.1	215.1	188.8	140.2

Low Fertility Projection

1980	100.0	100.0	100.0	100.0	100.0	100.0
1990	120.3	107.0	129.3	115.2	91.2	94.6
2000	145.3	112.8	153.4	128.6	90.4	90.6
2010	171.1	117.6	176.8	142.1	81.9	89.7
2020	184.0	122.4	233.1	154.3	78.4	82.9
2030	187.6	125.5	295.8	163.3	75.3	80.5

Source: F.T. Denton and B.G. Spencer, "Prospective Changes in the Population and their Implications for Government Expenditures," in *Ottawa and The Provinces: The Distribution of Money and Power* (Toronto, 1985), Tables 2–4.

a. Refers to productivity growth assumption, see text.

of the projection period. In the base case scenario, this ratio increases gradually until the end of the century and beyond.

Education

Of the four Statistics Canada population projections, only in the high fertility, high immigration case does the share of the population aged 0–14 not significantly decline. Similarly, in the first three projections, the annual rate of growth of this age group is either negative or negligible. The share of the population aged 15–24 declines substantially in all the Statistics Canada projections and in the CPP projections as well. The decline in the share of the young in the total population presents some opportunity for expenditure savings in education that may counteract expenditure pressures on programs for the elderly.

Denton and Spencer (1985) indicate that, for both the low and medium fertility assumptions, constant quality expenditures on education will decline. As can be seen in Table 5-12, for elementary and secondary, and for post-secondary education, constant quality expenditures are lower throughout the projection period than they were in 1980 in all but the high fertility scenario. Under the standard demographic projection, the elementary and secondary expenditure levels in 1990 are 8.5 percent lower than they were in 1980. There is a slight increase between 1990 and 2000 which is consistent with the minor increase in the number of people aged 0–14 years over this decade associated with the "baby boomlet" (or echo of the baby boom). After 2000 there is a further decrease in this expenditure category. For post-secondary education there is a decrease of 5.4 percent over the period 1980–90, and, by 2030, the cumulative decrease is 11.4 percent.

In the low fertility projection, the decrease is, not surprisingly, more substantial, while in the high fertility projection, real expenditures decrease until 2000 and rise thereafter. This latter development occurs because of the assumption in this scenario that the fertility rate will rise to 3.0 after 1991. Even in the high fertility case, real output growth is greater than the growth in constant quality expenditures on education.

Foot, instead of projecting educational expenditures, uses projected enrolments as an indicator of the future demand for education. He finds that elementary-secondary enrolments will decline until the mid-1980s, reaching a level approximately 20 percent below the peak levels of the early 1970s (Foot, 1982, p. 178). There will then be a slight rise in the 1990s as a result of the baby boomlet, after which enrolments will continue to decline. In addition, he finds that university enrolments will decline somewhere between 3 and 12 percent while non-university post-secondary enrolments will decline to a much greater extent.

Other Expenditures

For other expenditure categories in Denton and Spencer (1985), constant quality expenditures are projected to grow at less than the rate of growth of population and, with few exceptions, less than the rate of growth of real GNP. These include expenditures in transportation and communications, and the environment. Expenditures in these categories are, of course, less sensitive to the changing age structure of the population and are more likely to increase because of changes in the quality change component. In large part, it is because of this fact that Denton and Spencer find that total constant quality expenditures (those related to changes in the age structure) will be manageable in the future.

Some International Comparisons

Table 5-13 presents data comparing anticipated demographic pressures in selected European countries, in Canada and the United States. The measure presented for Canada, the United States and Italy is defined as the ratio of the working-age population to the population of retirement age, while the other measures presented are defined as the ratio of actual workers to actual retirees. Further, the data are not strictly comparable because of differences in definitions of the components of the measure and differences in underlying assumptions, in particular, assumptions concerning fertility and participation rates. Nevertheless, the data do permit some approximate comparisons and reveal anticipated trends for the individual countries.

With an average participation rate of 65 percent for Canada in 1980 (giving a ratio of 3.9 of workers to retirees), Table 5-13 indicates that Canada was in a comparatively advantageous position, relative to the other countries, with respect to the number of workers supporting its retirees. The apparent exception is Sweden, but the high level of the Swedish ratio is related to differences in definitions and to the fact that the Swedish program is far from maturity. Assuming a similar participation rate to that assumed for Canada, the ratio of workers to retirees for the United States would have been 3.5 in 1980. The Canadian advantage diminishes considerably by the year 2000 under both the low and high demographic projections compared to the other analogous projections. However, Canada's low fertility rate (1.4) is significantly lower than the assumed low fertility rate for the United States (1.7), the United Kingdom (1.8), and France (1.8). Assuming again a participation rate of 65 percent (for both Canada and the United States), the Canadian ratio of workers to retirees by the year 2000 (which reaches 2.9 for the low projection and 3.0 for the high projection) is in the approximate range of the United Kingdom and Switzerland. It is below the not entirely comparable ratio in Sweden, somewhat higher than the ratio in the United States (which is 2.7 for the low projection and 2.9 for the high projection), and it is above the ratios of France, Germany and Italy. This remains true for moderate increases in the Canadian participation rate

TABLE 5-13 Ratio of Population of Working Age to Population of Retirement Age (or Ratio of Workers to Retirees) for Canada, United States and Selected European Countries

Year	Canada[a]		United States[b]		United Kingdom[c]		France[d]		Germany[e]	Sweden[f]	Italy[g]	Switzerland[h]
	I	II	I	II	I	II	I	II				
1970	6.50	6.50	5.44	5.44	2.84	2.84	3.14	3.14	N.A.	N.A.	3.53	N.A.
1975	6.37	6.37	5.29	5.29	N.A.	N.A.	2.66	2.66	2.40	8.21	N.A.	N.A.
1980	5.99	5.99	5.13	5.13	2.76	2.76	N.A.	N.A.	2.19	6.84	3.50	3.6
1985	5.65	5.65	4.90	4.95	N.A.	N.A.	2.82	2.82	2.15	5.69	N.A.	3.6
1990	4.89	5.13	4.52	4.65	2.87	2.87	2.70	2.70	2.11	4.85	3.10	3.6
2000	4.52	4.65	4.10	4.42	2.99	3.03	2.49	2.50	1.83	4.55	2.76	3.2
2010	4.08	4.37	3.75	4.24	2.84	2.99	2.24	2.33	1.56	4.07	N.A.	2.8
2020	3.00	3.55	2.80	3.30	2.41	2.66	1.86	2.01	1.37	3.44	N.A.	2.2
2030	2.17	2.87	2.10	2.65	2.04	2.40	1.64	1.87	1.12	N.A.	N.A.	1.8
Index 1980-100												
1970	108.5	108.5	106.0	106.0	102.9	102.9	114.6	114.6	109.6[i]	120.0[i]	101.0	N.A.
1980	100.0	100.0	100.0	100.0	100.0	100.0	100.0[i]	100.0[i]	100.0	100.0	100.0	100.0
2000	75.5	77.6	79.9	86.2	108.3	109.8	90.9	91.2	83.6	66.5	78.9	88.9
2020	50.1	59.3	54.6	64.3	87.3	96.4	67.9	73.4	62.6	50.3	N.A.	61.1
2030	36.2	47.9	40.9	51.7	73.9	87.0	60.0	68.3	51.1	N.A.	N.A.	50.0

Sources: Statistics Canada, "Historical Statistical Compendium," prepared for the Royal Commission on the Economic Union and Development Prospects for Canada (Ottawa, 1984), 1.7; Statistics Canada, *Population Projections for Canada, Provinces and Territories, 1984–2006*, Cat. No. 91–520 (Ottawa, 1985). Data other than for Canada are from various articles in Jean-Jacques Rosa, ed., *The World Crisis in Social Security* (San Francisco, 1982).

a. This ratio is defined as the population aged 20–64 divided by the population 65 or older and is calculated from Statistics Canada projections presented in Tables 5-2 and 5–5. Ratio I is based on the low fertility, low immigration case, where the fertility rate is assumed to be 1.4 and immigration is assumed to be 50,000 per annum; ratio II is based on the high fertility, high immigration case, where the fertility rate is assumed to be 2.2 and immigration 100,000 per annum. Actual years presented are 1971, 1976 and 1981.

b. The ratio is defined as the number of people aged 20–64 divided by the number of people in the population aged 65 or older. Ratio I assumes an average fertility rate of 1.7 and ratio II assumes an average fertility rate of 2.1. The recent average is 1.8.

222   *Green, Gold & Sargent*

c. Actual years presented are 1971, 1981, 1991, 2001, 2023 and 2032; the ratios are defined as that of working population to pensioners, and no further details for the exact age are provided. Ratio I assumes a fertility rate of 1.8 and ratio II a fertility rate of 2.1.

d. The ratios are defined as the overall ratio of workers to retirees where the participation rate is assumed to be the rate observed in 1978. Ratio I assumes a fertility rate of 1.8 and ratio II assumes a fertility rate of 2.1, the rate in 1980 was 1.95.

e. The ratio is defined as that of workers to retirees (excluding public pensions for the Beamte category of civil servants). Assumed fertility rate is 1.30 (inferred from the text), no information is given about the participation rate assumption.

f. The ratio is defined as that of workers to ATP Pensioners not including survivors' and disability pensioners (the ATP is the supplementary pension system and is a major part of the public pension system in Sweden). The ratio of workers paying into the system to retirees receiving benefits is rather high in the early years because the system will only reach maturity in 1990. The participation rates for groups between 16 and 65 years of age are assumed to remain constant for men (90 percent) and to increase for women (from 73 percent in 1980 to 81 percent in 2020). The assumed fertility rate underlying the projections is not given.

g. The ratio is defined as the population aged 15–59 divided by the population aged 60 and older, no information on the assumed fertility rate is given. Actual years presented are 1971, 1981, 1991 and 2001.

h. Ratio is defined as that of workers to retirees, no further information is given.

i. Index for 1975.

j. The average of 1975 and 1985 values is used in place of the unavailable 1980 value.

(to about 70 percent); the ratio of workers to retirees will be higher the larger the increase in the participation rate.

By the year 2030, Table 5-13 indicates, Canada (again assuming a 65 percent participation rate, the Canadian ratio of workers to retirees would be 1.4 in the low projection and 1.9 in the high projection) is likely to be right in the middle of the range with the United Kingdom at the high end and Germany at the low end.[3] Canada is very likely to have a ratio of workers to retirees similar to that for the United States and France.

The larger decline in the Canadian index (presented in the latter part of Table 5-13), compared to the declines of the indexes of other countries, reflects Canada's loss of its current advantageous position with respect to the share of its working-age population. As stated above, increases in the participation rates, though not affecting the ratio of working-age population to retirees, will reduce the sharpness of the decline in the ratio of workers to retirees.

A Warning as to Uncertainties: Stone and Fletcher

In reviewing the conclusions of the studies surveyed, it is useful to keep in mind some concerns expressed by Stone and Fletcher (1984, pp. 474–84). To begin with, they maintain that it is only possible to make useful forecasts of the total population for the next 5–20 years. In support of this view, they argue that it is difficult to forecast future fertility trends of persons currently not yet born or distant from their childbearing years, particularly since there are many competing theories as to the factors determining fertility. They recommend the use of a wide range of assumptions for the future fertility rate, suggesting that a range from 1.2 to 2.7 would be appropriate.

Stone and Fletcher also assert that we cannot rule out substantial increases in life expectancy in the future. As people become increasingly aware of the type of lifestyle and environment which will enhance their lifespan, mortality rates could fall more than projected in many studies. Conversely, mortality rates could rise dramatically owing to wars of plagues. To Stone and Fletcher, the level of international migration for Canada in the long term in an enigma. It could, however, affect significantly the future ratios of pensioners to workers. They also note the possibility that revolutionary production technologies could emerge over the next fifty years, generating high productivity growth and thus resources to pay for pensions and other demography-related expenditures. Another factor to consider is that the age at which most people retire could change significantly.

In conclusion, Stone and Fletcher state that there is no scientific basis to support the claim that there is an impending demography-induced crisis. They suggest, instead, that there should be an emphasis in government policy on the improvement of flexibility and innovative skills among persons and institutions and on the development of systems and tools for early warning and analysis.

Conclusions

This paper has reviewed alternative projections of the Canadian population and their implications for the population's age structure. Different assumptions within what is viewed as a reasonable range as to the key determinants — fertility and net immigration rates — affect the pace and extent of change but leave intact the basic result of a substantial increase in the share of the population of those over 64. In the Statistics Canada high scenario, that is, a fertility rate of 2.2 and net immigration of 100,000 per annum, the share of the population aged 65 and older almost doubles from 1981 to 2030, while the share of the population between the ages of 14 and 65 declines by 10 percent during the same period. In the low scenario, that is, fertility rate of 1.4 and net immigration of 50,000 per annum, the share of the population aged 65 and older almost triples between 1981 and 2030 while the population share between the ages of 14 and 65 declines by 9 percent.

Different authors have come to rather different conclusions as to the overall consequences of the aging of the Canadian population for government expenditures. Assuming a constant real level of per capita expenditures for age-specific programs (equal to that prevailing in the mid-1970s), Foot calculates hypothetical expenditure profiles from 1940 on and shows that, in fact, the growth rate of demographic-related total government expenditures will decline after 1981–90 to 2011–21, at which time the growth rate increases as the baby boom generation moves fully into the over 64 category. Foot notes that, despite the minor increase in the growth rate of total demographically related government expenditures in the periods 1981–90 and 2011–20, these rates of growth are substantially below the rates that would have been experienced historically. Foot does note that, unless there is some reallocation of government revenues or expenditures between the three levels of government, the federal government will experience fiscal imbalances as a result of the aging population.

Denton and Spencer (1985) present the most optimistic conclusions based on an analysis that separates all changes in government expenditures into two components: those directly related to changes in population size and structure, and all other "quality" changes which they related to the growth of income. They estimate that, for the period from 1981 to 2030 as a whole, even if there is no productivity growth, demographically induced expenditure growth will be lower than population growth and only slightly higher than GNP growth. This would imply that the share of demographically related expenditures in GNP will hardly change in the no-productivity-growth case, and, in the case of the other productivity-growth assumptions, the share of demographically induced expenditures in GNP will decline. The Denton and Spencer study seems to suggest that, if there proves to be a problem with growing government expenditures, its sources will be basically non-demographic.

In contrast, Hamilton and Whalley (1984) and the Economic Council of Canada (1979) conclude that demographic effects will constitute much more of a problem. Both these studies focus on the fact that employee and employer contributions to CPP and QPP rates will need to begin to increase by the end of this decade, a process that will continue until almost 2030 by which time contribution rates may be of the order of three times that of current rates. These conclusions are broadly consistent with the official CPP actuarial projections made by the Department of Insurance (SAR). Furthermore, taxation rates will have to increase to support growing OAS and GIS expenditures as well as higher medical costs. However, there are factors that could counteract the pressures of the aging population on expenditures. First, as the CPP/QPP mature, the need for GIS will decline. Second, the trend of increased participation of women in the labour force is also likely to reduce GIS payments. Third, increased participation rates will also reduce the burden on the working population of supporting pension benefits, which could be further reduced by voluntary postponement of retirement. Finally, the reconsideration of the universality of OAS, as suggested by Hamilton and Whalley (1984, p. 132) and raised as a possibility by the Economic Council of Canada (1979, p. 91), and/or a slower growth in real OAS benefits than in productivity, would also significantly reduce the need for future tax rate increases.

Even the more pessimistic analyses, these presented by the Economic Council of Canada and Hamilton and Whalley, are not necessarily indicative of fiscal crises. As the Economic Council indicates, the projected share of retirement benefits in GNP for most middle-of-the-road scenarios are of the magnitude observed in many of the European countries at the beginning of the 1970s. By the time Canada reaches this point it is likely to be enjoying much higher per capita real GNP than that observed for the European countries in the 1970s.

Notes

This study was completed in December 1984.

We wish to thank, without implicating, Dr. M.V. George of Statistics Canada for his comments and for making available supplementary material, and Paul-Henri Lapointe of the Department of Finance for his comments.

1. Statistics Canada (1985); and unpublished projections to the year 2030 obtained from the Population Projection Section, Demographic Division, Statistics Canada. Five official projections are available; they are identified as Series 1 to 5, where:
   - Series 1 assumes a fertility rate of 1.4, net immigration of 50,000 per year and internal migration pattern A;
   - Series 2 assumes a fertility rate of 1.4, net immigration of 50,000 per year and internal migration pattern B;
   - Series 3 assumes a fertility rate of 1.6, net immigration of 50,000 per year and internal migration pattern A;
   - Series 4 assumes a fertility rate of 1.6, net immigration of 100,000 per year and internal migration pattern A;
   - Series 5 assumes a fertility rate of 2.2, net immigration of 100,000 per year and internal migration pattern C;
   and where the assumption concerning internal migration patterns are:
   - A, continuation of current trends;
   - B, gradual return to westward flow; and
   - C, recent rates (average of 1981–83) remain constant for the projection period.
   The paper discusses projection series 1, 3, 4, and 5. The assumptions concerning internal migration patterns have little impact on total population and age structure, though these different assumptions are important to the regional distribution of employment.

2. "Base case" refers to the projection of future population corresponding to the set of assumptions which the agency in question judged to be most likely or most representative of the width of the range of possible outcomes.

3. There are no projections for the Swedish ratios in the year 2030, but, given the projections for the year 2020, Sweden may well have the highest ratio in 2030. As stated in the text, however, the high level of the Swedish ratio seems related in part to definitional differences. The German fertility rate assumption is the lowest, at 1.3.

Bibliography

Canada. 1982. Department of Insurance. *Canada Pension Plan Statutory Actuarial Report No. 8. as at December 1982*. Ottawa: The Department.

Denton, F.T., and B.G. Spencer. 1983. "Aging and Future Health Costs." *Canadian Public Policy* 9 (June): 155–64.

_____. 1985. "Prospective Changes in the Population and Their Implications for Government Expenditures." In *Ottawa and the Provinces: The Distribution of Money and Power*, edited by Thomas J. Courchene, David W. Conklin and Gail C.A. Cook, pp. 44–95. Toronto: Ontario Economic Council.

Economic Council of Canada. 1979. *One in Three: Pensions for Canadians to 2030*. Ottawa: Minister of Supply and Services Canada.

Foot, David K. 1982. *Canada's Population Outlook*. Ottawa: Canadian Institute for Economic Policy.

_____. 1984. "The Demographic Future of Fiscal Federalism in Canada," Working Paper Series Number 8410. Toronto: University of Toronto and Institute for Policy Analysis.

Hamilton, Colleen, and John Whalley. 1984. "Reforming Public Pensions in Canada: Issues and Options." In *Pensions Today and Tomorrow: Background Studies*, edited by David W. Conklin, Jalynn H. Bennett and Thomas J. Courchene, pp.62–137. Toronto: Ontario Economic Council.

Rosa, Jean-Jacques, ed. 1982. *The World Crises in Social Security*. San Francisco: Institute for Contemporary Studies.

Statistics Canada. 1985. *Population Projections for Canada, Provinces and Territories, 1984–2006*. Cat. No. 91-520. Ottawa: Minister of Supply and Services Canada.

Stone, Leroy O., and Susan Fletcher. 1984. "Why We Should Be Cautious in Accepting Forecasts of the Dependency Ratios in the 21st Century." In *Pensions Today and Tomorrow: Background Studies*, edited by David W. Conklin, Jalynn H. Bennett and Thomas J. Courchene, pp.474–86. Toronto: Ontario Economic Council.

Michael G.S. Denny is Professor in the Department of Economics, University of Toronto.

A.R. Dobell is President of the Institute for Research on Public Policy, Victoria, and is Adjunct Professor in the School of Public Administration and the Department of Economics, University of Victoria.

Judith Gold, a former member of the Royal Commission economics research staff, is an economist with the Department of Finance, Ottawa.

Douglas Green, a former member of the Royal Commission economics research staff, is a student at Carleton University, Ottawa.

John F. Helliwell is Professor in the Department of Economics, University of British Columbia, Vancouver.

Gregory V. Jump is Associate Professor in the Department of Economics, University of Toronto.

Bruce R. Kennedy is a doctoral candidate at the School of Public Administration, University of Victoria, and a researcher with the Victoria office of the Institute for Research on Public Policy.

Mary E. MacGregor is a researcher at the Institute for Policy Analysis, University of Toronto.

Tim Padmore is Research Associate in the Department of Economics, University of British Columbia, Vancouver.

John Sargent, Research Coordinator for the Macroeconomics section of the Economics Research Area of the Royal Commission, is Assistant Deputy Minister, Financial Sector Policy Branch, Department of Finance, Ottawa.

Thomas A. Wilson is Professor in the Department of Economics and Research Associate for the Institute for Policy Analysis, University of Toronto.

THE COLLECTED RESEARCH STUDIES

Royal Commission on the Economic Union and Development Prospects for Canada

ECONOMICS

Income Distribution and Economic Security in Canada (Vol.1), *François Vaillancourt, Research Coordinator*

Vol. 1   Income Distribution and Economic Security in Canada, *F. Vaillancourt* (C)*

Industrial Structure (Vols. 2-8), *Donald G. McFetridge, Research Coordinator*

Vol. 2   Canadian Industry in Transition, *D.G. McFetridge* (C)
Vol. 3   Technological Change in Canadian Industry, *D.G. McFetridge* (C)
Vol. 4   Canadian Industrial Policy in Action, *D.G. McFetridge* (C)
Vol. 5   Economics of Industrial Policy and Strategy, *D.G. McFetridge* (C)
Vol. 6   The Role of Scale in Canada–US Productivity Differences, *J.R. Baldwin and P.K. Gorecki* (M)
Vol. 7   Competition Policy and Vertical Exchange, *F. Mathewson and R. Winter* (M)
Vol. 8   The Political Economy of Economic Adjustment, *M. Trebilcock* (M)

International Trade (Vols. 9-14), *John Whalley, Research Coordinator*

Vol. 9   Canadian Trade Policies and the World Economy, *J. Whalley with C. Hamilton and R. Hill* (M)
Vol. 10   Canada and the Multilateral Trading System, *J. Whalley* (M)
Vol. 11   Canada–United States Free Trade, *J. Whalley* (C)
Vol. 12   Domestic Policies and the International Economic Environment, *J. Whalley* (C)
Vol. 13   Trade, Industrial Policy and International Competition, *R. Harris* (M)
Vol. 14   Canada's Resource Industries and Water Export Policy, *J. Whalley* (C)

Labour Markets and Labour Relations (Vols. 15-18), *Craig Riddell, Research Coordinator*

Vol. 15   Labour-Management Cooperation in Canada, *C. Riddell* (C)
Vol. 16   Canadian Labour Relations, *C. Riddell* (C)
Vol. 17   Work and Pay: The Canadian Labour Market, *C. Riddell* (C)
Vol. 18   Adapting to Change: Labour Market Adjustment in Canada, *C. Riddell* (C)

Macroeconomics (Vols. 19-25), *John Sargent, Research Coordinator*

Vol. 19   Macroeconomic Performance and Policy Issues: Overviews, *J. Sargent* (M)
Vol. 20   Post-War Macroeconomic Developments, *J. Sargent* (C)
Vol. 21   Fiscal and Monetary Policy, *J. Sargent* (C)
Vol. 22   Economic Growth: Prospects and Determinants, *J. Sargent* (C)
Vol. 23   Long-Term Economic Prospects for Canada: A Symposium, *J. Sargent* (C)
Vol. 24   Foreign Macroeconomic Experience: A Symposium, *J. Sargent* (C)
Vol. 25   Dealing with Inflation and Unemployment in Canada, *C. Riddell* (M)

Economic Ideas and Social Issues (Vols. 26 and 27), *David Laidler, Research Coordinator*

Vol. 26   Approaches to Economic Well-Being, *D. Laidler* (C)
Vol. 27   Responses to Economic Change, *D. Laidler* (C)

* (C) denotes a Collection of studies by various authors coordinated by the person named.
  (M) denotes a Monograph.

POLITICS AND INSTITUTIONS OF GOVERNMENT

Canada and the International Political Economy (Vols. 28-30), *Denis Stairs and Gilbert R. Winham, Research Coordinators*

Vol. 28 Canada and the International Political/Economic Environment, *D. Stairs and G.R. Winham* (C)
Vol. 29 The Politics of Canada's Economic Relationship with the United States, *D. Stairs and G.R. Winham* (C)
Vol. 30 Selected Problems in Formulating Foreign Economic Policy, *D. Stairs and G.R. Winham* (C)

State and Society in the Modern Era (Vols. 31 and 32), *Keith Banting, Research Coordinator*

Vol. 31 State and Society: Canada in Comparative Perspective, *K. Banting* (C)
Vol. 32 The State and Economic Interests, *K. Banting* (C)

Constitutionalism, Citizenship and Society (Vols. 33-35), *Alan Cairns and Cynthia Williams, Research Coordinators*

Vol. 33 Constitutionalism, Citizenship and Society in Canada, *A. Cairns and C. Williams* (C)
Vol. 34 The Politics of Gender, Ethnicity and Language in Canada, *A. Cairns and C. Williams* (C)
Vol. 35 Public Opinion and Public Policy in Canada, *R. Johnston* (M)

Representative Institutions (Vols. 36-39), *Peter Aucoin, Research Coordinator*

Vol. 36 Party Government and Regional Representation in Canada, *P. Aucoin* (C)
Vol. 37 Regional Responsiveness and the National Administrative State, *P. Aucoin* (C)
Vol. 38 Institutional Reforms for Representative Government, *P. Aucoin* (C)
Vol. 39 Intrastate Federalism in Canada, *D.V. Smiley and R.L. Watts* (M)

The Politics of Economic Policy (Vols. 40-43), *G. Bruce Doern, Research Coordinator*

Vol. 40 The Politics of Economic Policy, *G.B. Doern* (C)
Vol. 41 Federal and Provincial Budgeting, *A.M. Maslove, M.J. Prince and G.B. Doern* (M)
Vol. 42 Economic Regulation and the Federal System, *R. Schultz and A. Alexandroff* (M)
Vol. 43 Bureaucracy in Canada: Control and Reform, *S.L. Sutherland and G.B. Doern* (M)

Industrial Policy (Vols. 44 and 45), *André Blais, Research Coordinator*

Vol. 44 Industrial Policy, *A. Blais* (C)
Vol. 45 The Political Sociology of Industrial Policy, *A. Blais* (M)

LAW AND CONSTITUTIONAL ISSUES

Law, Society and the Economy (Vols. 46-51), *Ivan Bernier and Andrée Lajoie, Research Coordinators*

Vol. 46 Law, Society and the Economy, *I. Bernier and A. Lajoie* (C)
Vol. 47 The Supreme Court of Canada as an Instrument of Political Change, *I. Bernier and A. Lajoie* (C)
Vol. 48 Regulations, Crown Corporations and Administrative Tribunals, *I. Bernier and A. Lajoie* (C)
Vol. 49 Family Law and Social Welfare Legislation in Canada, *I. Bernier and A. Lajoie* (C)
Vol. 50 Consumer Protection, Environmental Law and Corporate Power, *I. Bernier and A. Lajoie* (C)
Vol. 51 Labour Law and Urban Law in Canada, *I. Bernier and A. Lajoie* (C)

The International Legal Environment (Vols. 52-54), *John Quinn, Research Coordinator*

Vol. 52 The International Legal Environment, *J. Quinn* (C)
Vol. 53 Canadian Economic Development and the International Trading System, *M.M. Hart* (M)
Vol. 54 Canada and the New International Law of the Sea, *D.M. Johnston* (M)

Harmonization of Laws in Canada (Vols. 55 and 56), *Ronald C.C. Cuming, Research Coordinator*

Vol. 55 Perspectives on the Harmonization of Law in Canada, *R. Cuming* (C)
Vol. 56 Harmonization of Business Law in Canada, *R. Cuming* (C)

Institutional and Constitutional Arrangements (Vols. 57 and 58), *Clare F. Beckton and A. Wayne MacKay, Research Coordinators*

Vol. 57 Recurring Issues in Canadian Federalism, *C.F. Beckton and A.W. MacKay* (C)
Vol. 58 The Courts and The Charter, *C.F. Beckton and A.W. MacKay* (C)

FEDERALISM AND THE ECONOMIC UNION

Federalism and The Economic Union (Vols. 58-72), *Mark Krasnick, Kenneth Norrie and Richard Simeon, Research Coordinators*

Vol. 59 Federalism and Economic Union in Canada, *K. Norrie, R. Simeon and M. Krasnick* (M)
Vol. 60 Perspectives on the Canadian Economic Union, *M. Krasnick* (C)
Vol. 61 Division of Powers and Public Policy, *R. Simeon* (C)
Vol. 62 Case Studies in the Division of Powers, *M. Krasnick* (C)
Vol. 63 Intergovernmental Relations, *R. Simeon* (C)
Vol. 64 Disparities and Interregional Adjustment, *K. Norrie* (C)
Vol. 65 Fiscal Federalism, *M. Krasnick* (C)
Vol. 66 Mobility of Capital in the Canadian Economic Union, *N. Roy* (M)
Vol. 67 Economic Management and the Division of Powers, *T.J. Courchene* (M)
Vol. 68 Regional Aspects of Confederation, *J. Whalley* (M)
Vol. 69 Interest Groups in the Canadian Federal System, *H.G. Thorburn* (M)
Vol. 70 Canada and Quebec, Past and Future: An Essay, *D. Latouche* (M)
Vol. 71 The Political Economy of Canadian Federalism: 1940-1984, *R. Simeon and I. Robinson* (M)

THE NORTH

Vol. 72 The North, *Michael S. Whittington, Coordinator* (C)

COMMISSION ORGANIZATION

Chairman
Donald S. Macdonald

Commissioners

Clarence L. Barber	William M. Hamilton	Daryl K. Seaman
Albert Breton	John R. Messer	Thomas K. Shoyama
M. Angela Cantwell Peters	Laurent Picard	Jean Casselman-Wadds
E. Gérard Docquier	Michel Robert	Catherine T. Wallace

Senior Officers

Executive Director
J. Gerald Godsoe

Director of Policy Alan Nymark	*Senior Advisors* David Ablett	*Directors of Research* Ivan Bernier
Secretary Michel Rochon	Victor Clarke Carl Goldenberg Harry Stewart	Alan Cairns David C. Smith
Director of Administration Sheila-Marie Cook	*Director of Publishing* Ed Matheson	*Co-Directors of Research* Kenneth Norrie John Sargent

Research Program Organization

Economics	Politics and the Institutions of Government	Law and Constitutional Issues
Research Director David C. Smith	*Research Director* Alan Cairns	*Research Director* Ivan Bernier
Executive Assistant & Assistant Director (Research Services) I. Lilla Connidis	*Executive Assistant* Karen Jackson	*Executive Assistant & Research Program Administrator* Jacques J.M. Shore
Coordinators David Laidler Donald G. McFetridge Kenneth Norrie* Craig Riddell John Sargent* François Vaillancourt John Whalley	*Coordinators* Peter Aucoin Keith Banting André Blais Bruce Doern Richard Simeon Denis Stairs Cynthia Williams Gilbert R. Winham	*Coordinators* Clare F. Beckton Ronald C.C. Cuming Mark Krasnick Andrée Lajoie A. Wayne MacKay John J. Quinn
Research Analysts Caroline Digby Mireille Ethier Judith Gold Douglas S. Green Colleen Hamilton Roderick Hill Joyce Martin	*Research Analysts* Claude Desranleau Ian Robinson *Office Administration* Donna Stebbing	*Administrative and Research Assistant* Nicolas Roy *Research Analyst* Nola Silzer

*Kenneth Norrie and John Sargent co-directed the final phase of Economics Research with David Smith